THE CROWN
AND THE
MONEY MARKET
1603–1640

Oxford University Press, Amen House, London E.C.4

GLASGOW   NEW YORK   TORONTO   MELBOURNE   WELLINGTON
BOMBAY   CALCUTTA   MADRAS   KARACHI   KUALA LUMPUR
CAPE TOWN   IBADAN   NAIROBI   ACCRA

THE CROWN
AND THE
MONEY MARKET
1603–1640

BY

ROBERT ASHTON

LECTURER IN ECONOMIC HISTORY IN
THE UNIVERSITY OF NOTTINGHAM

OXFORD
AT THE CLARENDON PRESS
1960

TO THE MEMORY OF
MY MOTHER

PREFACE

My interest in the financial history of the early Stuart period began when as a postgraduate student at the London School of Economics I worked for a doctoral degree under the guidance of Professor R. H. Tawney and Professor F. J. Fisher. To both of them I owe an incalculable debt, not only for starting me off upon what I hope has been a fruitful line of research, but also for the generous encouragement which they have given to me during the whole of the ten years which I have devoted to this topic. It was my good fortune to begin working on the subject of royal finance at a time when Professor Tawney was turning his attention to this subject in connexion with his interest in the career of Lionel Cranfield. I have benefited enormously from his advice and criticism, from his unrivalled knowledge of the economic and social history of the period, and, most of all, from his example, which has encouraged me to try to look beyond the rather narrow boundaries of economic history and to regard the non-economic implications of my work as an important call upon my attention. To Professor Fisher also I owe more than I can adequately express, for his constant readiness to give advice, his unfailingly fertile suggestions, and, not least, for subjecting my work to vigorous criticism which was sometimes devastating, but always salutary.

I am also deeply indebted to Professor H. J. Habakkuk and Mr. Lawrence Stone for valuable advice, criticism, and information; to Dr. C. D. Chandaman for his willingness to enter into a detailed and involved correspondence with me on problems relating to the Exchequer tally, which was of great value to me in writing the section dealing with this subject; to Dr. G. E. Aylmer, both for our discussions of seventeenth-century problems and for permission to quote from a document which he cites in his own published work; to Mr. T. F. Reddaway and Mr. G. Hammersley for valuable information; to Professor J. C. Smith for his generous advice on the legal problems which are so important to the historian of finance; to Professor J. D. Chambers and Mr. R. S. Smith for suggesting amendments which are designed to make this book more palatable to the reader who is not well versed in the technicalities of early Stuart finance; to the officials of the Public Record Office and the British Museum and to Mr. P. E. Jones and Mr. M. J. Chandler of the Records Office of the Corporation of London for their unfailing help and courtesy; to the Masters and Wardens of those Livery Companies who kindly allowed me access to their records; to Miss V. A. Robinson for assistance in typing, and to Mr. R. B. Outhwaite and other members of Nottingham University for their help in proof-reading. The greater part of this distasteful but essential drudgery has fallen upon my wife, but this is the very least of the debts which I owe to her.

R. A.

Nottingham
November 1959

CONTENTS

NOTE ON DATING AND ABBREVIATIONS

1. All dates are old style except for the fact that the year is taken to begin on 1 January.

2. The following abbreviations are used in the footnotes:

Amer. H.R.	*American Historical Review.*
A.O.	Audit Office.
A.P.C.	*Acts of the Privy Council.*
B.I.H.R.	*Bulletin of the Institute of Historical Research.*
B.M.	British Museum.
Cal. S.P.D.	*Calendar of State Papers Domestic.*
Cal. S.P.E. Indies	*Calendar of State Papers East Indies.*
Cal. S.P. Ven.	*Calendar of State Papers Venetian.*
Camb. Hist. J.	*Cambridge Historical Journal.*
C. of L.R.O.	Corporation of London Records Office.
Coll. Sign Man.	Collected Sign Manual Grants and Warrants.
D.N.B.	*Dictionary of National Biography.*
Econ. Hist. Rev.	*Economic History Review.*
Econ. J.	*Economic Journal.*
Eng. Hist. Rev.	*English Historical Review.*
Exchequer K.R.	Exchequer King's Remembrancer.
Exchequer L.T.R.	Exchequer Lord Treasurer's Remembrancer.
Hist. MSS. Comm.	Historical Manuscripts Commission.
J. Mod. Hist.	*Journal of Modern History.*
J. Pol. Econ.	*Journal of Political Economy.*
L.Q.R.	*Law Quarterly Review.*
MS. Cal. of Sackville MSS.	Manuscript Calendar of Sackville MSS. (Newton's transcripts).
P.C.R.	Privy Council Register.
P.R.O.	Public Record Office.
R.C.E.P.	Royal Contract Estates Papers.
Roy. Hist. Soc. Trans.	*Transactions of the Royal Historical Society.*
S.P.	State Papers (Domestic).
S.P. Foreign	State Papers Foreign.

INTRODUCTION

No one who has even the most superficial knowledge of the constitutional conflicts which culminated in the Great Rebellion can fail to be aware of the central position which is occupied in this field by problems of government finance. Indeed, one of the consequences of the fact that financial problems have forced themselves upon the attention of political and constitutional historians has been to make the examination of such problems something of a handmaid to the study of constitutional development. Royal finance in the sixteenth and early seventeenth centuries has been studied from the constitutional, political, and administrative points of view, and almost every aspect of the subject has been extensively exploited except the economic.[1] This emphasis is both understandable and healthy, in so far as it has served to emphasize the interdependence of financial and political history, for the tendency in recent historiography to divide historical studies vertically into watertight compartments, while responsible for many spectacular additions to historical knowledge, must also bear some of the responsibility for obscuring the relationship between analytically distinct, but historically related, aspects of historical development. The link between economic and political history is a vital one, the importance of which has recently been emphasized by Professor R. H. Tawney's great study of *Business and Politics under James I.* Nevertheless, all aspects of the subject need to be explored before a proper understanding of its historical significance can emerge, and it is the economic aspect which has suffered most from neglect. It follows from this fact that interest in the economic aspects of royal finance must not be confined to the economic historian alone.

---

[1] An outstanding exception is, of course, W. R. Scott, *The Constitution and Finance of English, Scottish and Irish Joint Stock Companies to 1720* (Cambridge, 1912) (hereafter cited as *Joint Stock Companies*). Scott sought to examine, *inter multa alia*, the repercussions of royal finance on the economic life of the country. Although the financial information then available to him was very meagre, and his attempt was, to that extent, premature, the pioneering quality of this aspect of his great book has not received the attention it deserves, and it is astonishing that subsequent economic historians have not notably exploited this particular field of inquiry.

In no century are economic and political factors more closely inter-
twined than in the seventeenth, and no one these days would
attempt a serious explanation of the causes of the Civil War without
giving very serious attention to the economic background to political events. Although it is perhaps regrettable that many of the
more fruitful and stimulating of recent attempts to grapple with
this problem have been couched in terms of an *exclusively* economic
causation, the economic approach to political problems need not
be identified with economic determinism. Its function is rather to
attempt to provide that economic and social background to politics
which is the essential pre-condition of a truly integrated interpretation of events. In the evolution of such an interpretation the
study of royal finance has an important part to play, but its significance is by no means exhausted by the reiteration of traditional
arguments about the parliamentary attitude to arbitrary taxation.
It is indeed quite impossible to appreciate the historical—and even
the more narrowly political—importance of royal finance until more
is known about its economic aspects.

There are many cases in which further intensive study of the
stock problems of royal finance seems likely to yield diminishing
returns. As things stand at present, Professor Dietz's general study[2]
seems unlikely to be replaced, and in these circumstances is likely
to remain for many years an indispensable, if sometimes rather
erratic, guide to the general development of the royal finances.
Nor is it likely that anything which could be added to the study of
the constitutional aspects of royal finance would succeed in doing
more than dot the i's and cross the t's of the arguments of the
incomparable Gardiner. But in those cases where the economic
aspects of royal finance are most prominent, there still remain
important gaps to be filled. One of these gaps is the study of the
incidence of taxation, for, in the absence of a systematic study of
this intricate and immensely difficult problem, any examination of
the impact of royal finance upon the economy as a whole—and,
through the economy, on political life—is inconceivable. Another
is the question of royal indebtedness, which, in the periods before
the emergence of the national debt, has received scant attention
from historians. And, finally, there is the closely related topic of the
Crown's relations as a borrower with the business world, which is
the subject of this book. At this point the study of royal finance not

[2] F. C. Dietz, *English Public Finance (1558–1641)* (New York, 1932).

only touches the subjects of revenue, expenditure, and royal indebtedness, and the wider problems of political organization, but seeks also to explore the relationship between the needs of the State and the development of finance in general.

Two factors have helped to obscure the essential fact that the true significance of the economic policies of the Tudors and the early Stuarts—of which financial policy forms a part—is to be found, as Dr. Coleman has recently suggested,[3] in the impact of a relatively highly developed apparatus of State power upon a relatively undeveloped economy. The first of these factors is the quite illogical and unwarranted connexion between economic history and that economic interpretation of history which emphasizes the historical dependence of particular forms of government upon the prevailing mode of material production. The second is the familiar fact that the ends of government economic policy were too ambitious in relation to the administrative means which were at the disposal of Tudor and early Stuart governments. In a sense this book provides a case history of the impact of the financial demands of a relatively highly organized State upon a relatively undeveloped business community—of a super-borrower upon a financial world which was equipped to meet demands which were different both in kind and in size from those of the Crown. The problems which are raised by these circumstances are further complicated by the political and legal context in which they were set, a fact which makes the working out of these problems a further case study in arbitrary finance, though in a less familiar environment than that which is provided by the study of financial expedients such as the Impositions, Ship Money, and Fiscal Feudalism, in which terms the financial problems of a monarchy which was neither completely arbitrary nor limited in the modern sense are usually discussed.

The fact that a systematic study of the problems with which this book is concerned has not been attempted before reflects, among other things, the curious and unnatural dichotomy which has arisen between the study of royal and that of private finance in this period. It is almost as if constitutional and economic historians had set their seals to a sort of historiographical contract, assigning to one another mutually exclusive spheres of interest in the historical study of finance. Be this as it may, the former have poured forth

[3] D. C. Coleman, 'Labour in the English Economy of the Seventeenth Century', *Econ. Hist. Rev.* 2nd ser. viii (1956), 295.

their ideas of the constitutional aspects of the subject, together with occasional, and often highly valuable monographs and papers on different branches of the revenue, while the latter have made signal contributions to the history of changing—and unchanging—attitudes to usury, the development of credit techniques, and the growth of financial institutions. Yet until the appearance of Professor Tawney's book in 1958 the mysterious country where the one aspect of the subject impinges upon the other had been almost entirely unexplored. The history of the money market *per se* in the centuries before the foundation of the Bank of England will probably never be written, and, indeed, it is possible that the absence of institutionalized finance and the prevalence of individual and personal financial relationships precludes systematic historical treatment of this topic. But in the study of the Crown's relations with the money market—the term has been deliberately preferred to that of capital market, which is not especially appropriate in connexion with this period—there is a manageable problem, which is at once both narrower and wider than this; narrower in that it is concerned with unique circumstances and with a specific and limited set of financial relationships—though these are the relationships with the money market of what was by far the most important source of demand for funds; but wider, in that such a study affords the twin opportunities of bringing together the studies of public and private finance, and of providing a link, however tenuous, between finance and politics. It is upon this shadowy borderland between public and private finance, and, though perhaps to a lesser extent, between economic and political history, that this book seeks to shed some light.

I

THE ORGANIZATION OF THE MONEY MARKET

By the accession of James I an active money market had developed in London, but it was still hardly thirty years since the Crown had ceased to raise its largest and most important loans abroad. It is hardly surprising, therefore, that in 1603 the London money market was geared to the needs of private individuals rather than to those of the Crown. Although the history of the private sector of the money market in Elizabethan and early Stuart times has yet to be written, the researches of a number of scholars have revealed the existence both of a highly developed bill market in which extensive credit operations in the purchase and sale of commercial paper had for a long time been well established, and of varied expedients for meeting the demands of the non-mercantile borrower.[1] The central problem of this study is to be found in the fact that, in a period when the Crown was thrown back preponderantly upon native resources of loanable funds, it could make only limited use of the facilities which existed for the private borrower. This important fact can most conveniently be illustrated by a brief description of these facilities.

That the moneylenders of early Stuart England were drawn from almost every occupation and social class and that moneylending was viewed by most of them, whether business men, officials, lawyers, or landowners, 'not as a profession, but a bye-employment',[2] are commonplaces whose importance in contrasting the money

---

[1] See especially, T. Wilson, *A Discourse upon Usury* (1572), ed. with an Historical Introduction by R. H. Tawney (1925) (hereafter cited as Tawney, *Introduction to Wilson*); M. E. Finch, *The Wealth of Five Northamptonshire Families 1540–1640* (Oxford, 1956); R. de Roover, *Gresham on Foreign Exchange* (Cambridge, Mass., 1949); R. H. Tawney, *Business and Politics in the Reign of James I* (Cambridge, 1958), pp. 113–20; L. Stone, 'The Anatomy of the Elizabethan Aristocracy', *Econ. Hist. Rev.* xviii (1948), 1–41, and 'The Elizabethan Aristocracy—A Restatement', ibid. 2nd ser. iv (1952), 302–21; H. R. Trevor-Roper, 'The Elizabethan Aristocracy: An Anatomy Anatomized', ibid. 2nd ser. iii (1951), 279–98.

[2] The phrase is borrowed from Professor R. H. Tawney, *Introduction to Wilson*, p. 21.

market of these times with that of the present day has perhaps been overstressed. Such lenders had become accustomed to dealing in a wide range of financial instruments, each of which was suited to the different needs of different types of borrower, and afforded varying kinds and degrees of security to the lender, whose requirements might therefore be varied according to the credit-worthiness of different clients.

Borrowing upon bills of exchange and bills obligatory were credit techniques which were admirably suited to the needs of the business world. In such cases the personal reputation of the borrower was the prime element of security, though in the case of the bill of exchange, the essence of which is the notion of transference of funds in terms of place, this was supplemented by the reputation of the person on whom the bill was drawn. In the case of bills obligatory, however, no such transfer of funds was involved, and the bill was a simple promise on the part of the borrower to repay the lender at a specified date. As such, it has obvious affinities with the more modern promissory note, except for the fact that it lacked the important attribute of legal negotiability.[3]

Both types of bill seem to have enjoyed some degree of transferability by assignment, but the widespread development of this practice, which, by lessening the risk of the lender, would have made lending money on bills an even more widely accepted practice, was limited by a number of factors. In the first place, bills were usually made out for inconvenient amounts rather than round sums. Moreover, the financial status of the debtor, even when it was well known to the original lender, might not be familiar to the business world as a whole. And, finally, there were formidable legal difficulties. The assignability of bills obligatory was still not recognized by the common law, and, in the case of the bill of exchange, the legal position of a holder or indorsee remained dubious and obscure so long as his possession of such a bill was not deemed to be sufficient proof that he had given value for it, and so long as he had no legal redress if he had acquired it from someone whose title was defective.[4]

---

[3] According to Malynes, both bills obligatory and bills of exchange were extensively used for purchases of goods on credit (G. de Malynes, *Consuetudo vel Lex Mercatoria* (London, 1622), p. 71). It was, however, probably more usual for such credits to be unsecured by bill.

[4] The common law did not recognize the right to sue either of an indorsee or of a holder of a bill payable to bearer even when the latter could provide proof

The emphasis which has frequently been laid upon the use of the bill of exchange as a means of evading the usury laws has tended to obscure its primary significance as an essentially mercantile credit instrument. It was clearly convenient for a merchant to be able to borrow in the place where he bought, and repay in the place where he sold. In such cases he would make use of the bill of exchange rather than the bill obligatory, since the latter had to be repaid in the place where the money was borrowed. Moreover, in the vast majority of cases the profits of lending were not the sole, or even the main, advantage obtained by the purchase of a bill of exchange. The merchant in London who lent money by purchasing a bill of exchange on Amsterdam might be as concerned to effect a transfer of his funds to Amsterdam as was the borrower to obtain money in London. No doubt the fact that the lender not only obtained his required transfer, but also made an additional profit, made the transaction doubly satisfactory to him, but the profits of lending were subsidiary to his main aim of obtaining a transfer of his funds. These important facts have often been obscured by a failure to emphasize the vitally important facts that most of the operators on the bill market were merchants whose primary interest lay in commodity trade rather than in finance, and that the great exchange specialist was very much the exception rather than the rule.

At some time during the early seventeenth century the scope of the exchange mechanism was widened by the development of the inland bill of exchange, by which means the legitimate use of the exchanges became no longer confined to those borrowers whose potential or actual sources of funds lay abroad.[5] For a long time before this, however, it had been possible for borrowers who had no such sources of funds either at home or abroad to use the foreign bill of exchange as a means of raising money. This was done by

that he had given valuable consideration for it. On the development of the legal negotiability of bills in the seventeenth century see W. Holdsworth, *A History of English Law* (3rd edn., 1922), viii. 140–70; J. M. Holden, *The History of Negotiable Instruments in English Law* (1955), pp. 30–70, and 'Bills of Exchange during the Seventeenth Century', *L.Q.R.* lxvii (1951), 230–48.

[5] Malynes (op. cit.), writing in 1622, makes no mention of inland bills. John Marius, in his *Advice Concerning Bills of Exchange*, written in 1651, specifically mentions them (Holden, op. cit., pp. 38–39, 47). As early as the first two decades of the seventeenth century, however, the inland bill drawn upon local dealers who wished to transfer cash from their London sales to the provinces was frequently used by landowners as a means of transferring rents to London. I owe this information to the kindness of Mr. Lawrence Stone.

means of the perverted exchange contracts known as *dry* and *fictitious exchange*. These were essentially devices by which the element of transferability of funds in point of place was adapted to situations in which transferability was not required, and, as such, they were purely and simply methods of evading the usury laws. In the case of *dry exchange* an actual transfer of the bill was made, the pretended drawee being either a fictitious character or the agent of the lender, on whom fell the duty of making out a second bill for rechange on London. If the original bill was at *usance*—that is, one month between London and the Low Countries—the original transfer and the rechange operation meant that in effect two months' credit was allowed before the money became due to the lender in London. *Fictitious exchange* was even further removed from the pure exchange contract, for the use of this expedient did not even involve the transfer of a bill. It was, in fact, simply a straightforward loan whose element of interest was disguised either in the prevalent market rate of exchange or in an artificial rate agreed upon by the parties to the loan.[6]

Despite the effective legalization of a limited degree of interest after 1571, recourse to *dry* and *fictitious* exchange was by no means uncommon after that date. An important factor which helped to prolong their life after the conditions which provided their main *raison d'être* had disappeared was undoubtedly the recurrent periods of stringency in the money market, when lenders might be able to impose their own terms, since, as Professor de Roover has pointed out, lenders 'often expected a larger profit by delivering money on the exchange'.[7] On the other hand, borrowers might elect to use the dry exchange mechanism in cases where it was cheaper to do this than to borrow on other securities.[8] Moreover, the small merchant who could not afford to employ a factor abroad, and whose circle of contracts in foreign business centres was extremely limited, might find in the dry exchange mechanism a convenient method of obtaining short-term credits.

It must by now be clear that the bill market was of little use to the

---

[6] For *dry* and *fictitious exchange*, see Tawney, *Introduction to Wilson*, pp. 73–75, 80–81; de Roover, op. cit., pp. 161–5, and 'What is Dry Exchange?', in *J. Pol. Econ.* lii (1944), 250–69.

[7] Op. cit., p. 164.

[8] This statement runs counter to Malynes's belief that it was always dearer to take up money by exchange than by other methods (Malynes, op. cit., p. 253). Malynes, however, was something of an exchange crank.

Crown which was wedded to the necessity of raising its loans at home, and had no desire to enter into the additional complication of repaying them abroad. Moreover, lending to the government offered no attractions to those merchants whose chief object in purchasing bills of exchange was to obtain transfers of their funds for subsequent use in commodity trade, since the Crown required longer credit than such lenders would have found it convenient to grant. Finally, since very few bills seem to have been for more than £200,[9] they related to sums smaller than those which were required by the Crown. It was not in the least attracted by the prospect of entering into the tortuous complexities of *dry* and *fictitious* exchange, since it was not bound by the usury laws which it was the chief object of these devices to evade. It is true, however, that while the Crown does not appear to have used the foreign exchange mechanism on its own account, terms on the bill market might be affected by its demands either through the diversion of resources from the bill market into the provision of funds for loans to the Crown, or through the sale of bills by lenders in order to raise such funds. The outstanding example of this connexion is to be found in the operations of the great financial specialist, Philip Burlamachi, who made extensive use of the bill market in connexion with the financial services which he rendered to the government.[10]

Borrowing on bills was by no means the only credit technique employed by the mercantile community of early Stuart London. That rich storehouse of early seventeenth-century commercial and financial practice, the Cranfield papers, records a wide variety of commercial loans on securities ranging from notes of hand to the mortgage of a life assurance policy.[11] Among these transactions those concerned with borrowing upon various types of bond are especially prominent.[12] The bond was a financial instrument which was better

---

[9] I owe this information and a number of other points relating to the foreign exchanges to conversations with Professor F. J. Fisher.

[10] For a fuller treatment of this aspect of Burlamachi's activities see R. Ashton, 'The Disbursing Official under the Early Stuarts: The Cases of Sir William Russell and Philip Burlamachi', in *B.I.H.R.* xxx (1957), 167–8.

[11] *Hist. MSS. Comm., Sackville MSS.* i, *passim.*

[12] For these purposes it has not been thought necessary to draw a sharp distinction between bonds and Statutes Staple, since both instruments rendered the defaulting borrower liable to a monetary penalty. Differences between the two instruments as to methods of enforcement are, however, important, not least in the sense that the Statute, by providing recourse to distraint on real property as a means of defraying the penalty, was especially suitable as a security against loans made to landowners (see also G. Jacob, *A New English*

suited to the needs of borrowers who required longer-term loans. It was usually, though not always, made out for a period of six months or a year, and was easily renewable provided that the lender was willing to consent to prolongation. It is true that there was nothing in the nature of a bill to prevent it from being renewed, but, as we have seen, most buyers of bills—and especially of bills of exchange—desired to employ their funds in commodity trade, and were therefore concerned only with the granting of short-term credits. The bond was, therefore, a more convenient instrument for the lender who desired to make a longer-term investment. Moreover, it has already been emphasized that the personal credit of the borrower was a vitally important factor in the case of loans on both bills obligatory and bills of exchange. No prudent lender could be expected to accept the bill of a borrower with a reputation for anything less than the strictest commercial integrity, or of a stranger whose credit was an unknown quantity in business circles. He would prefer to lend upon bond, because as will appear, this credit instrument offered him a security which was more tangible than that of the borrower's reputation. It is not surprising, therefore, that this credit technique was not confined to commercial circles, but was resorted to by lenders and borrowers of all types.

The precise nature of the more definite security offered by a bond lay in the fact that the penalty for the failure to observe the condition of the bond—in this case the repayment of principal and interest at a specified date—was far larger than the principal debt and the accrued interest. It may be argued that if the borrower were completely bankrupt, this sanction would afford to the lender nothing more tangible than the malicious satisfaction of immuring his debtor in prison. While it is unlikely that lenders would make extensive loans on bond to persons without adequate resources in real or personal property, which might be distrained to pay the penalty on the borrowers' default, it was to guard against this eventuality that they frequently demanded that borrowers should obtain the collateral security of other persons as guarantors of repayment, the sureties being liable for the whole of the penalty in case of default. For example, on 14 January 1618 Sir Francis Jones, the customs farmer, entered into a bond with his partner, Sir

Law Dictionary (ed. T. E. Tomkins), (1797): Bond, Recognizance, Statute Merchant, Statute Staple); W. West, Symboleography (1622 edn.), pt. i, sects. 103–9.

Nicholas Salter, and Sir John Wolstenholme, in penalty of £1,000, the condition of the bond being that Jones would pay £525 to Samuel Hare on 6 July. By doing this, Jones would cancel the bond in penalty of £800 which Salter and Wolstenholme had given to Hare as sureties of Jones, guaranteeing that Jones would repay him the £525.[13]

Although the bond offered to lenders a more tangible type of security than the bill,[14] for the cautious moneylender the pledge was an even safer security. There is, of course, a basic similarity between bonds and pledges, in that the value of a pledge, like the penalty stipulated in a bond, greatly exceeded the principal and accrued interest for the agreed period of a loan. But rather than accept as security a borrower's liability to pay a large sum of money in case of default, some lenders preferred to receive a pledge, either of real or personal property which would become their own property if the borrower failed to meet his obligations. The researches of Mr. Stone and Professor Trevor-Roper have clearly shown that many landowners borrowed on bond. But, whereas this method of borrowing was common to borrowers of most classes, the pledging of real and personal property was designed primarily, though by no means exclusively, to meet the demand of the non-commercial borrower. It is true that recent controversies on the respective fates of the nobility and gentry in this period have emphasized that the distinction between landowners and business men is to some extent an abstraction—that many business men invested in land, and many landowners engaged in business activities. Nevertheless, although those whose preponderant economic interest lay in land may have borrowed for other purposes than 'to meet the current expenses of their establishments, to stave off creditors, or to renew debts',[15] more often than they have sometimes been given credit for, in the context of credit techniques it is not unreasonable to distinguish between their demands and those of borrowers who were primarily city men rather than landowners. For it was natural enough in an age when aristocratic and gentry inclinations to save generally took the form of investment in land, or the hoarding of plate and jewels, that the needs of the landowning class in times of economic stress

---

[13] P.R.O. S.P. James I, 95/7.
[14] Although bonds, unlike bills obligatory, were recognized by common law, they were not legally negotiable (Holden, op. cit., p. 20).
[15] Tawney, *Introduction to Wilson*, p. 31.

should largely manifest themselves in attempts to render these resources liquid, and a mortgage market and large-scale pawn-broking facilities had arisen to meet these needs. If such borrowers could raise money on bonds they did so, but failing this there were usually lenders who were prepared to make advances on the mortgage of land or the pledge of personal property. In the latter category is comprised almost every conceivable item from family jewels to the pawning by a peer of his parliamentary robes.[16]

The commonest type of mortgage of land was that in which the land was forfeit on the default of the borrower, but in which any income from the land for the duration of the loan was enjoyed by him and not by the lender. These mortgages took the form of deeds of bargain and sale to the lender to take effect from the date at which repayment fell due, and containing a saving clause that if the condition of the mortgage—that is the repayment of the principal with interest at the contracted date—were observed, the contract should be null and void. So long as the mortgagee's title became absolute on the non-observance of the condition by the mortgagor, this type of borrowing remained unpopular with borrowers. Professor Trevor-Roper has emphasized that to the Elizabethan land-owner borrowing on mortgage security was always 'a desperate expedient' to be avoided where possible.[17] However, during the next two reigns the mortgage was to undergo a major transformation which was largely due, as Dr. Finch has recently demonstrated, to the development of the mortgagor's equity of redemption. At first applied tentatively by Chancery to special cases of hardship, the right of any mortgagor to redeem his property on the payment of the principal sum became a generally accepted doctrine of equity, and, with astonishing rapidity, there developed the further notion that he might keep possession of his land after default, provided his payments of interim interest were made promptly. This remarkable transformation seems to have been completed by the fourth decade of the seventeenth century.[18] Thereafter, borrowing on mortgage ceased to be an expedient which was feared, and, as far as possible, shunned, by all landowners, and became an admirable method of

[16] Stone in *Econ. Hist. Rev.* xviii (1948), 23.
[17] *Econ. Hist. Rev.* loc. cit., pp. 296–7.
[18] Finch, op. cit., pp. 32–33, 168–9; Holdsworth, op. cit. v. 330–2; vi. 663–5; R. W. Turner, *The Equity of Redemption* (Cambridge, 1931), pp. 24–37. On this topic I would like to acknowledge my indebtedness to conversations with Professor H. J. Habakkuk.

financing agricultural improvement or of providing for sudden needs for money capital for other purposes out of future improvements which might yield incomes sufficient not only to discharge the interest but also to amortize the principal.[19] But these changes could hardly have been welcomed by lenders, to whom they offered no compensating advantages. Under the older practice, the lender was not denied the opportunity of making a long-term investment, for a short-term mortgage could easily be prolonged. From the lender's point of view, the only change brought about by the introduction of the equity of redemption was the undesirable one of removing his option of entering into possession of the lands or prolonging the loan. Thus mortgages ceased to be attractive to those lenders for whom this type of investment was, in part at least, a form of speculation on the likely default of the borrower. In these circumstances there may well have been some movement of funds from mortgages into bonds and statutes. Accordingly, while the introduction of the equity of redemption may explain an increase in the demand for mortgages, it is not unreasonable to assume that it would be accompanied by a decrease in the number of lenders willing to lend money on this security, unless its effects were counteracted by developments in the mortgage market, such as the growth of the assignability of mortgages. Such developments still require further research.

It must now be asked to what extent the Crown was able to compete for funds with the private borrower by offering similar securities in the money market. It has already been shown that there were serious obstacles to its use of the bill market. While it is true that its Privy Seal notes of hand and its tallies struck upon a drawee who was a collector of some branch of the royal revenue[20] were financial instruments analogous to the bill obligatory and bill of exchange respectively, this analogy is designed to gladden the heart of the historian of credit technique rather than throw any significant light upon the realities of the royal financial situation. And in its failure to use the bill market, the position of the Crown was no different from that of the ordinary non-mercantile borrower. Like any private gentleman, however, it could raise loans both on bonds and on

[19] Mr. Lawrence Stone informs me that despite these legal changes and Dr. Finch's examples of their utilization he has found no striking increase in the use of the mortgage by landowners before 1640. The generalized increase in its use may well have been a very gradual process.

[20] For these royal securities, see below, pp. 47–53.

pledges of real and personal property.[21] But the basic similarity between royal financial instruments and their private equivalents tends to obscure one vital difference between the position of the private and that of the royal borrower. The royal immunity from the ordinary legal processes which were open to any lender in claiming redress from a defaulting debtor undoubtedly reduced the attractiveness of royal securities as a financial investment, a factor whose importance was by no means entirely offset by the fact that, again by virtue of its unique position, the Crown was also the fountain head of privilege. These considerations, therefore, go some way towards an explanation of the inadequacy of the private money market to meet the royal needs. But the fact remains that, even if the early Stuart kings had been able to offer gilt-edged securities against their loans, the ordinary resources of the money market would have been incapable of meeting their demands. For, in the first place, the sums involved were enormously larger than those required by the private borrower, while, in addition to this, the Crown usually required these sums to be forborne over relatively long periods.[22] Each of these factors, and especially the first, created special difficulties to discuss which it is necessary to turn from problems of credit techniques to those of credit machinery. It is in this sphere, far more than in that of credit techniques, that the reasons for the inadequacy of the money market to the needs of the early Stuarts, and the contrast between it and the money market of more recent times, become most apparent. For the highly organized banking and credit institutions which characterize the modern financial world were almost unknown to the early Stuart investor. As Professor Tawney has pointed out in another connexion, it was this absence of an impersonal and institutional credit mechanism and, in consequence, the very personal nature of the financial relationship between creditor and debtor, which was in no small measure responsible for exacerbating these relations and making the problem of usury one of the most inflammable social issues of the age.[23]

---

[21] For a detailed discussion of these royal securities, see below, pp. 53–67.

[22] Most royal borrowings were nominally short-term, but the term was very frequently extended by prolongation. See R. Ashton, 'Deficit Finance in the Reign of James I', in *Econ. Hist. Rev.* 2nd ser. x (1957), 26–28.

[23] Tawney, *Introduction to Wilson*, pp. 23–24. Professor Tawney writes here of provincial transactions, but his remarks are hardly less applicable to the capital.

It is not suggested that in early Stuart London there was a complete absence of financial machinery for bringing lenders and borrowers into contact with one another, but simply that in this period such machinery was relatively rudimentary and much less all-pervasive and impersonal than that with which twentieth-century lenders and borrowers are familiar. This is especially true of the most commonly employed type of financial intermediary, the broker, who, in return for a commission fee, put borrowers in touch with lenders without himself performing any specifically financial functions. Such duties were often part of the scrivener's stock-in-trade, but most London 'brokers' were probably engaged in business of a more occasional nature. For this a rough knowledge of particular aspects of the demand for and the supply of loanable funds was the only necessary qualification, and the broker's function might thus be performed by any person with contacts with the financial world. Thus the merchant-financier, Lionel Cranfield, might arrange a loan from a London goldsmith to Lord William Howard, or a highly placed government official like Sir Michael Hicks might find money for Fulke Greville, probably by using the services of his brother, the famous usurer and silkman, Baptist Hicks, or one of Baptist's associates.[24] One need for such intermediaries is aptly demonstrated by Greville's letter to Michael Hicks, thanking him for his services, 'wherein I was the more willing to troble you because I am very loth to have my name in question amongst them that practice in this kind uppon the exchange'. But, in general, the economic utility of the broker derived from the more commonplace fact that many borrowers did not possess contacts with the London business world, and even in those cases where they did, the lenders within the limited range of contact of an unaided borrower might not always be able to provide the type of accommodation which he was seeking.

The royal need for the services of the broker was at least as great as that of the private borrower. But, although even in private transactions the loan-broker did not always possess that complete independence of both lender and borrower which the proper exercise of his function requires, the services which were performed for the Crown by experienced merchant-financiers such as Lionel Cranfield and Philip Burlamachi were more akin to those of the royal

[24] For Cranfield, *Hist. MSS. Comm., Sackville MSS.* i. 216, 229; for Hicks, B.M. Lansdowne MSS. 88, Nos. 61, 62.

financial agent than to those of the broker. Men of this type who rose to serve the government in official or semi-official capacities were able to use their first-hand knowledge of the money market to point out to the government where loans might be had on the best terms. That similar services might be rendered by the customs farmers is suggested by an Exchequer Order of September 1616 which required the farmers of the great customs to repay four merchants, each of whom had lent £2,000 direct to the King, for whom the farmers had originally negotiated this loan.[25]

While the broker confined his attention to bringing borrowers and lenders together in a physical sense, the role of the banker as financial intermediary operates through his acceptance of deposits from one set of customers for the purpose of relending them to another. There are, of course, a great number of variations on this basic financial theme, ranging from the raising of specific loans for the purpose of relending to specific borrowers to the acceptance of demand and time deposits, loan operations on a fractional reserve system and the creation of bank money by making advances in notes. That many of these more sophisticated and complex operations were unknown in early Stuart England is a commonplace, and there is no doubt that the most typical figure amongst the many financial middlemen whose activities bear certain similarities to those of the banker was the merchant-financier who borrowed money in order to meet the demands of specific borrowers. In such cases there is no question of deposits being accepted, there being a direct connexion between the raising of a loan and its specific re-employment. At the most it might be termed *ad hoc* banking, and was a very widespread practice, of which the papers of Lionel Cranfield are particularly rich in examples.[26] By the use of similar expedients the Crown itself was enabled to draw upon much wider sources of loanable funds than would otherwise have been available to it.[27]

Another type of neo-banking function was performed by those retailers of loans who lent out the moneys which were deposited

---

[25] P.R.O. Exchequer of Receipt, Order Book (Pells), E. 403/2735, fo. 176.

[26] *Hist. MSS. Comm., Sackville MSS.* i, *passim.* The practice need not, of course, be confined to merchants. Nicholas Trott, a lawyer, who lent substantial sums to Francis Bacon in the last decade of Elizabeth's reign, claimed that to supply Bacon's needs he had borrowed from another lawyer, 'whom I had no occasion to deale with but for the necessity of using him for Mr. Bacon's business' (B.M. Lansdowne MSS. 88, No. 21).   [27] See below, pp. 24–30.

with them on shorter term than that at which they borrowed. Such operations are nearer to modern investment banking than to deposit banking proper, in which business success depends not upon borrowing long and relending short, but on maintaining a safe ratio between cash held in hand and the demand of customers for the withdrawal of their deposits. The alien brokers, whom a State Paper of the mid-1620's describes as 'putting forth at interest the moneys both of English and strangers' may have engaged in the former type of business.[28] And it is conceivable that the scriveners, who are usually credited with originating deposit banking in this country, were in fact doing no more than borrowing deposits on long-term and relending on short. There is abundant evidence that many scriveners accepted deposits, and the fact that they paid interest to depositors indicates that they had acquired rights of use over these deposits. But on the crucial question of the terms on which deposits might be withdrawn the authorities are silent.[29]

These still unresolved problems suggest that there may be some truth in the old theory that English deposit banking proper originated in the banking business of the goldsmiths. Moreover, since it is clear that deposits were already being accepted by some goldsmiths at least as early as the 1630's, it is perhaps not unreasonable to question the authenticity of the familiar argument that goldsmith banking did not develop before 1640 at the earliest. But even if some goldsmiths did accept deposits and acquire rights of use over them early in the reign of Charles I, the historical significance of their activity is to be found in connexion with the morbid matter of the search for the origins of English deposit banking rather than in their quantitative importance in the financial world of Caroline London.[30] In contrast with this, by the Restoration goldsmith bank-

[28] P.R.O. S.P. Charles I, 14/23.

[29] On the scriveners, see Tawney, *Introduction to Wilson*, pp. 96–101; H. C. Gutteridge, 'The Origin and Historical Development of the Profession of Notaries Public in England', in *Cambridge Legal Essays* (Cambridge, 1926), pp. 123–37; R. D. Richards, *The Early History of Banking in England* (1929), pp. 15–18; A. V. Judges, 'The Origins of English Banking', in *History*, xvi (1931), 140.

[30] On the goldsmiths, see W. R. Bisschop, *The Rise of the London Money Market 1640–1826* (1910), pp. 39–67; Tawney, *Introduction to Wilson*, pp. 93–95; Richards, op. cit., pp. 23–91; Judges, *History*, loc. cit., pp. 142–3. For the origins of the theory, accepted by both Richards and Bisschop, that goldsmith banking developed out of certain events in 1640 and at the beginning of the

ing had developed sufficiently for it to be not only a familiar feature of the financial landscape, but also an important means of supplying the financial requirements of Charles II. It is true that both James I and Charles I occasionally borrowed small sums from persons such as George and James Heriot, John Williams, Sir William Herrick, and John Acton, all of whom were described as goldsmiths, but these men were jewellers rather than bankers, most of them being persons who from time to time sold jewels or plate to the royal family, for which services they were known by such titles as 'the King's goldsmith' or 'the King's jeweller'.[31] Even if it should prove to be true that a number of goldsmiths had developed modest deposit banking businesses in the reign of Charles I, it would be absurd to suggest that the role of the goldsmith banker assumed more than insignificant proportions in the money market of that time. As financial intermediaries they were almost certainly less important than the scriveners, whose services the Crown used not at all, and far less important than the numerous merchants who raised loans at low rates to meet the demands of borrowers. Moreover, in neo-banking activities profit-seeking collectors of royal revenue may well have been more prominent than either scriveners or goldsmiths. Their opportunity to engage in these practices arose from the interval between the date at which revenues had to be collected and that at which they had to be paid into the Exchequer. The practice of lending out these revenues was profitable, especially as the collectors who indulged in it obviously did not pay interest to the Crown whose moneys they lent; it was also safe, provided that the lender kept a safe amount of cash in hand, out of which government tallies drawn upon the revenue might be met, a practice which is one of the essential skills of the deposit banker. The putting out of portions of the customs revenue to loan by the syndicates of business men to whom that revenue had been farmed is less akin to banking than these operations of collectors of directly adminis-

Civil War, see *The Mystery of the New Fashioned Goldsmiths or Bankers* (1676), printed in J. B. Martin, *The Grasshopper in Lombard Street* (1892), pp. 287–92.

[31] For evidence of royal borrowing from and through goldsmiths, P.R.O. Exchequer of Receipt, Order Books (Pells), E. 403/2727, fo. 195(*b*); E. 403/2730, fo. 59; E. 403/2732, fos. 37(*b*), 49(*b*); E. 403/2750, fo. 192; S.P. James I, 80/60, 62; Docquets, James I, bk. vii; Coll. Sign Man. Jac. I, vol. xii, no. 85; *Cal. S.P.D. (1611–18)*, p. 275; *(1629–31)*, p. 62. No single advance from any goldsmith to the Crown seems to have exceeded the sum of £5,000.

tered revenue, since revenues in farm were, of course, alienated to the farmers by the terms of their contract.[32]

The ordinary machinery of the money market, though adequate to the needs of the private borrower, was of little or no use to the Crown, whose demands for loans were enormously greater than those of even the largest private borrower. It is a commonplace that the Tudors and early Stuarts had to administer a modern State with medieval methods of finance, and the royal demand for loans had expanded no less than the other financial needs of the Crown. In the mid-Tudor period this problem had been shelved by the frequent and more or less regular recourse of royal borrowers, from Henry VIII to Elizabeth, to the great money market of Antwerp, the period from the last years of the former's reign to the end of the second decade of the latter's being the age of external borrowing *par excellence*. Although the Elizabethan government and its advisers were not without appreciation of the dangers of undue dependence upon foreign financiers, 'who serve all princes at once', the sharp break which was made with the Antwerp money market was forced by events rather than the result of deliberate planning. The economic rivalries which had come to a head in the mutually recriminatory economic sanctions of the English and Netherlands governments in 1563–4 were themselves exacerbating Anglo-Spanish political relations, which took a sharp turn for the worse in 1568–9 with the incident at San Juan de Ulloa and Elizabeth's seizure of the Genoese treasure. In these circumstances the financial connexion with Antwerp, however tenuous it had now become, was fraught with a host of dangers, and both in 1570 and in the following year Gresham was reporting that the discriminatory measures of the Duke of Alva were drying up the supply of loans for the English Crown.[33] Thus the pressure of events forced Elizabeth to look elsewhere for her loans, a movement which would in any case have been brought about by the precipitous decline upon whose brink Antwerp now stood. But in the 1560's and 1570's there appear to have been official hopes that an alternative source of loans might be found in Germany.[34] In these years the movements

---

[32] For an example of the practices of revenue collectors, see A. P. Newton, *Hist. MSS. Comm., Sackville MSS.* i, Introduction, p. xxi; on those of the farmers, see Ashton, 'Revenue Farming under the Early Stuarts', in *Econ. Hist. Rev.* 2nd ser. viii (1956), 319–20.

[33] S.P. Elizabeth, 74/19, 77/61.

[34] S.P. Elizabeth, 74/19, 77/2, 30, 105/73; B.M. Cottonian MSS. Cleopatra

of the Merchant Adventurers from one precarious cloth staple to another were to some extent paralleled by the government's tentative attempts to tap sources of German wealth. These measures were almost certainly not designed to find a German equivalent to the Antwerp money market, but to provide a source of loans which could from time to time be used to supplement the now far greater volume of domestic borrowings. In other words, the government probably envisaged that, with its exclusion from a declining Antwerp money market, it would become preponderantly dependent upon the resources of London for its loans. But with the failure of its German experiments, this dependence was to become nearly absolute. The contrast between the vast foreign borrowings of the mid-Tudor era and the very exceptional and relatively small external loans which were raised by the first two Stuarts is both impressive and significant. Apart from the 300,000 rixdollars raised from Christian IV of Denmark in 1620–1, and the £58,400 borrowed by Charles I on the Amsterdam money market in 1626, the foreign borrowings of the early Stuarts are of negligible importance.[35]

That royal borrowing, when once confined predominantly to England, should be centred on London was both inevitable and convenient. The economic, social, legal, and political tendencies of the period all favoured the growth of the metropolis. Expanding as the centre of a government, the volume of whose business was increasing year by year, and as the hub of the legal universe in an age of increased litigation, it was also becoming, as Professor Fisher tells us, more and more important as a centre of fashion where provincial incomes were spent.[36] And most important of all is the familiar theme of the expansion of London's commerce at the expense of, or, at the very least, disproportionately to that of the

F. vi, No. 16; J. W. Burgon, *The Life and Times of Sir Thomas Gresham* (1839), i. 334, 337–47; ii. 418–19; W. R. Scott, *Joint Stock Companies* (Cambridge, 1911), i. 53; F. C. Dietz, *English Public Finance (1558–1641)* (New York, 1932), pp. 26–27.

[35] For the loan from Christian IV, repaid in 1632, see P.R.O. S.P. Foreign (Denmark), bdle. v, fos. 215–215(*b*), 217–18, 244, 261–2; bdle. xii, fo. 365; bdle. xv, fos. 153, 299–299(*b*); MS. Cal. of Sackville MSS. 1111, 6920–1; T. Rymer, *Foedera* (3rd edn., The Hague, 1735–45), vii, pt. iii, p. 208; S. R. Gardiner, *History of England, 1603–1642* (1883–4), iii. 386; iv. 180; Dietz, op. cit., p. 187. For the loan at Amsterdam, see below, pp. 64–65.

[36] F. J. Fisher, 'The Development of London as a Centre of Conspicuous Consumption in the Sixteenth and Seventeenth Centuries', in *Roy. Hist. Soc. Trans.* 4th ser. xxx (1948), 37–50.

outports. This tendency had become very marked as early as the first half of the sixteenth century, when the relatively open commerce which marked that period had become increasingly concentrated along the short-distance route between London and Antwerp. And the growth of the great whale at the expense of the little fishes was no less marked when the advent of the more restrictive commercial policies of the Elizabethan period gave greater powers to the restrictionist elements among the chartered companies with their headquarters in the capital.[37] Although the early Stuart period saw some relaxation in this respect, the restrictive practices as to membership of companies in the old-established trades did not cease, and it has been suggested by one authority that the parliamentary agitation for free trade which was a permanent feature of the reign of James I was little more than the envious rantings of the disgruntled and declining outports.[38] Be this as it may, the growing concentration of liquid wealth in the capital was a development which was not inconvenient to the government as a borrower. With the exception of the general Forced Loans on letters of Privy Seal dispatched to gentlemen all over the country, the Crown hardly bothered to look outside London for its loans. Provincial borrowings, such as the £12,000 raised in 1616 and a further £12,000 in 1621 from the Cornish moneylender and tin magnate, Richard Robartes, are sufficiently exceptional to prove this rule.[39]

It has been shown that the machinery by which early seventeenth-century borrowers and lenders were brought into contact with one another was not appropriate to the special needs of government borrowing. But many of the persons from whom the Crown borrowed money were sufficiently prominent to make the use of such machinery unnecessary. Among them noblemen and persons influential about the Court are sometimes to be found. Those whom the King delighted to honour might sometimes find the wherewithal to provide for the Crown's needs out of purses which were already swollen with the royal bounty which itself had often been the chief factor out of which these needs had arisen. Thus the

[37] On these tendencies, see F. J. Fisher, 'Commercial Trends and Policy in Sixteenth Century England', in *Econ. Hist. Rev.* x (1940), 95–117.

[38] A. Friis, *Alderman Cockayne's Project and the Cloth Trade* (1927), *passim*.

[39] P.R.O. Patent Roll, 19 Jac. I, pt. 14; *Cal. S.P.D. (1611–18)*, pp. 412, 427. I am indebted to Mr. G. Hammersley for drawing my attention to the reference on the Patent Roll.

profligate Somerset lent £25,000 to James I in 1613,[40] while his successor in the enjoyment of the royal favour, Buckingham, claimed to have made disbursements amounting in all to over £30,000 in connexion with the bizarre and fruitless mission to Spain in 1623 in search of a bride for Prince Charles. In 1624 he lent £10,000 towards naval charges, and in the following year, or at the beginning of 1626, appears to have negotiated a further £10,000 for the fleet from the well-known moneylender, Sir Paul Bayning.[41] Diplomats such as Lord Digby, and military commanders such as Sir Horace Vere, sometimes found that they were called upon to raise and disburse money.[42] Many collectors of government revenue and treasurers of great disbursing departments were appointed only on the understanding, tacit or expressed, that they were prepared to make advances when required. In discussing this last category of lenders we move towards the world of commerce and finance proper, for the financial services which the Crown required from many of its revenue collectors and disbursing officials were such as to require them to be wealthy men of business, although in the former case the letting of revenues to farm, rather than their direct administration, was an expedient more likely to secure large-scale advances for the Crown. The role of a highly placed official of a disbursing department in connexion with government borrowing is perhaps best exemplified by the career of the wealthy merchant-financier, Sir William Russell, who was Naval Treasurer from 1618 until 1627, and again from 1630 to 1642. When occasion demanded, Russell paid out money considerably above the sums which he received from the Exchequer for naval purposes, the balance being carried over as 'surplusage' from the account of one year to that of the next. In addition, he was a prolific lender in the more conventional sense, not only for the naval service, but also to meet the more private requirements of the Crown. The profits of moneylending from borrowing cheap and relending at the statutory maximum rate of interest were not the only financial return on the investment

[40] P.R.O. Exchequer of Receipt, Order Book (Pells), E. 403/2733, fo. 84.
[41] Ibid. E. 403/2747, fo. 52(*b*); Coll. Sign Man. Car. I, vol. vi, no. 36; S.P. Charles I, 145/7; *Cal. S.P.D.* (*1623–5*), p. 206; (*1625–6*), p. 557.
[42] Both of these loans were made abroad, and both were for military purposes, Digby's £10,000 being lent on his way home from a diplomatic mission to Vienna in 1621 (*Cal. S.P.D.* (*1619–23*), p. 300; Gardiner, op. cit. iv. 222–3). In 1631 the government reached a settlement with Vere, whose disbursements of £5,071 in the Palatinate had long been outstanding. Vere settled for a cash payment of only £5,000 (Coll. Sign Man. Car. I, vol. xii, no. 63).

which Russell had made when he purchased his office from Sir Robert Mansell in 1618, for like many revenue officials, he was presented with a source of working capital in those years when the naval charges were insufficiently heavy to require the expenditure of the whole of the revenue appropriated to them.[43]

Hardly less concerned with the government service in an age when many public duties were performed by private enterprise were the farmers of the various branches of the customs revenue, and notably the great customs, whose prolific advances and overdrafts far in excess of what the government might expect from collectors of a directly administered customs revenue provided the strongest argument in favour of the retention of tax-farming in the face of bitter opposition to the system.[44] Individual customs farmers such as Sir William Garway, the head of a dynasty of customs farmers and the chief figure in the syndicate which farmed the great customs from 1604 to 1621, and Sir Paul Pindar, who dominated the farming syndicates in the reign of Charles I, were also prominent as individual lenders quite apart from their activities as contributors to syndicated loans.[45] Among the other prominent individual lenders were concessionaires of one sort or another such as the notorious projector, Sir William Cockayne, who, both in the years before and long after his ill-fated cloth-finishing project lent at least £27,000 to James I, and at the very end of his life became a farmer of the customs.[46] And it is not surprising to find that many of those merchants whose livelihood was to some extent bound up with their ability to obtain government and Court contracts were prominent as lenders. Such a person was the famous silkman and moneylender,

[43] On Russell, see R. Ashton, 'The Disbursing Official under the Early Stuarts: The Cases of Sir William Russell and Philip Burlamachi', in *B.I.H.R.* xxx (1957), 162–6. That office of this kind was not always a source of profit, however, is shown by the unfortunate career of Sir Allen Apsley, a Surveyor of Marine Victuals in the early years of Charles I's reign, although his financial difficulties seem not to have been solely attributable to debts which he incurred in the royal service. See below, pp. 165–6.

[44] On the farmers, see below, pp. 79–112; and Ashton, *Econ. Hist. Rev.* 2nd ser. viii (1956), 310–22.

[45] Of the two, Pindar was by far the more important individual lender.

[46] P.R.O. S.P. James I, 40/42, 50/75; Warrant Book James I, ii, fos. 132(*b*)–3; Docquets, James I, bk. x; MS. Cal. of Sackville MSS. Lord Treasurer's Warrant Book (1621–2), pp. 4–5, 20–21; Exchequer of Receipt, Order Books (Pells), E. 403/2729, fos. 82(*b*), 105(*b*), 235; E. 403/2730, fos. 92, 227(*b*); E. 403/2731, fos. 84(*b*), 99; E. 403/2732, fos. 93(*b*), 194(*b*); E. 403/2733, fo. 202; E. 403/2735, fo. 164(*b*); E. 403/2741, fo. 52; *A.P.C. (1621–3)*, pp. 83–84, 92–93, 99–100.

Sir Baptist Hicks, who had already lent money to James before the union of the two Crowns, and who, after this event, provided the royal household and wardrobe with fine stuffs, proving himself to be a very accommodating creditor who was willing to deliver goods on long credit, as well as to prolong many of his numerous loans to the Crown.[47]

In the Crown's use of alien residents in London—or at least, in this case, of naturalized foreigners—there was nothing novel. The greatest of these successors to Palavicino and Spinola of the Elizabethan period and the Bardi, Peruzzi, and Ricardi of the Middle Ages was the mighty Philip Burlamachi, the greatest financier of the age. Burlamachi's financial services to the Crown, beginning in a modest enough way in the second decade of the reign of James I, attained spectacular dimensions in the 1620's, when the government was assuming an ever-increasing volume of military and diplomatic commitments on the Continent. Prominent as a negotiator on the bill market with correspondents in every notable centre of financial activity from Amsterdam to Madrid, Burlamachi performed invaluable services in lending his credit to the government, which instructed its agents abroad to raise the funds they required by drawing bills of exchange upon him. And in the more than likely event of his not being repaid when these bills fell due, they might be met by his sale of further bills. But such operations were neither the only nor the most important of his financial services. Especially after 1624, he made a number of prodigious loans to the government, and during the same period he frequently acted as paymaster to English expeditionary forces on the Continent, including the English troops in the service of the Dutch. In this capacity he was often called upon to pay out vast sums of money both in advance and in excess of his receipts from the government.

[47] P.R.O. S.P. James I, 26/103, 32/68, 36/42, 38/46–47, 60, 40/67; Coll. Sign Man. Jac. I, vol. viii, no. 15; MS. Cal. of Sackville MSS. M. 1047, Lord Treasurer's Warrant Book (1621–2), pp. 4–5, 20–21; Exchequer of Receipt, Order Books (Pells), E. 403/2727, fos. 69(b), 247(b); E. 403/2731, fos. 139(b), 160(b); E. 403/2733, fo. 64(b); E. 403/2737, fo. 100(b); E. 403/2738, fos. 130–130(b); E. 403/2740, fo. 134; E. 403/2741, fo. 52; E. 403/2745, fo. 177(b); E. 403/2746, fo. 131; B.M. Harleian MSS. 3796, fo. 22; Cal. S.P.D. (1625–6), p. 580; A.P.C. (1621–3), pp. 83–84, 92–93, 99–100; (1625–6), pp. 466–7; Hist. MSS. Comm., Salisbury MSS. xvi. 408–9. It can be established that Hicks lent at least £33,000 to James I and Charles I. This total does not include money owed for wares delivered on credit, nor a number of his substantial contributions to syndicated loans.

And in loans for the naval service he was second only to Russell. In the matter of government borrowing, the 1620's may, with little exaggeration, be called the era of Burlamachi, but the diminution of his usefulness to the Crown with the advent both of more pacific policies and of financial retrenchment after 1629 ultimately brought about his ruin, for the government's neglect to repay its long-standing obligations to him was the chief cause of his bankruptcy in 1633.[48] The fact that Burlamachi completely dwarfs the other alien lenders of the period reflects, however, the grandiose scale of his financial operations rather than the insignificance of theirs. For a number of other alien merchants performed services as lenders which were no less valuable than those of native-born moneylenders such as Hicks, Bayning, and Pindar. Such lenders were Sir Peter Vanlore, the Anglo-Flemish jeweller, speculator in licences and Crown lands and moneylender to fashionable Court and aristo-cratic circles, and Philip Jacobson, who was prominently associated with Burlamachi in a number of transactions involving the trans-mission of funds to the Continent and their disbursement there on behalf of the government.[49] Perhaps the most interesting of them all is Sir William Courteen, whose colourful career as a moneylender, as the financial expert in a family firm which was engaged in com-modity trade between England, the Low Countries, and France, as an illegal exporter of bullion, for which offence he, like Burlamachi and Vanlore, was fined in the great Star Chamber trial of 1619, as a colonizer in the West Indies, and as the originator of the enter-prise which caused the monopolists of the East India Company to

[48] On Burlamachi, see A. V. Judges, 'Philip Burlamachi: A Financier of the Thirty Years' War', in *Economica*, vi (1926), 285–300; and Ashton, *B.I.H.R.* loc. cit., pp. 167–74.

[49] It can be established that Vanlore lent more than £35,000 to James I, and at least £10,000 to Charles I (P.R.O. Exchequer of Receipt, Order Books (Pells), E. 403/2727, fos. 71–75, 87; E. 403/2729, fo. 88; E. 403/2734, fos. 94(*b*)–96(*b*); E. 403/2737, fos. 34–35, 87; E. 403/2740, fos. 175(*b*), 187–187(*b*); E. 403/2741, fo. 52; E. 403/2745, fos. 10(*b*), 21, 214(*b*); Issue Book, E. 403/1736, no foliation; S.P. James I, 40/67; Coll. Sign Man. Car. I, vol. i, no. 76; MS. Cal. of Sackville MSS. Lord Treasurer's Warrant Book (1621–2), pp. 4–5, 20–21, and M. 1047; B.M. Harleian MSS. 3796, fo. 22; *A.P.C. (1621–3)*, pp. 83–84, 92–93, 99–100). Jacobson's share in syndicated loans, as distinct from his continental disbursements, amounted to more than £15,000, which includes his share in the £8,000 lent with two other aliens in 1616, and in two loans totalling £26,000 made in conjunction with Burlamachi in 1621–2 (P.R.O. Coll. Sign Man. Jac. I, vol. viii, no. 15; Docquets, James I, bdle. xii; Exchequer of Receipt, Order Books, E. 403/2736, fo. 109; E. 403/2737, fo. 24(*b*); MS. Cal. of Sackville MSS. 7721).

quake in their shoes in the 1630's, is eminently worth the attention of the business historian. His loans to the Crown, though few in number, were substantial in amount. In 1613 and 1614 he lent £18,500 to James I, and Charles I borrowed a further £16,500 from him in the early years of his reign.[50] It is only when compared with the massive advances of Burlamachi that the services of such lenders as these appear small.

But important as such individual lenders were, their resources alone were quite inadequate to meet the needs of the royal borrower. Individual merchant-financiers might on occasion be capable of raising sums of between £5,000 and £15,000 without unduly straining their resources, while exceptional magnates like Burlamachi and Russell might have almost unlimited resources of credit. But the main point about these latter lenders is precisely that they were exceptional, and it has already been shown that the size and term of royal borrowings was frequently such as to be completely beyond the resources of the normal moneylender. One method of overcoming this difficulty was the use of loan syndicates. These might be simply informal *ad hoc* combinations of individual lenders such as the aliens Sir Noel de Caron, Robert de la Barre, and Philip Jacobson, who together lent £8,000 in January 1616,[51] or Hicks, Cockayne, and Vanlore, who lent £30,000 for the Palatinate in the summer of 1621.[52] On the other hand, they might be groups of merchants whose special position in one way or another rendered them an obvious source of loans. The loans from large syndicates of alien merchants, such as the £14,500 raised in 1607 from certain 'merchant strangers' in London, and the £20,000 from the Dutch merchants in London in 1617, the latter loan being negotiated through the good offices of the Dutch ambassador, the same Sir Noel de Caron who had himself lent money to the Crown in the previous year, are such examples.[53] But more significant and impor-

[50] P.R.O. Exchequer of Receipt, Receipt Books (Pells), E. 401/1890, 1892, no foliation; Order Books (Pells), E. 403/2733, fo. 163; E. 403/2745, fos. 11, 13(b), 22(b); E. 403/2749, fo. 109; S.P. James I, 115/115; S.P. Charles I, 4/128, 112/67, 286/43; Patent Roll, 12 Jac. I, pt. 12; *Cal. S.P.D. (1611–18)*, p. 197; B.M. Harleian MSS. 3796, fo. 22.

[51] P.R.O. Coll. Sign Man. Jac. I, vol. viii, no. 15; Exchequer of Receipt, Order Book (Pells), E. 403/2736, fo. 109.

[52] P.R.O. MS. Cal. of Sackville MSS. Lord Treasurer's Warrant Book (1621–2), pp. 4–5, 20–21; Exchequer of Receipt, Order Book (Pells), E. 403/2741, fo. 52; *A.P.C. (1621–3)*, pp. 83–84, 92–93, 99–100.

[53] B.M. Lansdowne MSS. 151, fo. 83; Lansdowne MSS. 165, fos. 282–3(b);

tant is the use which the Crown made of bodies of government concessionaires, whose privileges might make them all the more responsive to its financial demands. Of the greatest of these syndicates, the farmers of the customs, mention has already been made. More sporadically, the government raised loans from other groups, such as the members of a number of the syndicates of contractors for the purchase and resale of Crown lands, who lent £30,000 in the autumn and winter of 1609,[54] and the two successive groups of monopolistic soapboiling companies, which incurred such unpopularity in the 1630's, and whose advance payments of rent added to the financial advantages which the government undoubtedly derived from these monopolies.[55] Although the East India Company was occasionally called upon to lend money to the Crown,[56] it is at first somewhat surprising to find that the government apparently paid little attention to the possibility of extorting loans from the great chartered companies which dominated so large a part of the country's foreign trade. As will appear, it preferred to approach lenders through other channels.

The use of syndicates was, however, no more than a variation on the familiar theme of the direct relationship between borrower and lender. With it we move only one step further in the direction of royal utilization of wider sources of loanable funds than could be tapped via direct loans from individual merchants. But in heavy periods of government borrowing, these more obvious sources were patently inadequate, and, in such exigencies, what was needed above all else were intermediaries between the royal borrower and the money market, that is, not the few outstanding moneylenders for whom such machinery was obviously unnecessary, but the more widely diffused sources of loanable funds which, though individually unspectacular, were in their totality usually far more

---

P.R.O. S.P. James I, 91/1; MS. Cal. of Sackville MSS. M. 1047; *Cal. S.P.D.* (*1611–18*), p. 447.

[54] *Hist. MSS. Comm., Sackville MSS.* i. 183. Sometimes the syndicates themselves made advance payments of moneys due by them (P.R.O. Exchequer of Receipt, Order Books (Pells), E. 403/2728, fo. 252; E. 403/2732, fo. 32). For the method of disposing of Crown lands by the use of such syndicates, see especially R. H. Tawney, 'The Rise of the Gentry', in *Econ. Hist. Rev.* xi (1941), 30–31.

[55] P.R.O. S.P. Charles I, 294/62, 304/12, 311/38, 314/37; Docquets, Charles I, bk. xvii; Patent Roll, 13 Car. I, pt. 29; B.M. Harleian MSS. 3796, fo. 22.

[56] See below, pp. 171–2, 178–80.

considerable than the loans of individual merchants. It is a common-place of industrial and agricultural history that the function of the middleman becomes more important in proportion as the production of, or demand for, a particular commodity becomes more widely dispersed. As with industry and agriculture, so with finance. If the Crown was to exploit the resources of the money market to the full, it must raise its loans not simply from the few great lenders, whose concentrations of wealth and connexions with the government made them sitting targets, but also from smaller men, who were far more numerous and, for that reason, less easily accessible.

To a limited extent this problem was solved by the greater financiers themselves. For it would be absurd to assume, even if the evidence did not point to a contrary conclusion, that royal demands for loans from these financiers or syndicates of them were invariably met out of their immediately available cash resources. In many such cases it is quite certain that the circle of effective lenders was much wider than is suggested by the recorded names of the lenders, and that the greater financiers were often acting as intermediaries between the Crown and the money market. The evidence relating to such transactions is abundant, and it is necessary to give only a few examples. Many of the extremely substantial sums which were lent by that prolific lender, Sir William Russell, were raised by him by borrowing. The loan of £30,000 borrowed in equal contributions from Sir Baptist Hicks, Sir William Cockayne, and Sir Peter Vanlore in 1621, was raised by each of these lenders by further borrowing, while Hicks borrowed the whole of the further £10,000 which he lent to Charles I in 1626. It was claimed that a great part of the money which Sir William Courteen and Sir Paul Pindar lent to Charles I in the course of his reign had been borrowed by them from widows and orphans, a category into which many of the hard-pressed lenders to the Crown were apt to place their creditors when petitioning for repayment. Of the vast sum of £85,000 lent by Pindar in 1638–9 it was said that part was provided 'out of his own estate' and part out of 'moneys taken up on credit'. And a close examination of the principal sources of loanable funds utilized by the greatest loan syndicate of the period, the farmers of the great customs, yields similar conclusions. For by no means all of the advance payments of rent and the other loans which were made by the farmers could be provided out of current receipts of the revenue which had been leased to them. The flow of customs revenue was seasonal rather than regular, in which circumstances a royal demand for an advance from the farmers might not coincide with the availability of the necessary receipts of customs revenue, a difficulty which was aggravated by the fact that the farmers appear to have used the customs revenue as a source of working capital for private financial transactions. But, like other lenders, they were able to borrow from the money market in general, and re-lend to the Crown, probably at a profit. In these circumstances one of two alternative procedures might be adopted. The money might be provided by each member of the syndicate separately, either out of his own funds or by borrowing, or the syndicate as a whole might borrow upon its joint bond.[57]

The extent to which those individuals who frequently lent money to the Crown provided the sums required by borrowing, and thus in a real sense acted as intermediaries between the Crown and the money market, obviously varied with different lenders and circumstances. In the cases of prolific lenders such as Burlamachi, Russell, and, to a lesser extent, Hicks, such operations were common, which is hardly surprising since they were probably also profitable. Information about the terms at which these lenders were able to borrow to raise money to be re-lent to the Crown is meagre and in most cases it is impossible to state with any certainty whether they were able to make a profit out of the re-employment of borrowed funds. In this respect it is both interesting and significant that Russell's credit at the end of the period of Charles I's personal government was good enough for him to be able to borrow at 7 per cent. at a time when the statutory maximum rate of interest at which he invariably lent to the government was 8 per cent.[58] It seems probable that the customs farmers and other government concessionaires were able, by virtue of their concessions, to raise money cheaply in the city. The courtier, Lord Goring, who tried his hand at customs farming over the crucial years 1638–40, had previously claimed that 'it was the Kings farmes and not the farmers which

---

[57] For evidence in the cases of (i) Russell, see P.R.O. Coll. Sign Man. Jac. I, vol. xii, no. 20; vol. xvii, no. 17; Exchequer Order Books (Pells), E. 403/2739, fo. 156; E. 403/2743, fo. 62; (ii) Hicks, Cockayne, and Vanlore, S.P. James I, 124/33; A.P.C. (1621–3), pp. 99–100; (1625–6), p. 466; (iii) Courteen and Pindar, B.M. Sloane MSS. 3515, fo. 27, A Brief Narrative of the Cases of Sir William Courteen and Sir Paul Pindar, p. 9; (iv) the customs farmers, Ashton, Econ. Hist. Rev. 2nd ser. viii (1956), 319–22.

[58] S.P. Charles I, 441/7.

raysed credit to borrow money'.[59] Some of the more wealthy Livery Companies were sometimes able to borrow at well below the statutory maximum rate, presumably because their credit was good, but this fact did not always enable them to make a profit or even to avoid a loss out of their connexion with government borrowing.[60]

Although the financial contacts of these principal lenders were enormously wider than those of the Crown, in the times of its greatest need the latter turned also to another intermediary which was capable of delving still deeper into the sources of loanable funds which still remained to be tapped in the city. This was the municipal machinery of the Corporation of London, the traditional method which had been employed by Tudor and medieval governments to raise many of their largest loans in the city. This practice, which reflects one of the most characteristic features of Tudor and early Stuart administration—the centrally controlled use of local authorities—was to assume a far greater significance under the early Stuarts and to undergo further adaptation during the Interregnum.[61] The use of the Corporation as a loan contractor was, of course, simply one of many purposes to which the municipal machinery could be put, and in the matter of government borrowing, no less than in those of industrial policy and corn provision, the crux of the matter lay in the simple fact that there was no easy alternative approach to the citizens in general, save through their representatives, the Lord Mayor, aldermen, and common councilmen. Hence in all of the heaviest periods of government borrowing the Corporation of London played a prominent role.

The loans which were raised by the early Stuarts through the machinery of the Corporation are sufficiently important and well documented to merit two chapters to themselves, where the general observations which are outlined here are illustrated in some detail.[62] Royal negotiations for such a loan usually began with a polite and often flattering letter to the Lord Mayor and Common Council, informing them of the King's need for money and of his confidence that the Corporation, which had served the Crown so well in the past, would not fail it now. If the first request was met with excuses

---

[59] B.M. Stowe MSS. 326, fo. 51.

[60] For the rather exceptional circumstances arising out of the financial services of the Livery Companies, see below, pp. 115–17, 135–7, 140–1.

[61] For the Interregnum, see W. P. Harper, 'Public Borrowing (1640–60)' (Univ. of London. M.Sc., Econ. Thesis, 1927), *passim*.

[62] See below, pp. 113–53, 180–3.

and temporization, as in 1626 and 1640, or, if there was undue delay in raising the required sum, as in 1617, the tone of the government's letters became sharper and sometimes even abusive. Once the matter of terms had been settled, the onus of raising the money lay entirely with the Corporation. It might be provided by directly assessing the inhabitants of the different wards, using aldermen and common councilmen as collectors, a basic theme on which there were a number of minor variations. Alternatively the onus of raising the money might be transferred to the Livery Companies, each of which was rated to provide a proportion of the money in accordance with its wealth, its fixed assessment towards the provision of corn for municipal storage usually being the standard of judgement. Thus yet another intermediary might be interposed between royal borrower and ultimate lender, and the methods which were employed by the companies to raise the sums assessed upon them were various. They, too, could borrow by having recourse to a graded assessment of members, position in the company hierarchy being the criterion of relative affluence. When this expedient was inopportune, they might borrow on the security of their own bonds or of mortgage of their real or personal property, from a few of the richer members of the company or even from outsiders. Often enough a combination of several or all of these methods was employed.[63]

To these two methods employed by the Corporation of London in its capacity as loan contractor a third must be added. On occasions it raised loans for the Crown not by a general assessment of prominent citizens or of the Livery Companies, but by limiting the circle of contributors to the aldermanry. The occasional use of this additional method can probably be ascribed to the fact that there must have been occasions when a number of recent financial demands of this and a similar type rendered impolitic a more general approach to the citizens.[64]

The Crown's use of the machinery of municipal government in the city thus enabled it to tap sources of loanable funds which would hardly have been available to it without such assistance. But the financial services of the Corporation did not stop here. Many of the foreign borrowings of the mid-Tudor period had been secured on the Corporation's bonds, and, in most of the loans raised through

---

[63] For examples, see below, pp. 116, 116–17 note, 136–7, 140–1.
[64] For corroboratory evidence, see below, pp. 118–21, 129–31, 138–40.

the Corporation from 1617 onwards, this system was adapted for use in borrowing at home. Thus to the functions of loan contractor, which have been described above, the Corporation came to add those of loan guarantor. In contrast to the domestic loans of the pre-1617 period, it not only raised the money, but also lent its credit to the government; in contrast to the foreign loans of the mid-Tudor period secured on the Corporation's bond, it not only lent its credit, but also raised the money itself. While, therefore, the royal use of the Corporation of London in connexion with government borrowing was in a real sense a traditional financial expedient, it became a more highly developed and organized matter under the early Stuarts.

Parallel with this went developments in the use of the municipal treasury, the Chamber of London, in connexion with these loans.[65] Owing to the fact that the surviving Chamberlain's accounts do not pre-date 1633, it is impossible to tell how far these developments had been anticipated in the Tudor period or, indeed, before 1617. From this date onwards, however, it is possible, with the aid of the surviving accounts and associated documents,[66] to reconstruct the essential characteristics of the role of the Chamber in connexion with government borrowing. Although this role was to become more important during the Civil War and Interregnum, most of its functions, which have been described by Mr. Harper in his valuable study of government borrowing in this period,[67] were anticipated, albeit sporadically, under the early Stuarts. The first of these functions was to act as a place of safe deposit and receipt for contributions to loans in the interval between their collection and the date of their payment into the Exchequer or to disbursing departments. This was not, however, an invariable practice, since on some occasions individual lenders or companies paid their money into the Exchequer either directly or via specially appointed treasurers. Secondly, when the government's need for the loan money was too urgent to await the slow process of assessment and subscription, the Chamber sometimes made advances of portions of the loan

---

[65] For the importance of the Chamber, in municipal finance, see M. C. Wren, 'The Chamber of London in 1633', in *Econ. Hist. Rev.* 2nd ser. i (1948), 46–53.

[66] C. of L.R.O. City Cash Accounts, 1/1–1/4, Royal Contract Estates Papers, *passim*. The latter are documents relating to the conveyance of royal lands to the Corporation of London in satisfaction of the loans of 1617 and 1625 and further advances in 1628 (see below, pp. 132–5).

[67] W. P. Harper, op. cit., *passim*.

money before an equivalent amount had been received from contributors. Naturally, it reimbursed itself for these ways and means advances as contributions from individual lenders came into its hands, and, in so far as the funds out of which it had made these advances were moneys which had been deposited with it, and notably the Orphans' Fund, it was in a limited sense acting as a banker. Thirdly, on at least one occasion, that of the loan of £60,000 made to Charles I in 1625, the Chamber was required to make up the deficiency in the total sum provided by contributors, when this had fallen short of the required amount. This was a form of underwriting operation which had arisen out of the fact that the municipal authorities had originally undertaken to raise the whole of the money required by the Crown, and, on this occasion at least, were held responsible for any deficiency in the total sum subscribed. To its functions as a place of safe-deposit, a maker of ways and means advances, and an underwriter, the Chamber sometimes added that of a subsidizer of contributors, whether these were individual lenders or companies. Such subsidies were treated as interest-bearing loans to the contributors, and similar advances were sometimes made by the Livery Companies when loans were assessed upon them, and individual contributors were unable to raise their quotas except by borrowing. Finally, on one occasion, that of the much-prolonged loan of 1617, the Chamber made unilateral interest payments to lenders. This was the first loan of the period for which, as well as assuming the responsibility of raising the money, the Corporation also lent its credit to the government, which borrowed from the citizens not on the security of royal but of municipal bonds. These interest payments were unilateral in the sense that they were made to individual lenders out of the Chamber despite the fact that no such payments had been made to the Chamber by the Crown. Hence they throw into sharp relief the precise nature of the Corporation's role as loan guarantor which was, after 1617, more often than not added to its normal function of loan contractor. Although it was, as the municipal authorities repeatedly insisted, in no sense a principal debtor, its role being that of surety to the government, its bonds might be forfeit if interest payments were not observed. Moreover, while it would be technically incorrect from the legal point of view to describe the Corporation as borrowing from the citizens to relend to the Crown, in actual fact its functions lay somewhere between those of surety and banker, transcending those of the surety in the sense that it was responsible not only for guaranteeing loans but also for raising the money.[68]

It would be incorrect to assume that the Chamber necessarily performed all these functions in connexion with every loan which the Crown raised from the Corporation of London. For instance, although it made up the deficiency in the contributions to the loan of 1625, it had not done so in the case of that of 1617, when the contributions had fallen short of the total required by the Crown by a much larger amount.[69] Nevertheless, although there was no written body of financial procedure which formulated rules to be observed in the raising of loans for the government, by the end of the period certain methods had already been used frequently enough to be considered as standard measures for meeting given financial contingencies.

That the Crown's use of the Corporation of London for purposes of government borrowing was confined mainly to notable periods of deficit borrowing, which represent the peak periods of government borrowing in this period, is hardly surprising. The greater the volume of loans required in any given year, the greater was the inadequacy of the resources of the normal range of lenders from whom money could be borrowed directly, and consequently the greater the need for extraordinary machinery to raise the sums required. To this extent at least the Crown's choice of expedients in the matter of government borrowing was dependent upon the nature of its demand for loans, which is the subject of the chapter which follows.

[68] For examples of these functions performed by the Chamber, see below, pp. 120, 125–6, 128–9, 130, 137–9, 140, 141, 150–2.

[69] See below, pp. 125, 128.

II

THE ROYAL DEMAND FOR LOANS

GOVERNMENTS in all periods have found the need to borrow money both to render their revenue more flexible by making it available at the time when it is most needed, and to overcome difficulties arising out of the fact that on occasions the total volume of that revenue is physically inadequate to meet the required level of expenditure. In the chapter that follows, the former type of borrowing is described as *anticipation* and the latter as *deficit borrowing*, although it will be seen that, in certain of the financial operations of the government, the distinction between the two types of borrowing sometimes becomes blurred.

The need for the first type of borrowing has been aptly described by Adam Smith:

> Supposing that the sovereign should have, what he scarce ever has, the immediate means of augmenting his revenue in proportion to the augmentation of his expense, yet still the produce of the taxes, from which this increase of revenue must be drawn, will not begin to come into the treasury till perhaps ten or twelve months after they are imposed. . . . An immediate and great expense . . . will not wait for the gradual and slow returns of the new taxes. In this exigency government can have no other resource but in borrowing.[1]

The essence of the situation here described is the delay between the time at which the government requires the money and that at which it is available to it. In addition to these normal delays, in some cases early Stuart governments had to wait a considerable period of time before some of their revenues were available as the direct result of a definite stipulation made by the granting authority. Such delays were most marked in the case of parliamentary subsidies granted as extraordinary revenue. In face of the alarming but familiar fiscal phenomenon of the ossification of the subsidy, the granting of multiple subsidies had become the established rule by the accession of James I, but the collection of these subsidies was

---

[1] *Wealth of Nations* (Everyman edn.), ii. 392.

usually spread out over a matter of years, it often being stipulated that only part of the sum granted should be collected immediately.[2]

The difference between these two types of delay can best be illustrated by examples of loans which were made in anticipation of parliamentary subsidies. In June 1628 parliament voted Charles I the large supply of five subsidies, and on 8 June, a few days before this grant was made, certain members of the Privy Council lent £9,600 on the first of these subsidies for supply of the fleet intended to relieve La Rochelle. But it was not only the currently due subsidy which was anticipated, for, either in the same month or at the beginning of July, a loan of £5,000 was raised from John Bland and Hugh Perry, and was assigned upon the third of the five subsidies. The general purpose of both of these loans was the same—to render the subsidy available when needed. But the type of delay avoided was in each case different. In the case of the former loan, it was that normal administrative delay with which all students of the impact of the directives of Tudor and Stuart central governments upon local authorities are familiar; in that of the latter it was an expressed delay stipulated by the parliament, which had ordered that the five subsidies were to be payable over a period of rather less than two years. And even this delay was an improvement on the usual terms of parliamentary grants.[3]

Unlike the parliamentary subsidies, the ordinary revenue of the Crown was available in every financial year. Here the most usual type of anticipation was probably the loan made by a collector or farmer of a branch of the revenue in advance of the date at which he was obliged to pay the sum required into the Exchequer. In the case of a collector of the revenue the sums lent were simply an advance on his collections, while, in that of a revenue farmer, it was a portion of his rent which was anticipated. In each case these advance payments might be made either directly into the Exchequer or to assignees who presented tallies to the collector or farmer concerned. As in the examples which have been given of the anticipation of extraordinary revenue in the case of the parliamentary subsidies of 1628, ordinary revenue might also be anticipated by loans made by persons other than collectors or farmers of that revenue, and secured by a tally or tallies levied upon the relevant branch or branches of that revenue. It would, however, be incorrect to assume that all loans which were secured on particular branches of the revenue were designed specifically to anticipate that revenue. It would be dangerous to dichotomize between those loans against which a branch or branches of the revenue were pledged and those where this was not the case, in the hope that this distinction will afford some indication of the purpose for which the government raised any particular loan. In other words, it is not true that all loans which were raised on the security of revenue were anticipations, and that all other loans represent one form or another of deficit borrowing. In actual fact loans might be raised for the purpose of financing a deficit or managing the debt, but might nevertheless be secured upon a branch of the revenue falling due several years ahead. This mortgaging of the future might be done in the hope that the revenue of these future years might be sufficiently expanded or the expenditure sufficiently reduced for the government to be able to repay these loans out of future budget surpluses. Conversely, loans on every type of security other than that of revenue were frequently raised with the idea of anticipating revenue. As might be expected, the nature of the security offered in connexion with a particular financial transaction affords clues not so much to the purpose for which these particular loans were raised as to the prevailing state of the royal credit and the preference of a particular lender for a particular type of security.

The type of borrowing with which Adam Smith was particularly concerned in the passage which was quoted at the beginning of this chapter was the anticipation of revenue.[4] But when he indicates that the sovereign rarely has 'the immediate means of augmenting his revenue in proportion to the augmentation of his expense', he is clearly referring to a different type of situation in which borrowing is necessary. In other words, governments also need to borrow to deal with financial situations which have arisen out of the physical inadequacy of the revenue. Under the early Stuarts such deficit borrowing—as distinct from revenue anticipation—took two main forms. These were borrowing to bridge deficits and borrowing to manage the debt which arose out of these deficits. In the former case the government could deal with an existing gap between revenue and expenditure in either, or more usually both of two

---

[4] Smith's own definition of 'anticipation' was, of course, different from that interest and to achieve a gradual amortization of the principal (op. cit. ii. over a period of years, the sum pledged being sufficient both to discharge the interest and to achieve a gradual amortization of the principal (op. cit. ii. 394–5).

ways. It could virtually ignore the gap by allowing current bills to pile up unpaid, and this somewhat negative expedient was, of course, a form of borrowing; or it could bridge the gap by fresh borrowing of a more formal kind, an example of which is the loan of £69,000 which was raised through the Corporation of London in the early part of 1608. The purpose of this operation seems to have been the payment of a number of bills currently due on the half-year's ordinary account.[5] The deficits which were to be bridged, or, more usually, partially bridged, by such borrowing consisted chiefly of tradesmen's bills and debts due to government servants, officials, pensioners, and annuitants. In 1615 Lord Chief Justice Coke divided the royal debt resulting from these deficits into 'eating debts, such as were taken up at interest; the second crying debts, due to soldiers, mariners, tradesmen and such as live on labour, the third pressing debts, but named them not, nor explained not his meaning therein'.[6] Although the distinction between Coke's last two categories of royal debt is as obscure to the historian as it was to the mystified contemporary reporter, a careful analysis of the constituent items of the early Stuart debt suggests that the interest-bearing items of the debt consisted chiefly of formal loans taken up at interest. It is true that the debts to tradesmen usually contained an element of effective interest, but in most cases this seems to have been contained in the price of the wares, and was therefore based primarily upon the seller's estimate of the time which he would have to wait before receiving satisfaction.[7] In these circumstances it would appear that it was often cheaper for the Crown to leave unpaid bills to pile up rather than to borrow to pay off some or all of these bills which could not be met out of current revenue. In many cases this was done, but the government's frequent recourse to borrowing to bridge deficits, therefore involving itself in an

---

[5] B.M. Lansdowne MSS. 164, fos. 393–4, 433; P.R.O. S.P. James I, 34/20, 45/116; Warrant Book James I, ii, fo. 112; Exchequer of Receipt, Issue Book, E. 403/1707, no foliation; Order Book, E. 403/2728, fos. 42(b), 46, 124(b), 184; C. of L.R.O. Remembrancia, ii, No. 310 (hereafter cited as Remembrancia).

[6] J. Spedding, *The Life and Letters of Francis Bacon* (1861–74), v. 199.

[7] The difference between the price of goods sold to private customers and those which were sold for the royal use was often very considerable. Thus, early in Lionel Cranfield's career in the royal service, he resolved that 'the king shall pay no more than other men do, and he shall pay ready money; and if we cannot have it in one place, we will have it in another' (G. Goodman, *The Court of King James the First* (1839 edn., ed. J. Brewer), i. 309–10).

increased debt because of the element of interest on these borrowings, is explicable mainly in terms of the need to preserve the royal
credit, and perhaps in the circumstances that failure to act might
be reflected in a rise in the current price of wares purchased by the
Crown.

So far two elements of royal debt have been considered, those
comprising bills left unpaid and those consisting of the principal
and interest on loans which had been raised to pay off currently due
bills. To these two items of debt a third should be added, for the
process whereby these bills were paid by deficit-bridging loans was
not identical with the more sophisticated modern practice of fund-
ing the floating debt. The reason for this is that under the early
Stuarts most of these loans—though often prolonged—were short-
term obligations of six months or, at the most, a year. In these circumstances the need for further borrowing to manage the debt
becomes immediately apparent. Unlike the deficit-bridging borrowing which has just been described, borrowing for purposes of debt
management was not designed to pay off bills due on current
account, but to repay loans which had been raised to liquidate these
items, or to discharge those bills which had not been paid off either
out of revenue or by borrowing in the years during which they had
originally fallen due. The heavy borrowings which took place in
1607, of which the most important example is the loan of £120,000
raised from the farmers of the great customs in the latter part of
that year, were undertaken largely with this object in view.[8]

A further method of managing the debt was the renewal of existing obligations by prolongation. This is, in effect, what was involved
in the process of allowing bills to pile up, but it is applicable also to
borrowing both to bridge deficits and to manage the debt. Dis-
regarding Gresham's celebrated maxim of financial statecraft that
it is better to borrow to repay debts than to prolong them, the
government frequently turned its short-term debt into long by
repeated prolongation of maturing obligations. Some of the most
outstanding examples of this tendency are to be found in the use of
Forced Loans on letters of Privy Seal. The first of the Stuart Forced
Loans, which was raised in 1604–5, yielded £111,891 and although
it was ultimately repaid, £20,362 of this sum was still due as late as
December 1609.[9] But a more dismal fate befell the contributors to

[8] R. Ashton, 'Deficit Finance in the Reign of James I', in *Econ. Hist. Rev.*
2nd ser. x (1957), 26.   [9] P.R.O. S.P. James I, 50/75.

the Forced Loan of 1611–12. This loan yielded £116,381, but as late as July 1618 the sum of £112,000 still remained to be repaid.[10] Indeed, as the early Stuart period progressed, Forced Loans came to approximate more and more nearly to taxes, and, despite official protestations to the contrary, the famous Loan of Five Subsidies of 1626–7 was, as its name clearly implies, little more than a thinly disguised tax.[11] But hardly less striking examples of the Crown's delays in repaying its loans can be found in many of its more normal borrowings in the city. Such a case was the very large loan of £100,000 which was raised from the aldermen of London in 1610. Like most other loans of this type, this was originally raised for one year, but the government was able to turn short-term debt into long by persuading the lenders to concede two prolongations. But by far the best example of the technique of managing the debt by the repeated prolongation of maturing obligations is provided by the loan of £96,466. 13s. 4d. which was raised through the Corporation of London in 1617. This loan was not repaid until 1628, during which year royal lands were conveyed to trustees of the Corporation in satisfaction of this and later obligations incurred by Charles I. And the Crown's laxity in meeting its obligations extended not only to the matter of principal repayments, but also to the payment of covenanted interest. While interest had been punctually paid on the loan of 1610, in the case of that of 1617 only one such payment was made, the remainder of the interest being repaid with the principal sum in 1628. And meanwhile the Crown had secured all the real benefits of a conversion operation when the statutory maximum rate of interest was reduced to 8 per cent. in 1624.[12]

The practice of managing the debt by repeated prolongation of loans was not confined to Forced Loans and to those loans which were raised through the medium of institutions such as the Corporation of London. Examples of the same tendency occurring in the case of loans which were raised directly from private persons are numerous, but one must suffice. In the autumn of 1621, the three notable merchant-financiers, Sir Baptist Hicks, Sir William Cockayne, and Sir Peter Vanlore, combined to lend £30,000 to the government in connexion with the Palatinate. The date of Cockayne's repayment is uncertain, but neither of his two co-lenders

[10] P.R.O. MS. Cal. of Sackville MSS. M. 1047.
[11] Gardiner, *History*, vi. 143–4, 148–50, 154–8; Dietz, op. cit., pp. 235–7.
[12] On these loans, see below, pp. 118–27.

was repaid within the stipulated year. It was not until July 1625 that arrangements were made to repay Vanlore, while Hicks had to wait until May of the following year before receiving satisfaction. Moreover, the long overdue repayment of these two lenders was in effect no more than a disguised prolongation, for each of them had to provide a further £10,000 on security in return for receiving fresh assignments.[13]

None of the expedients of debt management which have been described above afforded a permanent solution to the problems of Stuart deficit finance, for each of them involved not the liquidation of the debt but its postponement. The ultimate redemption of the debt could come only from more permanent measures such as the application of parliamentary subsidies or other extraordinary windfalls, the liquidation of royal capital, or the utilization of budget surpluses for purposes of debt redemption.

The first two of these expedients may be treated fairly summarily, since they are only incidental to the main theme of this chapter.[14] Together they represent by far the most important measures of permanent debt reduction over the whole of the early Stuart period. In the great period of debt reduction which took place during the four years which preceded the momentous debates over the Great Contract of 1610, during which period the debt was reduced from about £735,000 to about £280,000, the sum of £453,000 was made available from the grant of three subsidies and six fifteenths and tenths which had been voted by parliament in 1606. Over the same period sales of royal land and woods yielded over £445,000 and the facts that the money available from extraordinary taxation and the sale of Crown lands amounted to a sum which was considerably in excess of the debt of 1606, and that this debt was even then by no means entirely liquidated by 1610, serve to indicate that the unbalance between revenue and expenditure which had caused the rise in the debt was not notably checked even during a period when the government was straining almost every nerve to reduce that debt to manageable proportions.

It is broadly true to say that during the first two decades of the reign of James I, and certainly down to 1618 at the earliest, this unbalance arose preponderantly out of the King's failure to 'live of

---

[13] Ashton, *Econ. Hist. Rev.* 2nd ser. x (1957), 27.

[14] For a more detailed account and for extensive citation of the evidence upon which these conclusions are based, see ibid., pp. 20–24.

his own', that is, as the phrase was then understood by most contemporaries, to meet his ordinary expenditure out of ordinary
revenue. It was largely this failure, then, which gave rise to the
temporary expedients of borrowing both to bridge deficits and to
manage the debt, and to the ultimate and more permanent solutions
both of capital liquidation and the use of extraordinary taxation to
reduce a debt which had arisen primarily out of a state of ordinary
unbalance. The Crown might deplore the expedient of using parliamentary grants to defray this debt, thereby inevitably inviting
parliamentary criticism of royal improvidence. But, needless to say,
its regret was more than matched by that of parliament itself. That
the extraordinary revenues which were voted by parliament should
be applied to defray extraordinary charges such as the cost of royal
funerals, weddings, coronations, and, above all, wars, was both
natural and proper, although, as the word 'subsidy' perhaps suggests to the modern reader, it was not considered necessary that the
yield of these extraordinary parliamentary revenues should be
sufficient to meet the *total* level of extraordinary expenditure. A
clear and familiar illustration of this is to be found in the financial
history of the later Elizabethan period, when the parliamentary
grants towards the expenses of the Spanish war and the Irish revolt
had to be supplemented by revenue from other sources.[15] That
extraordinary revenues should be used to defray debts which had
arisen out of the failure to balance the *ordinary* account was, however, a violation of the central dualism between ordinary and
extraordinary revenue and expenditure which lay at the heart of
financial policy. But there can be no doubt that this was what
happened under James I, when royal extravagance caused the level
of ordinary expenditure to rise disproportionately to any increase
in the ordinary revenue which was achieved through such measures
as the growth of the impositions, the more extensive adoption of
customs farming and the screwing up of the farmers' rents. Herein
lie the root causes of the rise of the Jacobean debt and the urgent
need for measures to manage or reduce it.

The 1620's, however, present a somewhat different picture. On
the whole, beginning perhaps with the Treasury Commission of
1618, but reaching its apogee under the Lord Treasurership of

[15] See the brilliant analysis of Elizabethan finance by W. R. Scott, *The
Constitution and Finance of English, Scottish and Irish Joint Stock Companies
to 1720* (Cambridge, 1912), iii. 485–544.

Lionel Cranfield, first Earl of Middlesex (1621–4), this seems to have been a period of greater economy on the ordinary expenditure.[16] But this decade, and especially the war years, 1624–9, was also a period of heavy extraordinary expenditure. Thus the rise of the debt in the later Jacobean period and especially in the first four years of the reign of Charles I can be attributed mainly to causes which were not dissimilar to those which operated in the later years of Elizabeth's reign. For this reason the circumstances of these years were more propitious than they had been in the early and mid-Jacobean period with regard to the possibility of obtaining financial assistance from parliament. 'Ordinary charges the Kinge should beare alone: but *ubi commune periculum, commune auxilium*. In extraordinary he may require releife.' Thus argued Sir Edward Coke in a speech in the Commons in 1625.[17] However, even if the parliamentary grants of the war years had been sufficient to meet all the extraordinary requirements of the government, some borrowing would still have been necessary because of the slowness of the yield of the taxes and the urgency of many of the charges, only some of which could be met by letting bills pile up. But even during the great patriotic war of the later Elizabethan period, parliamentary grants had been niggardly in the extreme. To the normal belief that the subsidy was a subvention, not a grant to cover all extraordinary charges, there was now added a large measure of parliamentary distrust as to the royal conduct of the war. Even the largest of the parliamentary grants of the war years, that of 1628, yielded only £275,000, most of which was not available until the latter part of 1628 and 1629. There can be no doubt that the government treated the Loan of Five Subsidies of 1626–7 as a tax rather than a loan. The contributors, like the unfortunate persons in the counties who had laid out money for the billeting of soldiers, could count themselves extremely fortunate if they were ever repaid. And the inadequacy of parliamentary grants as permanent deficit bridging or debt reducing measures serves to emphasize the importance of the second permanent expedient of debt reduction, the liquidation of royal capital by the sale of lands. The most important of these transactions was the famous Ditchfield Grant of

---

[16] On Cranfield's financial policy, see R. H. Tawney, *Business and Politics under James I* (Cambridge, 1958), pp. 184–228.

[17] *Debates in the House of Commons in 1625* (Camden Soc., ed. S. R. Gardiner) (1873), p. 32.

1627–8, whereby the government conveyed lands to trustees of the Corporation of London in satisfaction of a debt of £349,897. But out of this sum more than £158,000 was due to the creditors of the Crown for the satisfaction of obligations which had been incurred in 1617, long before the war years. This part of the debt was therefore a legacy from the period when deficit borrowing had been designed primarily to manage a debt which had resulted from frequent deficits on the ordinary account. However, the remainder of the money, that is the principal and interest of £50,000 advanced in 1625 and the further £120,000 which was paid in 1628 as the condition of the Ditchfield contract, was definitely owed in return for advances made in the service of war finance.[18] But, quite apart from the Ditchfield Grant, more than £292,000 was made available for the liquidation of the debt from the proceeds of other sales of royal lands during the first decade of Charles I's reign.[19]

From this brief analysis of the problems of war finance two salient features, which are of special importance in determining the role of deficit borrowing in this period, stand out. The first is the inadequacy of the parliamentary subsidies, and the second the fact that royal lands were sold to defray the debt and not to meet current charges as they arose. The reasons for this are obvious enough. The machinery of the land market was not capable of immediately absorbing such unwontedly large amounts of land, and, even if it had been, the result of attempting to sell off these large quantities all at once would have depressed the price catastrophically. Thus, as in the deficit finance of the decade after 1606, the role of sales of royal land was one of debt reduction rather than the bridging of deficits. The latter was done by borrowing, either by leaving bills unpaid or by raising loans to pay off current charges. In turn, many of these loans were later prolonged, like the Corporation of London's loan of 1625 and the £58,400 which was raised in Amsterdam in 1626, and was not repaid until 1636;[20] and many others were

[18] For full details of this grant and supporting references see below, pp. 132–5.

[19] Dietz, op. cit., p. 271, note. The total debt provided for by the Ditchfield Grant is incorrectly stated by Dietz.

[20] For the Corporation of London's loan, see below, pp. 127–9. For the loan at Amsterdam, P.R.O. Exchequer Declared Accounts, E. 351/1957; Exchequer of Receipt, Order Book (Pells), E. 403/2754, pt. ii, fos. 39(b)–40; P.C.R. (1628–30), pp. 368–9, 398; S.P. Charles I, 8/7, 11, 11/75, 12/10, 19/122–4, 20/60, 26/59, 60, 246/104, 285/91–92, 94, 290/66, 295/34, 523/116; Coll. Sign Man. Car. I, vol. ii, no. 18; Docquets, Charles I, bdle. xiii;

repaid by the raising of further loans. Thus the pattern of deficit borrowing which emerges in the 1620's is the familiar one whereby loans are raised both to bridge deficits and to manage the debt. The inadequacy of the parliamentary subsidies and the fact that liquidation of royal capital was designed to pay off the debt rather than to bridge deficits clearly demonstrates the need for deficit borrowing as distinct from borrowings which were, in effect, anticipations or ways-and-means advances on the subsidy money or other revenues. To some extent this distinction between these two types of borrowing is open to the criticism that it is of an *ex post facto* nature, for at the time when the government borrowed, it was by no means always certain either of the amount of expenditure which was required or of the amount of extraordinary revenue which would be available. Nevertheless, it seems reasonable to designate the two loans of 1628, which were cited earlier as advances on the subsidies voted in that year, as anticipations,[21] while the loan of £55,000 which was made by Philip Burlamachi and Sir Ralph Freeman late in 1624 and the £10,000 which was lent by Sir Peter Vanlore in 1625 are examples of the same genus.[22] On the other hand, there is every indication that much of the heavy borrowing of the years 1625–6, and notably the two loans in London and Amsterdam which have already been mentioned, and the £70,000 borrowed from the prolific Burlamachi in the autumn of 1627—'although wee have noe constant or apparent meanes to give satisfaccon'[23]—was occasioned by the lack of revenue rather than by the need to anticipate it. And the same argument is, of course, applicable to the Loan of Five Subsidies which brought in more than £264,000 between 1626 and 1628,[24] although, as has already been suggested, this was hardly a loan in anything but name.

Although the years of heavy war expenditure were succeeded by nearly a decade of peace, the royal finances never completely

Cal. S.P.D. (1625–6), pp. 123, 150, 178, 180, 255, 330; *(1629–31)*, 41, 44; *(1635)*, pp. 3–4, 469, 565, 582–3; *(1635–6)*, pp. 167, 228; *Cal. S.P.D. Addenda (1625–49)*, pp. 97–98; B.M. Additional MSS. 18,764, fo. 22; *Hist. MSS. Comm., XIIth Report*, pt. i, p. 255; pt. ii, pp. 129, 135, 143; T. Rymer, *Foedera*, viii, pt. iii, p. 60.

[21] See above, p. 32.

[22] For Burlamachi and Freeman's loan, *Cal. S.P.D. (1623–5)*, pp. 382, 387–8; for Vanlore's loan, P.R.O. Coll. Sign Man. Car. I, vol. i, no. 76; Exchequer of Receipt, Issue Book, E. 403/1736, no foliation; Order Book (Pells), E. 403/2745, fos. 10(*b*), 21, 214(*b*).

[23] S.P. Charles I, 8/26.   [24] Dietz, op. cit., p. 238, note.

recovered from the strain. In the first place, the debt had to be paid off, and the money from the sale of Crown lands was by no means sufficient to achieve this purpose. It was in these circumstances that one method of deficit finance, the large-scale hypothecation of future revenues, came to assume a pre-eminent importance. This rather haphazard expedient was not, of course, peculiar to the reign of Charles I. Early in the previous reign, Lord Treasurer Salisbury had fulminated against the worst abuses of this system, declaring that 'it is but a betraying of our owne reckoninges to cast debtes upon Receiptes which we know will fall short'.[25] Even if we accept the view that the Caroline government intended that this expedient should be, like the sale of royal lands, a permanent measure of debt reduction, we are bound to admit that the necessary corollary of this view, which is the notion that these charges could ultimately be paid off out of future revenue surpluses, shows an optimism which is both difficult to understand and impossible to condone. If such hopes were entertained, they proved in the event to be completely illusory, in which circumstances the disposal of a part of the war debt by the hypothecation of future revenues, far from being a permanent measure of debt reduction, proved to be the most characteristic method of debt management which was employed in the reign of Charles I. In other words, a large part of the existing debt was repaid only at the expense of incurring new debts. Despite increases in some branches of the revenue, the basic ingredients of the financial situation in the decade which succeeded 1628 were these. In so far as the current charges of the Crown were not reduced to the extent that its revenue was mortgaged in advance, these charges could, in a period when the Crown ruled without a parliament and in the absence of further sales of land, be met only by the expedient of assigning a part of the current charges on the revenues of future years or by borrowing to meet these charges, and, in turn, hypothecating future revenues against these borrowings. This was the essentially vicious circle of Caroline finance, and it raises some doubts about the validity of the familiar thesis that the years of personal government were a period of progressive financial improvement.[26] The situation is admirably summed up in a memorandum which was drawn up in 1641 for the benefit of the Earl of Bedford in connexion with that nobleman's proposed

---

[25] S.P. James I, 32/28; B.M. Lansdowne MSS. 164, fo. 427.
[26] For the best-known statement of this view, see Dietz, op. cit., pp. 257–88.

investigation of the royal financial position. Although the financial situation which it describes had worsened considerably as a result of the heavy extraordinary expenditure of the three previous years, its conclusions are nevertheless in essence perfectly applicable to the decade before 1638. Under the prevailing state of affairs, the burden of cumulatively hypothecated revenue made it impossible for the King to 'live of his own', in which circumstances, it might be added, statements of balanced or nearly balanced ordinary accounts are a positively misleading form of historical evidence. What was needed, concluded the author of the memorandum, writing at a time when the idea of parliament was no longer a rather indecent novelty, was a parliamentary grant to pay off these 'anticipations', and to make the whole of the current revenue available for the purpose of defraying current expenditure.[27] The burden of these charges was the legacy of the war years of the early part of Charles I's reign, and had not been significantly reduced by the time that a further war came in 1639.

The history of these developments can be briefly told in terms of their statistics. By 1628 that part of the debt which had been provided for by the hypothecation of future revenues had risen to more than £325,000, and the government had to have recourse to pledging the revenues not only of the following year, but also of the year after that. The early 1630's saw a very gradual reduction of the burden of hypothecation. That this reduction was by no means considerable can be seen from the fact that, whereas the amount of future revenue mortgaged in August 1630 stood at £277,680, it was still as high as £204,674 in May 1633. Another feature of these years is that, despite the fact that the total burden of these charges had gradually been reduced, it was also spread out over a longer period. By 24 August 1630 some of the revenues had been hypothecated down to 1637. In May of the following year this extended to Christmas 1642, though the assignments on the years 1640–2 were as yet negligible. From 1634 the total burden of assignations of future revenues rose alarmingly, reaching a peak of £315,816 at Michaelmas 1637 with one small branch of the revenue anticipated as far ahead as 1651. More significant is the fact that at this date the revenues of the two financial years ending at Michaelmas 1639 were hypothecated to the extent of £278,979, which was only slightly lower than the peak period of the war years towards the end of the

27 *Cal. S.P.D. (1640–1)*, pp. 565–7.

1620's. This sudden rise poses difficult problems for the fiscal historian, more especially in connexion with the argument that the 1630's were a period of marked improvement in the royal financial position, and it suggests the need for a radical re-examination of the financial policy of this decade.[28]

The blurring of the distinction between borrowing in anticipation of revenue and deficit borrowing, which was such a notable feature of royal finance in the 1630's, was further accentuated in the last two years of the personal government of Charles I, when the royal demand for loans was enormously increased in face of the dangers of the Scottish invasion and, after the Treaty of Ripon, the expense of maintaining the two armies. Although such borrowings as the £85,000 which was lent by Sir Paul Pindar in 1638–9 and the forced 'pepper loan' from the East India merchants in the autumn of 1640 were designated as 'anticipations', since they were assigned upon branches of the revenue falling due in subsequent years, it is more illuminating to regard them as deficit borrowings which were designed to meet current charges which could not be met out of revenue. The same argument is applicable to the massive advances which were made by the newly formed syndicate of customs farmers in the summer of 1640. Like the so-called 'anticipations' of the early and mid 1630's, all these loans were, in fact, hypothecations of future revenue, which, failing extensive land sales, extraordinary windfalls, or the unlikely achievement of enormous revenue surpluses in the future, could be repaid only by continuing and intensifying the now well-established and apparently inevitable process of cumulative hypothecation. However, in the case of these borrowings, much was to happen in the period between assignment and maturation which was to have the effect both of putting a stop to this process and of rendering the lenders' hopes of prompt repayment nugatory. The dates at which the lenders' assignments were due to mature provide a sufficient commentary on the latter observation. Pindar's loans were secured on several branches of the

---

[28] The figures in this paragraph have been obtained from the very numerous accounts of revenue 'anticipated' in the State Papers, all of which have been examined, and more especially, S.P. Charles I, 3/98, 32/46, 63/114, 112/64, 148/37, 166/34, 172/94, 190/19, 222/4, 238/29, 263/36, 294/62, 371/101, 450/30. In the calculations made from these accounts the year has been taken to run from Michaelmas to Michaelmas. Similar information, though relating only to the administration of Lord Treasurer Juxon (1636–41), is obtainable in the Bodleian, Bankes MSS. 5/45. I am indebted to Mr. Lawrence Stone for drawing my attention to this source.

revenue maturing between Michaelmas 1639 and Christmas 1645. In making their advances of 1640, the customs farmers, of whom Pindar was the most notable figure, were continuing, or, at least, renewing a tendency which had developed in the 1630's whereby they extended the term upon which they made advances of rent to the government, a process which was part of the general tendency of cumulative hypothecation which has been described above. But they were also well aware of the fact that there was a far greater risk involved in this practice in 1640 than there had been in the less exciting but safer days of Charles's personal rule. Their forebodings were fully justified when their lease was sequestered by the Long Parliament in 1641, an event which was also fatal to the hopes of full repayment entertained by the hapless East India merchants whose forced contribution in pepper had been assigned on the customs revenue falling due between March 1641 and December 1642.[29]

With the failure of the government's attempt to crush the Scots, and the prospect of prolonged expenditure on the maintenance and ultimately, as it was hoped, the disbandment of the two armies, the calling of parliament became inevitable. Thus from the end of 1639 onwards we find some loans being raised with the expressed purpose of anticipating such grants as parliament might make when it met. As soon as the King announced that parliament was to be convened on 13 April 1640, the government initiated a general loan with this end in view. As an anticipation, however, this loan, which began its career as a loan from the privy councillors and which yielded £232,530 between December 1639 and May 1640, was a very damp squib in view of the failure of the Short Parliament. In these circumstances its actual effect was simply to reinforce those other loans which were designed to bridge the current deficit. Between the end of the Short and the opening of the Long Parliament similar attempts were made to anticipate the hoped-for subsidies, and, in fact, the authorities of the Corporation of London would not countenance the raising even of the first £50,000 of the £200,000 demanded by the government until they were quite certain that parliament would be called. Once it had met, the need to anticipate its grants was as urgent as ever, and from the end of 1640

---

[29] For Pindar's loan, see below, pp. 175–6; for the loan from the East India Merchants, see below, pp. 178–80; for the advances of the customs farmers, see below, pp. 110–11.

onwards there was an extensive spate of borrowing in anticipation of the parliamentary subsidies which was begun by the loan of £50,000 rather reluctantly made by the customs farmer, John Harrison, at the end of the year.[30]

The calling of the Long Parliament saw the beginnings of parliamentary control of government borrowing and marks an obvious break in the history of the relations between the government and the money market. The subsequent developments, which fall outside the sphere of this study, saw a remarkable enhancement of the government's ability to borrow, but an enhancement whose essential condition was the growth of parliamentary influence over the course of political events. The new importance of parliament in connexion with the government's relations with the money market is reflected in the role played by the city members of parliament as intermediaries between the government and the city.[31] In the uneasy interval between the opening of parliament and the beginning of the Civil War the scale of government borrowing was enormously increased. But its general pattern remains familiar. Although the vast bulk of the borrowings of these years was designed to anticipate revenues such as the parliamentary subsidies and the Poll Tax of 1641, as well as the more normal anticipations of ordinary revenue, other loans were designed to bridge the gap arising out of the inadequacy of that revenue.[32] The scale of the government's financial operations, the conditions which governed its relations with the money market, and, indeed, the very nature of the government itself, were all changing. But the fundamental character of its demand for loans remained the same.

[30] For the 'general loan', see below, pp. 176–7; for the Corporation of London's loan, see below, pp. 180–3; for Harrison's loan, see below, p. 176.
[31] See W. P. Harper, op. cit., pp. 47, 215–22.
[32] Ibid., pp. 30–48.

III

THE PROBLEM OF INDUCEMENT

It was remarked earlier[1] that between the securities offered by the Crown and those of the private borrower there are certain marked similarities, but that these similarities of form conceal a more fundamental difference of legal and economic reality. The purpose of this chapter is to elaborate this theme and to examine the extent to which these differences are reflected in the terms upon which the Crown was able to borrow.

1. *The Royal Equivalent of Borrowing upon Bill*

It will be remembered that a significant feature of private bills obligatory and bills of exchange is to be found in the fact that they reflect the high financial standing of the borrower in that no penalty appreciably greater than the principal and the accrued interest of the sums borrowed was incurred by him in case of default. Since royal letters obligatory such as letters patent and letters of Privy Seal also carried no penal sanctions of this type, such securities represent the nearest royal equivalent to the private bill obligatory. Indeed the basic similarities between these instruments is immediately obvious from the most cursory examination, and one example will suffice to illustrate this point. On 1 May 1617 the prominent London merchant, Sir John Coteles, lent £2,000 to James I, and letters patent drawn up on that date indicate the fact of the loan, the royal promise to repay the lender with interest before 6 May 1618, and contain instructions to the officials of the Exchequer to see that this promise is carried out.[2] For our purposes, however, the really significant fact is not so much what these instruments contain as what they do not contain, for they make no mention of the borrower's liability to incur a penalty on default, and herein lies their basic similarity to the private bill obligatory. Nor did these royal letters obligatory provide a watertight

---

[1] See above, pp. 9–10. [2] P.R.O. Patent Roll, 15 Jac. I, pt. 8.

administrative guarantee that the machinery of issue would automatically be set in motion by payment in cash or by levying of tallies of assignment on the expiration of the loan and their presentation to the appropriate Exchequer official. In these circumstances it is hardly surprising that most lenders preferred to secure for themselves a place nearer to the head of the queue of creditors awaiting repayment. This could be done by obtaining a tally or tallies of assignment in return for a loan.

At this point a word of explanation about the use of tallies will perhaps be useful to the reader who is not acquainted with the technicalities of Exchequer practice.[3] All tallies were originally instruments of receipt, recording the payment of money into the royal Exchequer. But, as Sir Hilary Jenkinson and other scholars have demonstrated, quite early in its history the tally of receipt was adapted in such a way that it could be used for purposes of issue. The beauty of this device lay essentially in its simplicity. For if a tally purported the payment of money into the Exchequer by X, a collector of a branch of the revenue, it could when given to Y, a creditor of the Crown, serve as a cheque drawn upon X in favour of Y for part of the money due by X to the Crown. The position of X was thus analogous to that of the drawee of an inland bill, and the tally served, like the bill of exchange and the later cheque, to economize the use of currency.

The simple medieval dichotomy between the tally of *sol*, which denoted a straightforward receipt of money into the Exchequer,

---

[3] Considerations of space preclude a full bibliography on the history of tallies. The most fundamental work has been done by historians of medieval finance, and notably by H. Jenkinson, 'Exchequer Tallies', *Archaeologia*, lxii (1911), 367–80, and in a note supplementary to this paper in *Proceedings of the Society of Antiquaries of London*, 2nd ser. xxv (1913), 29–39, and 'Medieval Tallies, Public and Private', *Archaeologia*, lxxiv (1925), 289–351. The valuable and pioneering researches of Mr. A. Steel, contained in a number of articles, are summed up in A. Steel, *The Receipt of the Exchequer 1377–1485* (Cambridge, 1954), especially pp. xxix–xl, 4–36, 371–406. See also J. F. Willard, 'The Crown and its Creditors (1327–1337)', *Eng. Hist. Rev.* xlii (1927), 12–19; E. B. Fryde, 'Materials for the Study of Edward III's Credit Operations, 1327–48', *B.I.H.R.* xxii (1949), 127–9, and ibid. xxiii (1950), 7–12; G. L. Harriss, 'Fictitious Loans', *Econ. Hist. Rev.* 2nd ser. viii (1955), 187–99. On the early modern period see F. C. Dietz, *The Exchequer in Elizabeth's Reign* (Northampton, Mass., 1923), p. 91, and *The Receipts and Issues of the Exchequer during the Reigns of James I and Charles I* (Northampton, Mass., 1928), pp. 120–4. And for an admirably lucid description of post-Restoration practice see C. D. Chandaman, 'The English Public Revenue 1660–88' (unpublished Ph.D. thesis, London University, 1954), pp. 26–42.

and the tally of *pro*, which denoted an anticipation of such a receipt in the manner described above, was breaking down in the early Stuart period. Certainly by the 1620's the use of the latter instrument had become confined to cases where, for one reason or another, the Crown desired to convey to the assignee its legal title to the revenue which it pledged. An account of the causes of this development, which involved a notable diminution in the use of tallies of *pro*, is to be found in an undated document which was certainly written after 1612, and probably between 1618 and 1620.[4] This is a complaint by the Clerks of the Tally Court against the growth of what they call 'a new Invencion contrary to the Course of the Exchequer', in consequence of which the decline in the use of the tally of *pro* was accompanied by a most significant expansion in the use of the tally of *sol*. No longer employed simply and solely as an instrument of receipt, it was increasingly used also as an instrument of anticipation in precisely the same manner as the tally of *pro*, except for the fact that the Crown's right to the revenue pledged was not formally conveyed to the assignee. This last fact tended perhaps to make the tally of *sol* a less safe form of security than the tally of *pro*, for in the latter case the lender clearly had the right to sue the accountant upon whom the tally was drawn in cases where the latter had sufficient funds to honour the draft, but refused to do so. However, the tally of *sol* had certain compensating advantages. For whereas in the later Middle Ages a tally of *pro* was not inscribed with the name of the assignee,[5] the entry, 'pro Y', being confined to the Receipt Roll, the seventeenth-century practice was to give these details on the tally as well. By contrast, when the tally of *sol* was used as an instrument of anticipation, the name of the assignee was not recorded on the tally, in which circumstances it was the more easily negotiable, a fact which gave it an obvious advantage as a credit instrument. This is not to say, however, that

[4] P.R.O. Exchequer Miscellanea, E. 407/71/29. My attention was first drawn to this reference by Chandaman, op. cit., p. 29, note. A perusal of the document as well as a study of Dr. Chandaman's pioneering treatment of post-Restoration Exchequer practice, to which I am heavily indebted, led me to a re-examination of the Pells of Receipt and Issue for the early seventeenth century, on which sources this account of the use of tallies is primarily based. I am also greatly indebted to Dr. Chandaman for his opinion on a number of technical points.

[5] This statement is based on the account given by Mr. Harriss (*Econ. Hist. Rev.* loc. cit.). It has been criticized by J. E. D. Binney, *British Public Finance and Administration 1774–92* (Oxford, 1958), pp. 225–6, note.

the older practice was superseded entirely by the end of the period. It was applied for example in 1638–9 in the case of the £50,000 part of a larger sum lent by Sir Paul Pindar and secured upon a number of branches of the revenue maturing in 1639.[6] But from the 1620's onwards the practice which had met with the displeasure of the Clerks of the Tally Court, whose fees were sensibly reduced thereby —the practice which they described as 'Anticipations by the way of the Tellors', involving the use of the tally of *sol*—became more and more prominent. The £5,000 lent by Sir William Russell in August 1620, secured by tallies on the farm of the great customs, the £2,300 advanced by the same lender on similar security in April 1621, the £3,000 lent by Peter Vanlore in July 1621 secured by tallies on two collectors of the new impositions, and the £5,000 lent by Lord Digby in March of the following year, secured by tallies on the great farm, are all examples of this process.[7]

Moreover, there developed a frequent, but by no means universal practice, whereby the tally of *sol*, while retaining its peculiar advantages as an easily negotiable financial instrument, could be made to carry the same advantages in terms of liability of the assignee to honour a draft drawn upon him which we have seen obtained in the case of the tally of *pro*. This device was to accompany the levying of tallies with the drawing up of bonds by the accountants or collectors concerned. The first of Russell's two advances mentioned above was secured in this way, while, in October 1626, when Philip Burlamachi agreed to make over £21,610. 13s. 6d. by bills of exchange towards the pay of the 6,000 men who were serving under the Dutch government, he received as security assignments on the great customs, backed up by the bonds of the farmers.[8]

[6] Patent Roll, 14 Car. I, pt. 44; S.P. Charles I, 410/108; Exchequer of Receipt, Receipt Book (Pells), E. 401/1925, no foliation.

[7] Exchequer of Receipt, Receipt Books (Pells), E. 401/1904, 1906, 1907, no foliation; Issue Books (Pells), E. 403/1726, 1728, 1729, no foliation; Order Books (Pells), E. 403/2739, fo. 156; E. 403/2740, fos. 96, 175(b); E. 403/2741, fo. 87(b).

[8] A.P.C. (1626), pp. 319–20. Dr. C. D. Chandaman has suggested to me that this practice was probably confined to the period when the use of the tally of *sol* as an instrument of anticipation was in its infancy, and it is certainly more prominent in the reign of James than in that of Charles. That it need not be confined to the tally of *sol* is suggested by its use as early as 1610, in connexion with the £100,000 borrowed from the aldermen of London in that year (P.R.O. Close Roll, 11 Jac. I, pt. 21; MS. Cal. of Sackville MSS. 178, M. 98; C. of L.R.O. Repertory of the Court of Aldermen, xxix, fo. 225).

Since it is obviously important to establish the precise legal relationship between the farmers or collectors and the lenders whose advances had been quartered upon the revenues in their trust, it is particularly unfortunate that a detailed search of Chancery enrolments for such obligations did not yield any significant fruit. Nevertheless, even without the backing of evidential proof, it can be asserted fairly confidently that these bonds were not a species of collateral security by which the farmers or collectors concerned incurred an obligation to pay a large penal sum in the event of there being insufficient revenue available to honour the assignments. The fact that no record of pleading on these bonds has survived in the records of the Exchequer of Pleas is evidence only of a negative order, and therefore not conclusive. But all the circumstances of such cases suggest that the interpretation which is advanced here is the correct one. For revenue officials were far too well acquainted with the frequent royal practice of over-assigning revenues to be likely to concur with any arrangement whereby they stood liable to forfeit large penal sums to lenders whose tallies had been dishonoured as a result of such royal malpractices. Writing on 5 November 1627 to the Duke of Buckingham, Lord Goring observed that, in the circumstances of financial stringency then prevalent in London, even the best securities were of dubious worth in the eyes of cautious lenders, for 'all the revenue is anticipated for the next whole year, which being so, the farmers' and such like bonds are little worth, for the King may break all those assignments at his own will, and where then shall they be paid?'[9] Now if the bonds in question had been in the nature of collateral security, they would clearly have been by no means worthless in these circumstances, since the lenders could sue the farmers or collectors for the penalties if there had been no revenue available to meet the assignments. Such bonds seem, therefore, to have been obligations merely to honour tallies if, and only if, the required revenue was available. The farmer or collector, in fact, undertook to obtain his receipt from a creditor of the Crown rather than pay his revenues into the Exchequer and receive his receipt there. In other words, the use of the collector's bond was a device by which the use of the tally of *sol* as a credit instrument, while retaining its own peculiar advantages in respect of negotiability, was assimilated to that of the tally of *pro*.

[9] *Cal. S.P.D. (1627–8)*, p. 422.

The common element in both sorts of operation was, of course, the securing of lenders not against the general expectations of the Exchequer, but against specific branches of the revenue. There is a measure of truth in the argument that this practice reflects the prevalence of a relatively undeveloped sense of public credit in that lenders felt that their money was safer when their loans were secured against definite receipts of revenue. More significantly, however, it reflects the administrative peculiarities of the medieval and early modern financial system, a notable feature of which was the fact that a large proportion of the royal revenue was anticipated in advance and therefore never reached the Exchequer. In these circumstances it was surely natural for creditors to seek such assignments for their loans. But having obtained them, they were by no means certain of receiving prompt repayment, even when their claims were strengthened with additional safeguards such as have been described above, though the position of lenders who had acquired such safeguards was obviously much stronger. Students of medieval finance have long been familiar both with the hazard of over-assignment which confronted all creditors of the Crown, whose claims had been met by the issue of tallies and with the administrative processes to which these contingencies gave rise.[10] In essence, their account requires little modification in considering the practices of the early Stuart period. Such a lender might have to wait until such time as his tally could be honoured, or alternatively, he might be fortunate enough to secure reassignment either of the whole of his loan or of that part of it which could not be repaid. Then again he might have his tally discounted by someone who was sufficiently influential to secure a good reassignment for himself. There is, however, evidence that, on some occasions at least, collectors of the revenue were required to honour tallies which were directed upon them even if the requisite revenues were not available. Thus in the case of the tallies for £7,000 on several branches of the revenue which were struck in favour of Burlamachi in May 1628, it was ordered that the assignees should make up any deficiency which might occur out of their own pockets and that 'satisfaccion shalbe made unto the said collectors, who shalbe ingaged for the said sommes above said, of so much as shall fall short of the whole somme for which they shalbe respectively engaged, out of

---

[10] Jenkinson, *Proceedings of the Society of Antiquaries of London,* loc. cit.; Steel, op. cit., *passim*; Harriss, *Econ. Hist. Rev.* loc. cit.

any other of His Majestie's revenue, such as they approve and like well of'. A similar provision was made at the end of 1639, when the Earl of Northumberland lent £5,000 to Charles I on the security of the impositions on cambrics and lawns for 1640 and 1641. If the proceeds of these collections should prove to be insufficient to honour Northumberland's tallies, the collectors were to make up the deficiency out of their own resources and to reimburse themselves out of the first receipts coming into their hands in the following year.[11]

Frequent over-assignment undoubtedly detracted greatly from the value of the tally of assignment as a royal security, and, when practised on an appreciable scale, as was the case in the early seventeenth century, was bound to lead to a sensible deterioration of the royal credit. Nor can it be asserted with any confidence that the malpractice of over-assignment was less developed in England than in France, where it was a notorious abuse. Of the French practice under Mazarin, Professor Martin has shown how the cardinal insisted on sound assignments for his favoured associates, which put a premium on his favour as a means of obtaining a safe form of financial security. More recently Mr. G. L. Harriss has demonstrated how in late medieval England certain strategically placed individuals, such as Exchequer officials and court favourites, were able to do a lucrative business in the discounting of dishonoured tallies, because they were more favourably placed than the original holders of the tallies to secure a sound reassignment of the dishonoured debt.[12] The difference between the expedients which are described by these two historians is one of technique rather than of substance. Early Stuart England with its notorious combination of administrative corruption and backstairs influence, together with a royal financial improvidence which rendered over-assignment inevitable offered a fruitful field for the exercise of both practices.

2. Borrowing Upon Bond

At first sight the similarity between royal and private financial instruments in the early seventeenth century is even more striking

[11] *A.P.C. (1627–8)*, pp. 441–2; *Cal. S.P.D. (1639–40)*, p. 191. Northumberland's advance was part of a more general loan made by members of the nobility and prominent officers of State in 1639–40. See below, pp. 176–7.

[12] G. Martin, *Histoire du crédit en France sous le règne de Louis XIV* (Paris, 1913), i. 8; Harriss, *Econ. Hist. Rev.* loc. cit., pp. 196–7.

in the case of the bond[13] than in those of the other securities which have been discussed above. The essence of the obligation of royal, as of private, bonds is to be found in the undertaking to observe a specified 'condition'—in this case the payment of the principal and the accrued interest of a loan at an agreed date—with a liability to forfeit a sum appreciably greater than the principal and interest in case of default. The date at which this penalty was enforceable could be deferred by the Crown's obtaining prolongation, which was usually done by the cancellation of the old bond and the issuing of a new.[14]

Two examples of the use of royal bonds may be cited to illustrate the above description. The citizens of London who lent £63,000 to James I in 1608 were secured by a royal bond in penalty of £100,000 while the loan of £100,000 made by the aldermen of London in 1610 was secured by a royal bond in penalty of £150,000.[15] The reader who is acquainted with cases of private borrowing upon bond will probably have observed that in the transactions cited here the penal sum is rather smaller in relation to the principal borrowed than was normally the case in equivalent private transactions.[16] This is probably explicable by the fact that in each of these two cases of borrowing upon royal bond, the bonds represented only a part of the security offered, for the lenders also received revenue assignments.

This last fact is not without significance, for it suggests that, in some circumstances at least, neither the royal bond alone nor revenue assignments alone were deemed sufficient security by lenders. The defects of the latter have already been examined, and it is necessary only to turn to the defects of royal bonds in order to explain this phenomenon. It seems highly probable that, despite their carefully worded penal sanctions, the chief significance of royal bonds as securities is to be found in the fact that they were, like letters patent, solemnly expressed obligations given under the Great Seal. If the financial worth of a security were dependent upon

---

[13] For private bonds, see above, pp. 5–7.

[14] As in the case of the two renewals of the loan of £100,000 originally made by the aldermen of London in 1610 (C. of L.R.O. Repertory of Court of Aldermen (hereafter cited as Repertory), xxx, fos. 108(b), 240, 296(b); ibid., xxxi, pt. i, fo. 70(b)).

[15] Cal. S.P.D. (1603–10), p. 415; Close Roll, 11 Jac. I, pt. 21.

[16] On the relation of penalty to principal in private transactions, see Trevor-Roper, Econ. Hist. Rev. loc. cit., pp. 282–3.

its diplomatic form, there is no doubt that royal bonds would be all that the Venetian ambassador claimed for them in his description of the securing of the citizens of London for their loan of 1608.

> . . . each contributor receives a bond under the great seal guaranteeing repayment, that is to say the very highest security they can possibly desire, and one which is seldom given by the Sovereign.[17]

But between diplomatic form and economic reality and between theory and practice there was a great gulf fixed, and few of those who had experience of lending their money to the first two Stuarts would have endorsed the ambassador's appraisal of the worth of royal bonds. For their ultimate value in the city was in the last resort dependent not upon the language in which the royal obligation was couched nor the seal under which they were issued, but on the more prosaic consideration of the lender's ability to sue for the penalty on the default of the royal borrower. And here the crucial point is the fact that, while the law provided ample redress for the creditor of a defaulting private borrower, there was no way by which the Crown could be sued by a private person, whose only remedy—if remedy it can be called—was procedure by Petition of Right. Indeed, as late as the last decade of the century, the issue of whether it was proper for an Exchequer court to command payment of creditors out of the royal treasury was still a matter of legal dispute, as is shown by the famous 'Case of the Bankers'.[18] It is certainly no exaggeration to say that, in the earlier period which is here under review, a lender was entirely dependent upon the royal word for the honouring of a bond, or, for that matter, of any other obligation. It is difficult, therefore, to resist the conclusion that, whereas in private credit transactions, the issue of whether the bond should be forfeit or the loan prolonged turned entirely upon the willingness or reluctance of the lender to wait longer for his money, in the case of government borrowing this is a factor of relatively minor significance. The Venetian ambassador was correct in writing of the royal bond as a financial instrument which was infrequently used, but incorrect in the explanation which he gives of

---

[17] *Cal. S.P. Ven (1607–10)*, p. 97. The ambassador's account is, strictly speaking, inaccurate. Two lenders who provided £3,000 apiece received separate bonds; the remainder, who lent £63,000 received a joint bond.

[18] *A Complete Collection of State Trials* (ed. T. B. Howell) (London, 1816), xiv. 1–114.

this fact. It is true that the revenue assignments, which were by far
the most common type of security, were subject to the hazards of
over-assignment, but they did at least provide the lender with a
claim, and in some cases with something approaching a prior claim
—on a specific branch of the revenue. By contrast, the sum total of
the security which was contained in a royal bond was a penalty
which in the last resort could not be enforced at law. No doubt the
King never technically broke his solemn word as expressed in a
royal bond. No doubt, in all those cases where the Crown was
unable to pay up, the lenders appear to have yielded gracefully to
its polite requests for prolongation. But what alternative had they?
It is true that to some creditors prolongation of loans bearing interest at 10 or 8 per cent. might represent a reasonable return on
capital, but the essential reality which lies behind the forms of
prolongation of most royal bonds is normally to be found in the
legal impotence of the lenders, who were denied recourse to en-
forcing the one real sanction afforded by a private bond—that of
suing for the penalty if the borrower was unable to pay up, and the
lender was unwilling to grant a prolongation. In these circumstances royal bonds, unlike their private counterparts, were of no
greater value to lenders than those other royal writings obligatory
to which no penal sum was attached.

It was shown earlier[19] that some lenders preferred to accept the
collateral bonds of sureties who were known to them as men of
some substance and credit rather than accept the bond of a principal debtor whose financial reputation was an unknown or doubtful quantity. The argument of the preceding pages suggests that if
lenders found this practice useful in connexion with private transactions, it presented even more obvious advantages in connexion
with royal borrowing. For the legal inviolability of the Crown did
not extend to those private persons who consented to act as its
guarantors. There were many cases in which royal pressure could
be brought to bear upon private individuals who, although unwilling or unable to lend money themselves, might be induced to offer
their services as sureties. In the sixteenth century it had not been an
uncommon practice for royal bonds to be subscribed by a number
of peers of the realm, who thus incurred the obligation of ensuring
that the loans would be repaid when they fell due. For example, in
September 1566 Gresham wrote to Cecil from Antwerp that the

---

[19] See above, pp. 6–7.

royal bonds for the borrowing of £100,000 should be subscribed by as many peers as possible.[20]

A security of this nature which had been more frequently used in connexion with the raising of loans abroad in the Tudor period was the bond of the Corporation of London under its common seal. In 1595, long after the hey-day of external borrowing, Sir Horatio Palavicino described this security as 'the first to-day in Europe'.[21] Although Palavicino's personal experience of the worth of such bonds had not been altogether happy,[22] there is no doubt that they had found ready acceptance abroad by reason of the easily enforce-able penalty which the surety incurred in the event of the borrower's default, the lenders being able to demand the penal sums 'either from the State of this Cittie, having given assurance under there Common Seale, or from som private person'. If the bonds were prosecuted in England, a legal action would be commenced against the Corporation; if such action were taken abroad—and this was often the more convenient method—then the holders of the bonds might satisfy themselves by the simple expedient of legal distraint on the goods of any London merchant.[23]

The end of extensive external borrowing by the Crown after 1570 brought a temporary cessation of the use of the Corporation's bonds as securities against royal borrowing. It is true that, during the remainder of the reign of Elizabeth, the Corporation still had an important part to play in connexion with government borrowing, but its role seems to have been confined to that of loan contractor and not to have extended to the *guaranteeing* of loans.[24] The same is true of James I's early loans from the city, but from 1617 onwards the most important of the loans raised by him and his successor through the mechanism of the Corporation of London were secured upon the bonds of that body. But the improvement in the position of the lenders who were secured in this way was in practice more apparent than real, and the royal failure to repay the loan of 1617 until 1628, though it resulted in many complaints and even

---

[20] J. W. Burgon, *The Life and Times of Sir Thomas Gresham* (1839), ii. 156.

[21] *Hist. MSS. Comm., Salisbury MSS.* v. 462.

[22] See L. Stone, *An Elizabethan: Sir Horatio Palavicino* (Oxford, 1956), pp. 66–97.

[23] *Hist. MSS. Comm., Salisbury MSS.* x. 315–16; Remembrancia, ii. 203; iii. 6, 7. For examples of threatened and actual confiscation in the case of the Palavicino debt, see Stone, op. cit., pp. 77–78, 87–88, 91–93.

[24] I owe this information to the kindness of Mr. R. B. Outhwaite.

occasioned legal actions by the more outraged lenders against the Corporation, does not seem to have resulted in any tangible loss to the surety other than the inevitable loss of its credit. The vast bulk of the lenders seem to have been as little inclined to sue the Corporation as they were the Crown, and in view of the fact that a small minority of them were paid off before the end of the reign of James I and interim interest payments were made to a few of the others, it seems likely that the Corporation settled out of Court with the most persistent of the lenders. But, for the remainder, loyalty to the Corporation, whose assumption of financial responsibility on the royal behalf had been by no means a matter of free choice, together with the fact that, however secured, this was just another loan to the Crown with all its attendant inconveniences, seem to have outweighed the fact that for once they had a clear legal redress in case of default. Thus they appear to have accepted, albeit reluctantly, the argument that they must wait until the Crown was in a position to make repayment, which, it was alleged, was high on the list of its financial priorities.[25]

Among the other most obvious candidates as sureties for royal borrowings were high officials of State. Thus we find members of the Privy Council giving their bonds for the repayment of a loan of £5,000 made by Peter Vanlore in 1615 and for £20,000 negotiated by Sir Noel de Caron in 1617, while the Corporation of London received the bonds of certain peers of the realm as security for the first £50,000 of the £200,000 which it consented to negotiate for Charles I in 1640. And on occasions when those merchant-financiers who were among the most regular lenders to the Crown were unable to supply cash, they sometimes did the next best thing by lending their credit. Early in 1625 Burlamachi offered to stand security for the raising of money abroad in connexion with the Palatinate, 'a man of his vocation sometimes adding credit to an affair'. Burlamachi and his brother-in-law, Philip Calandrini, were involved in a similar business in the following year, when the Crown raised £58,400 in Amsterdam on the security of jewels. In this case the jewels alone were not deemed to be sufficient security, for the lenders demanded in addition 'the Caution of some Merchants that the Jewelles shall be redeemed within three years at the furthest'. On the royal failure to get the municipality of Amsterdam to pro-

---

[25] Remembrancia, vi. 1, 54. 125, 140. For full details, see below, pp. 126–9, 162–3.

vide this guarantee, Burlamachi and Calandrini stepped into the breach by offering their bonds as additional security, 'which is but a superabondant Caution, since the Jewells are sufficient paunes'.[26]

Those who acted as sureties for the Crown usually received the King's own bond or, at least, some other form of written assurance as counter-security that the King would, in the eloquent contemporary phrase 'save them harmless'. Thus the Corporation of London received counter-bonds, both from Elizabeth for its services in securing Palavicino, and from James I in connexion with the citizens' loan of 1617. So did the fourteen privy councillors who secured Caron in 1617. When a number of peers of the realm offered to stand security for Charles I's loan from the citizens of London in 1640, the King declared his willingness 'to sell himself to his shirt for their indemnity'. But normal royal counter-security proved sufficient even at this desperate juncture.[27]

It is in the expedient of borrowing the credit of sureties that the closest parallel between royal and private securities is to be found. The cases which have been described above all arose essentially out of situations in which ordinary royal obligations were not deemed sufficient security by lenders, in which circumstances the Crown borrowed the credit of other persons or institutions who were either unable or unwilling to act as principal lenders themselves. In return they accepted the royal bonds which the lenders had refused.

3. The Pledging of Real and Personal Property

In private borrowing transactions the pledge was generally reckoned to be the safest of all securities, since the lender established a conditional claim on a definite piece of property which became his on the default of the borrower. There was no uncertainty about the latter's ability to pay a large penal sum on default, and, of course, in the case of the pledging of personal property, the lender kept possession of the pawn until repayment was made. In

[26] For security by privy councillors, S.P. James I, 91/1, 122/43(i); Exchequer of Receipt, Order Book (Pells), E. 403/2737, fos. 34–35; by the peers, Cal. S.P.D. (1640–1), p. 128; Remembrancia, viii. 233; B.M. Harleian MSS. 1219, fos. 166–73; by Burlamachi and Calandrini, Cal. S.P.D. (1623–5), p. 448; S.P. Charles I, 19/122–4.

[27] For the Corporation, Hist. MSS. Comm., Salisbury MSS. xiv. 118–19; Repertory, xxv, fo. 8; ibid., xxxiii, fos. 80, 94, 161(b), 220; Remembrancia, i. 393, 499, 513; ii. 56; iii. 7; Patent Roll, 15 Jac. I, pts. 8, 14, 15, 18; A.P.C. (1616–17), pp. 203–4; for Caron, S.P. James I, 91/1, 122/43(i); for the peers, Cal. S.P.D. (1640–1), p. 128.

these circumstances recourse to borrowing on the security of pledges will reflect in many cases the relatively poor financial standing of the borrower. There is consequently a real measure of truth in Professor Trevor-Roper's argument that borrowing on mortgage as distinct from borrowing on bond or statute was 'a desperate expedient',[28] though to assume that this was invariably the case would imply the existence of much more highly developed facilities for the marketing of different financial securities than was, in fact, the case. And, of course, before the end of our period the development of the mortgagor's equity of redemption had robbed the mortgaging of lands of many of its terrors for borrowers.[29]

To some extent the history of royal borrowing appears to bear out the view of the mortgage as a security to be resorted to only in extreme cases. For instance, when James I borrowed £96,466. 13s. 4d. from the citizens of London in 1617, he raised the money on bond, or rather, as we have seen, on the bonds of the Corporation of London, which in return received the royal bond as counter-security. Only a very small portion of that loan had been repaid by 1625, when Charles I demanded a further loan of £50,000 from the citizens. The Corporation consented to lend its credit to the Crown as before, but the loan was now secured not by royal bonds but by the mortgage of lands sufficient in value to act as security for both the old and the new loans.[30] It may well be true, therefore, that, as this case suggests, the Crown, like the aristocratic borrowers, whose operations have aroused such fierce controversy in recent years, resorted to the mortgage of its lands only as a last resort.

But it may be doubted whether the natural corollary of this proposition holds good for the loans raised by the Crown as it does for those raised by aristocratic and other private borrowers. In other words, while it may be true that the Crown avoided borrowing on mortgage wherever possible, the explanation of this fact is to be found in its personal distaste for this expedient rather than in the intrinsic value of the mortgage to its creditors. For however much the Crown may have disliked the idea of pledging lands against its borrowings, there is no reason to believe that, from the lender's

---

[28] Trevor-Roper, *Econ. Hist. Rev.* loc. cit., pp. 296–7. Borrowers' lands could, of course, be extended for debt in the case of loans on Statutes Staple.

[29] For the equity of redemption, see above, pp. 8–9.

[30] See below, p. 127.

point of view, the pledge of royal property had significantly greater value than any of the other royal securities which have been described in this chapter. For if the Crown might refuse to pay the penalty of its bonds on default, and if there was no effective legal method of forcing it to pay, might it not also impose equally effective barriers in the way of foreclosure on its mortgages or, for that matter, the confiscation of pledges of personal property? The validity of this argument seems to be borne out by an examination of the principal cases of royal borrowing on mortgage security. That there were a very few examples of foreclosure is true, but far more striking are those cases in which lenders who themselves were hard pressed for funds, did not foreclose at or after the default of the royal borrower. Moreover, even in those cases where a form of foreclosure took place the transactions seem to have been governed by special circumstances in which the lands concerned were very obviously of far greater utility to the mortgagee than they were to the Crown. Such a case was the mortgage in May 1628 of Hatfield and certain other manors in the 'drowned lands' of Yorkshire, Lincolnshire, and Nottinghamshire, to the famous Dutch engineer Sir Cornelius Vermuyden in return for a loan of £10,000 for four months. Vermuyden's mortgage and subsequent foreclosure appears, in fact, to have been effectively little more than a form of indirect sale in which the purchaser made an advance payment of the purchase money before it was due.[31]

To draw conclusions from cases of this type about the value of royal mortgages as security would obviously be a highly questionable procedure, even if the history of royal borrowing on mortgage from other lenders, and, more especially, the loans negotiated by the Corporation of London, did not suggest quite opposite conclusions. For neither the loan of £60,000 which Elizabeth raised through the Corporation in January 1599 on the mortgage of lands nor that of £60,000 obtained by Charles I in May 1625 from the same source and on similar security was repaid on time. Both of these loans had originally been on short term, in the former case for seven, and in the latter for five months. In each case the loan had to be prolonged—that is, in effect, the Crown defaulted; in each case the lenders had ultimately to wait for several years before they were repaid; and in neither case did the lands become forfeit to the

[31] Patent Roll, 4 Car. I, pts. 9, 13; Close Roll, 4 Car. I, pts. 14, 17; Docquets, Charles I, bk. xiv; Coll. Sign Man. Car. I, vol. vii, no. 54.

mortgagee. Among the possible explanations of these facts, some weight may perhaps be attached to the Corporation of London's natural preference for repayment to be made in cash, thereby avoiding the cumbersome process of having to sell lands to pay off the creditors. However, in view of the abundant evidence of the urgent necessities of many of the lenders, and of the fact that ultimately—in 1628—the Corporation was prepared to accept conveyance of lands in repayment of the debt, it is reasonable to assume that the predominant factor in the situation was the pressure which the government was able to exert to obtain an unwilling but unavoidable prolongation of its loans, and thereby to avoid the necessity of foreclosure.[32]

All the cases of borrowing upon mortgage which have been described above are examples of the most normal type of mortgage transaction, taking the form of a conveyance of the lands to the lender, but with a saving clause that if the condition of the mortgage—that is, the repayment of the principal and accrued interest at the contracted date—were observed, the conveyance was to be void. In such cases it was the borrower and not the lender who enjoyed possession of the lands for the duration of the loan. However, one example of a less common type of mortgage, in which the mortgagee entered into conditional possession of the lands which were pledged to him and appropriated a part of the rents to pay the interest charges, has survived in the records. The other remarkable fact about this unusual transaction is the relatively long-term nature of the loan. As we have seen, it was the frequent practice of the government to turn short-term loans into long by prolongation. Originally, however, such loans were rarely for more than a year's duration, and, more often than not, for from three to six months. The transaction now to be considered relates to a loan whose original term was two years, and there is every reason to assume that there was a connexion between the unusually long term of the loan and the unusual type of mortgage by which it was secured.

In February 1628 Sir Francis Crane, the Chancellor of the Order of the Garter, lent £7,500 to Charles I, receiving as security a mortgage of Grafton and other manors in Northamptonshire with an annual rent roll of £650. The mortgagee was to enter into possession

---

[32] Close Roll, 41 Elizabeth I, pt. 16; Patent Roll, 1 Car. I, pt. 4; *Hist. MSS. Comm., XIth Report*, vii. 133; S.P. Charles I, 1/66; C. of L.R.O. Journal (of Court of Common Council), xxxiii, fos. 85(*b*)–86, 107; Repertory, xxxix, fo. 227.

of these lands immediately and to appropriate to himself rents to the annual value of £600 to defray interest at the statutory maximum rate of 8 per cent. The remainder of the rents was to go to the Crown, to which, by the usual 'indenture of defeasance' contained in the agreement, the lands were to be reconveyed on the repayment of the principal sum at the end of two years. Repayment was not made at that time, but Crane was persuaded not to foreclose, and the loan was prolonged. In addition to this, however, a curious bargain was struck, whereby Crane was to pay the Crown a further £6,000 in return for the absolute sale to him of a part of these lands of the annual rental of £200, of which half was to be devoted to the establishment of the manufacture of tapestries at Grafton. Crane had long been connected with the production of tapestries at Mortlake and clearly desired to extend production outside the Home Counties. But the King later changed his mind, deciding that the lands should not be sold to Crane, who, in the meantime, however, on 22 February 1630, had already paid in £5,000 of his purchase money. Since this was not returned to him, the principal debt of Charles I to Crane was now £12,500. Moreover, no provision was made for the payment of interest on the advance of 1630, other than a Privy Seal which was not honoured. Not unnaturally Crane became increasingly aggrieved as the prospect of repayment diminished, but his threat that he would foreclose could not have been taken very seriously by the Crown, since foreclosure would not help him in the least to recover his second advance of £5,000. In these circumstances the borrower clearly held the whip-hand, and that Crane appreciated the realities of the situation is clear enough from the terms in which his rather feeble threat to foreclose was couched. He would do so, he asserted, only 'if such be his Majesty's good pleasure', strange terms for a mortgagee to use when addressing a defaulting debtor, except in circumstances when that debtor was the Crown. Although one of Crane's local enemies, Sir Robert Osborne, later claimed that Crane was acting as if foreclosure had already taken place and that he had enclosed some of the lands and raised some of the rents, this charge drew a spirited denial from Crane, who stated emphatically that there had been no foreclosure, that to fail to exact increased rents when leases fell in 'would have byn ill husbandrye', and that in any case he was accountable to the King for any increase in rents. The controversy ended with the repayment of Crane's loan at a date which is uncertain, though it is clear that the mortgaged lands had been redeemed by May 1638.[33]

Cases of royal borrowing on pledges of personal property were even rarer than those of borrowing on the mortgage of land. Although technically the pledge would become the absolute property of the lender on the default of the borrower, there is every reason to believe that the types of pressure which could be exerted to induce the lender to prolong the loan rather than to confiscate the pledge were as much in evidence in cases where personal property was pledged as they were in cases of mortgages of land. This may be true even of one of the most important of the very few foreign loans which were raised in this period, the £58,400 borrowed at Amsterdam in 1626 on the security of jewels, even though it is difficult to see exactly how effective pressure could be applied in the case of loans raised on a foreign capital market, and it may be that at least some of the lenders were not averse to prolongation. Nevertheless, fears that prompt repayment was unlikely probably deterred many lenders at Amsterdam, for it had originally been planned to raise £300,000 on this count. The hesitancy even of those who finally consented to part with their money was due not only to their suspicions that it was contrary to English constitutional practice for the Crown to pawn its jewels without parliamentary consent, but also to their fears that repayment would be anything but prompt. Their attitude had two important consequences, the first of which was their refusal to lend without first receiving collateral security that the jewels would be redeemed within three years, an apparently vain expedient.[34] The second was the withdrawal of many of the jewels from the projected operation, so that in the end the vast bulk of the money was raised on the pawn of the jewels of the Duke of Buckingham. Since Buckingham had owed everything to the royal favour, it is not unlikely that many of the jewels which he now so obligingly consented to pledge on the royal behalf had originally come into his possession as gifts from the Crown. Nevertheless, the withdrawal of so many of the royal jewels lessened the value of the security, a factor which, together with the widespread reluctance of many of the Amsterdam financiers to risk their capital,

[33] Patent Roll, 3 Car. I, pt. 1; Coll. Sign Man. Car. I, vol. vi, no. 2; vol. xiii, no. 33; S.P. Charles I, 180/42, 307/17–18, 342/3, 4, 4(i), 5, 390/40, 41. I am indebted to Mr. Lawrence Stone for information about Crane's interest in the manufacture of tapestries.

[34] See above, pp. 58–59.

ensured that the loan was anything but the spectacular relief for the royal financial necessities which had originally been contemplated. Of the £58,400 which was ultimately provided, £11,400 was raised from the Elector Palatine, the so-called King of Bohemia, who in all probability raised the money himself by borrowing at Amsterdam. Thus the Crown had descended to the depth of borrowing from its chief remittance man. Besides this loan, it was able to raise only £7,000 from lenders who did not object to the royal jewels as security, while the remainder, including the Elector's loan and the largest single loan of £13,000 raised from Gerard van Schonhoven and Francis van Hove, was borrowed on Buckingham's jewels. During and after 1629, when the loans fell due, an unsuccessful attempt was made to provide the capital to redeem the jewels by the sale of English ordnance in the Low Countries, but this plan was frustrated by an alarming fall in the prices of munitions, caused, if John Brown, the King's gunfounder is to be believed, by the policy of dumping adopted by the Swedish armaments firm, Trip and Company, as part of its successful plan to drive English ordnance out of the Dutch market. None of the paltry sum of £18,532 obtained from the sale of ordnance could be employed in debt redemption, and by September 1633 there still remained more than £28,000 due to the lenders in principal alone. However, at least the most clamorous of them had been paid off, and the remainder had to wait until 1636 before they were repaid.[35]

Jewels were not simply the most obvious type of personal property to be pledged against loans, but in the case of royal borrowing, the only type. An obvious source of the smaller domestic loans on this security was the official royal jewellers, who from time to time sold jewels to members of the royal family, and whose skill in valuation especially fitted them both for the role of lenders on this security and for that of intermediaries in arranging such loans from other lenders. Thus the London goldsmith, John Williams, consented to

[35] S.P. Charles I, 8/7, 11, 11/75, 12/10, 19/122–4, 20/60, 26/59–60, 246/104, 285/91–94, 290/66, 295/34, 523/116; *Cal. S.P.D. (1625–6)*, pp. 123, 150, 178, 180, 255, 330; *(1629–31)*, pp. 41, 44; *(1635)*, pp. 3–4, 469, 565, 582–3; *(1635–6)*, pp. 167, 228; *Cal. S.P.D. Addenda (1625–49)*, pp. 97–98; Coll. Sign Man. Car. I, vol. ii, no. 18; Docquets, Charles I, bdle. xiii; P.C.R. (1628–30), fos. 368–9, 398; (1630–1), fos. 456–7; (1631–2), fos. 83, 284–5, 490–1; Exchequer of Receipt, Order Books (Pells), E. 403/2754, pt. ii, fos. 39(*b*)–40; Exchequer K.R. Declared Accounts, E. 351/1957; B.M. Additional MSS. 18764, fo. 22; *Hist. MSS. Comm., XIIth Report*, pt. i, p. 255; pt. ii, pp. 129, 135, 143; T. Rymer, *Foedera* (The Hague, 1735–45), viii, pt. iii, p. 60.

lend £3,000 to James I in September 1621 on condition that jewels were pledged with him to act as security not only for this loan but for an additional £2,000 which was owed to him by the King. In March 1615 Sir John Spilman, also an official royal jeweller, as well as a celebrated manufacturer of paper, was able to find a loan of £3,000 from six city merchants for James's queen, Anne of Denmark, on the security of some of her jewels, one of which, pawned by Spilman to a certain Gideon de Lawne for £500, was not redeemed until 1621.[36]

The loans which were made to Charles I by James Maxwell, a groom of the bedchamber, provide a fitting conclusion to the discussion not only of royal borrowing on the security of jewels but to the whole problem of royal securities, for in this case are to be found a number of the most significant features which characterize the general problem of inducement which is the subject of this chapter. Courtiers such as Maxwell were not only the most favourably placed of all subjects as potential recipients of the royal bounty. Those whom the Crown had made wealthy might themselves be called upon to aid it when necessary. We have already seen how Buckingham provided the bulk of the security for the loan at Amsterdam in 1626, and in 1628 he was to be of further service in finding a lender for the King. In the summer of that year Charles assigned to him two large diamonds on which he was instructed to raise money 'for our speciall service'. He pawned the diamonds to Maxwell in return for a loan of £6,000. The agreement between Buckingham and Maxwell was framed in the usual manner in the form of a deed of bargain and sale of the jewels to the latter, with a saving clause that if the principal together with the accrued interest of £240 were paid to him on 18 December 1628, the jewels were to be redeemed. In November Maxwell lent a further £4,300, and expressed willingness to prolong the old loan for a further six months. No additional security was granted to him for his new loan, and the same jewels were to remain in pledge for both sums, the King accepting responsibility for Buckingham's part in the business, since the Duke had been assassinated in the meantime. Both principal sums together with the interest on the old loan were now combined to form a new principal of £10,490. 18s., which was to be

[36] Patent Roll, 19 Jac. I, pt. 7; S.P. James I, 80/60–63; *Cal. S.P.D. (1611–18)*, p. 275; Docquets, James I, bk. xii; Coll. Sign Man. Jac. I, vol. xii, no. 85; Exchequer of Receipt, Order Book (Pells), E. 403/2741, fo. 18.

repaid with interest on 15 May 1629 on pain of the forfeiture of the jewels. At the end of this period, however, Maxwell consented to a further prolongation for yet another six months. The jewels were by now so obviously insufficient to cover the value of the debt, let alone act as reasonable security, that he was allowed to surrender them and to receive in their place other jewels valued at £12,554. The transaction was not finally closed until 26 January 1630, when an agreement was concluded whereby Maxwell was to have the jewels outright, not as a forfeiture, but in repayment of the royal debt to him. In these circumstances he was compelled to pay into the Exchequer the sum of £1,056. 13s. 4d., the difference between the debt due to him and the estimated worth of the jewels.[37]

No moneylender would have considered accepting such terms from a private borrower. Either the debt would have to be paid or the pledge confiscated without compensation. Why then was Maxwell willing to consent to a final settlement which was so favourable to the royal borrower? It may be, of course, that willingness did not enter into the picture at all, for his position at Court certainly made him particularly susceptible to royal pressure. At the same time, however, it might make him the potential recipient of coveted Court and other privileges. Strongly exerted pressure to accede to the royal terms, the bait of further advancement at Court, the part-payment for financial services in kind as well as in cash—he received a licence to export calf-skins in November 1628[38]—all provide likely and plausible explanations of Maxwell's position in this case, and it is to the more general consideration of such supplementary methods of inducement that we must now turn our attention.

4. Privilege and Pressure

The outstanding fact which emerges from the foregoing discussion of royal securities is that, as a consequence of the unique position of the Crown, such securities were of less value to lenders than their private equivalents. Not only the tally of *sol* used as an instrument of anticipation but even the tally of *pro* and the tally of *sol* backed up by the bonds of the collectors concerned were subject to the hazards of over-assignment, while the apparent value of each of

---

[37] Patent Roll, 4 Car. I, pt. 32; 5 Car. I, pts. 11, 21; S.P. Charles I, 159/19, 21; *Cal. S.P.D. (1628–9)*, p. 176; *(1629–31)*, pp. 178, 216–17.
[38] Patent Roll, 4 Car. I, pt. 24.

the other types of royal security, despite their superficial identity with their private equivalents, was, in fact, vitiated by the lack of provision of legal processes against a defaulting royal borrower. The use of private sureties for royal debts offered a possible way out of the impasse, but the fate of the contributors to the Corporation of London's loan of 1617 does not suggest that all lenders on such security gained substantially in practice, and, moreover, the number of persons who were prepared to accept royal counter-security in return for offering themselves as sureties on behalf of the Crown was obviously limited.

In these circumstances the credit-worthiness of the Crown was absolutely dependent upon its refusal to take advantage of its special position and upon its determination to be as punctilious in the observance of its financial obligations as the most respected private borrower. Such was the lesson which Gresham had been at pains to teach the government in the early Elizabethan period, and the practice of it was well exemplified by his policy of raising new loans to pay off old rather than prolonging the latter, and in his insistence on the punctual payment of covenanted interest.[39] The fruits of his policy were to be seen in the rise under his tutelage of the credit of the English Crown at Antwerp, both in absolute terms and in comparison with that of the other crowned heads who competed for loans there. Moreover, Gresham was well aware that his maxims were even more applicable to domestic than they were to foreign borrowing for the obvious reason that the opportunities and temptations for the Crown to abuse its special position as a borrower were infinitely greater in circumstances when the lenders were not foreigners but its own subjects. From the argument of the preceding pages it is abundantly clear that even if the point of Gresham's lessons was appreciated by the Crown's advisers, circumstances in the early seventeenth century made it difficult or impossible to apply. The succession of unwillingly prolonged loans, dishonoured assignments, and unforeclosed mortgages suggests, indeed, that a harsher verdict may not be inappropriate.

In these circumstances there is every reason to expect that the terms that the Crown would have to offer in order to make its securities a sufficiently attractive financial investment to bring forth the money which it required would be a good deal more onerous than

[39] See R. Ehrenberg, *Capital and Finance in the Age of the Renaissance* (trans. H. M. Lucas) (1928), pp. 253–4.

those which lenders required of most private borrowers. The most obvious index of such terms is, of course, the rate of interest, and it is at first a little disconcerting to find that both James I and Charles I almost invariably raised their loans at the statutory maximum rate of interest of 10 per cent. down to 1624 and 8 per cent. thereafter, the same rate as seems to have been paid by the vast majority of private borrowers whose credit was certainly better than that of the Crown. Such additional payments as were occasionally made to lenders over and above the stipulated rate of interest represent, almost without exception, compensatory payments in cases where they had borrowed in order to lend money to the Crown, and when the date of these borrowings preceded that at which they re-lent the money.

In attempting to explain this failure of royal interest rates to reflect adequately, if at all, the difference between royal and private credit, it is first necessary to inquire into the significance of the statutory maximum rate of interest in this context. It is highly unlikely that this was fixed without any reference to the financial needs of the government. The statutory maximum rate was, in fact, the official view of the rate at which most lenders might be expected to supply funds to most private borrowers, and the rate at which it was hoped that the Crown also might be able to raise funds. As far as private transactions were concerned, the fact that official calculations concerning the desirable level of interest rates were by no means absurd or wholly uninformed, and the force of convention, which tended to make the level of interest rates far less responsive to changes in financial conditions than it is today, combined to produce a result in which there was a remarkably high correspondence between the statutory maximum and the market rates of interest. While there is ample evidence that private borrowers whose credit was good could raise money at appreciably lower rates, there can be no doubt that the Crown's estimate of its own financial reputation in ranking itself even with the least credit-worthy private borrower erred very much on the side of optimism. Nevertheless, it is not unreasonable to assume that, in times when its demand for loans was not unusually heavy or the financial conditions in London not unusually stringent, there would be lenders to be found who would be willing to meet its demands on these terms. This, however, offers no more than a very partial solution to the problem, for there undoubtedly were many occasions when this favourable juncture of circumstances obtained only partially or not at all.

The problem, therefore, cannot be solved by reading present economic conditions back into the early seventeenth century, and the vital factor in the situation is not the rate of interest, which has already been used as a key with which to unlock too many historical doors, but once again the special position of the Crown as a borrower. For if it is of the essence of that position that the Crown could apply pressure to unwilling lenders to obtain loans or prolongations, there is no reason why similar pressure might not be exerted to make them lend on terms dictated by the borrower. Moreover, there is another and at least equally important side to the unique position of the royal borrower. The Crown was the source not only of all coercive authority, but also of privilege, circumstances which enabled it to dangle before lenders a varied assortment of carrots as well as to wield an appropriately formidable stick. While the application of royal pressure to lenders makes the rate of interest an unreliable determinant of the royal credit, the frequent connexion of royal loans with the grant of privileges afforded vitally important and statistically imponderable additions to that rate.

In the connexion between government borrowing and the acquisition of economic privileges there was nothing novel. Many years ago Eileen Power convincingly demonstrated the connexion between royal borrowing and the monopolistic privileges which were granted in connexion with the wool export trade in the late Middle Ages.[40] By the Tudor period cloth had replaced wool as the main English export commodity, and while recent research has thrown important light on the government's many non-fiscal motives in its support for the Merchant Adventurers' Company in the reign of Elizabeth, this has served to supplement rather than to confute the description of the intimate connexion between commercial policy and royal financial needs which we owe to Unwin.[41] To this con-

[40] E. Power, *The Wool Trade in English Medieval History* (Oxford, 1941), pp. 63–85, and 'The Wool Trade in the Fifteenth Century', in *Studies in English Trade in the Fifteenth Century* (ed. E. Power and M. M. Postan) (1933), pp. 72–79; W. I. Haward, 'The Financial Transactions between the Lancastrian Government and the Merchants of the Staple from 1449 to 1461', ibid., pp. 293–320. But see also K. B. McFarlane, 'Loans to the Lancastrian Kings: the Problem of Inducement', *Camb. Hist. J.* ix (1947), 51–68; E. B. Fryde, *B.I.H.R.* xxii (1949), 119–20.

[41] See G. Unwin, *Studies in Economic History* (ed. R. H. Tawney) (1927),

nexion Gresham's advice to the government in the summer of 1560 when contemplating the use of the Merchant Adventurers to pay the Queen's debts at Antwerp, that '. . . for licence of long cloths, the Queene's Majesty to grant them liberally, and to let them suffer another way' bears sinister but eloquent testimony.[42] Nor is it only earlier periods that are prolific in examples. The date at which modern history begins and medieval ends has often been the subject of fierce and not especially fruitful controversy, but in the sphere of government finance, and, more particularly, that of government borrowing, the crucial turning-point is surely to be found in the foundation of the Bank of England in 1694. And here, too, the connexion between economic privileges and government borrowing was notoriously prominent. For the celebrated 'Recompenses and Advantages' in the form of the banking privileges which the Bank received in its charter were conditional upon its performing financial services to the government, and it was to its ability to mobilize large-scale loans for the government that it owed its very existence.[43]

Perhaps the most obvious example of the connexion between loans and privileges in the early Stuart period is provided by the case of the farmers of the great customs, whose credit operations are treated in the next chapter. Their regular provision of loans was at once the main *raison d'être* to the government of the system of farming and the main method by which the farmers sought to make themselves indispensable. But the farmers provide only the most obvious and outstanding example of this connexion. Since the bulk of those who lent money regularly to the Crown were business men of one sort or another, it is not surprising to find that their loans were frequently tied up with the acquisition or maintenance of economic concessions. Indeed, there is a strong likelihood that the number of such cases greatly exceeds those for which a definite connexion can be adduced from the evidence. It is of course in the very nature of such transactions that such a connexion is often extremely difficult to establish. There is, for instance, a very real possibility that Maxwell's licence to export calf-skins in 1628 was not unconnected with his accommodating attitude to Charles I's

pp. 149–67; F. J. Fisher, 'Commercial Trends and Policy in Sixteenth Century England', *Econ. Hist. Rev.* x (1940), 95–117; L. Stone, 'State Control in Sixteenth Century England', ibid. xvii (1947), 103–20.

[42] J. W. Burgon, *The Life and Times of Sir Thomas Gresham* (1839), i. 336.

[43] J. H. Clapham, *The Bank of England* (Cambridge, 1944), i. 17–18. See also E. L. Hargreaves, *The National Debt* (1930), p. 10.

financial demands, but evidentially the connexion is a tenuous one. A similar case is that of the grant made in June 1617 to the aliens Philip Burlamachi and Giles Vandeputt, conferring upon them the right to trade, paying the customs duties of native Englishmen, a concession which was made in return for 'many good services' among which was certainly the loan of £4,500 which they had made in 1615. Again, there can be no doubt whatever that there was a connexion between the loans which were made by the notorious Westminster soapmakers in the years 1633–5 and the continued retention of their privileges in face of widespread opposition. When public disgust and private influence finally resulted in their being supplanted by a rival company in 1637, part of the price which the latter had to pay for its success was an undertaking to advance £10,000 to the Crown before entering on its monopoly.[44]

Lenders were, however, sometimes unsuccessful in their attempts to tie up their loans with the acquisition of economic privileges. The Privy Council refused the request of those alien merchants who had lent £20,000 to James I in 1617 that a licence to export ordnance should be granted to them 'by way of gratificacion' in return for their consent to the prolongation of this loan for another year.[45]

Needless to say, the connexion between loans and privileges was not always so direct as might appear from the cases described above. To explain James I's consent in and after 1614 to the cloth-finishing scheme and commercial policies which are associated with the name of Sir William Cockayne solely in terms of Cockayne's services as a lender would be to invite well-justified ridicule. The abrogation of the long-established privileges of the Merchant Adventurers and the ultimate plunging of the English export economy into chaos were immensely too great a price to pay for the loans from that magnate, which, between 1608 and 1616, probably amounted to no more than £17,000. Nevertheless, there is every reason to concur with the opinion of the historian of the project who sees these loans as investments whose value to the lender cannot be summed up

[44] For Maxwell, see above, pp. 66–67; for Burlamachi and Vandeputt, *A.P.C. (1616–17)*, p. 284; Exchequer of Receipt, Order Book (Pells), E. 403/2735, fos. 77, 89; for the soapmakers, Patent Roll, 13 Car. I, pt. 29; S.P. Charles I, 294/62, 304/12, 311/38, 314/37; Docquets, Charles I, bk. xvii; B.M. Harleian MSS. 3796, fo. 22; W. H. Price, *The English Patents of Monopoly* (Cambridge, Mass., 1906), pp. 119–28; Gardiner, *History*, viii. 71–76, 284.
[45] *A.P.C. (1618–19)*, p. 69.

solely in terms of the interest which they yielded. It is, in fact, not unlikely that they helped both to keep Cockayne in the notice of official circles and at the very least to secure for him a sympathetic hearing once his long maturing plans were ready to be put into effect.[46]

The most characteristic privileges associated with monarchical government are, however, social rather than economic, and it has long been established that the early Stuarts exploited the social ambitions of their subjects both as a means of increasing revenue by selling titles of honour direct and of saving expenditure by conferring upon courtiers the right to peddle such honours, the latter expedient being a further variation on the familiar theme of expenditure reduction via the simple process of making grants in kind rather than in cash.[47] The Crown's motives were, as usual, mixed. As Mr. Stone has recently shown, the financial harvest which it reaped from these measures was by no means inconsiderable, but its subsidiary political motive of creating sources of political support was less successful, for the excessive sale of titles brought the grantor no less than the titles themselves into disrepute. Moreover, it not only fostered a vastly increased amount of jealousy between the old-established families and the parvenus, but also helped to create a dangerous disequilibrium between the number of titled claimants to office and the number of offices available.[48] Among the recipients both of baronetcies and peerages were two of the most notable lenders of the period, Sir Baptist Hicks, who became the first Viscount Campden in 1628, and Sir Paul Bayning, who in the same year was granted first a barony, and, ten days later, a viscountcy.[49] It is impossible to say how far these awards were made in return for their services as lenders or for cash payments

---

[46] A. Friis, op. cit., p. 236. Cockayne's advances during these years may have amounted to £23,000 in all, but it is uncertain whether one loan of £6,000 was in fact a prolongation. These figures do not include contributions to syndicated loans (S.P. James I, 40/42, 50/75; Warrant Book James I, vol. ii, fos. 132(b)–3; Docquets, James I, bk. x; Exchequer of Receipt, Order Books (Pells), E. 403/2729, fos. 82(b), 105(b), 235; E. 403/2730, fos. 92, 227(b); E. 403/2731, fos. 84(b), 99; E. 403/2732, fos. 93(b), 194(b); E. 403/2733, fo. 202; E. 403/2735, fo. 164(b)).

[47] On the sale of titles see C. R. Mayes, 'The Sale of Peerages in Early Stuart England', J. Mod. Hist. xxix (1957), 21–37; L. Stone, 'The Inflation of Honours 1558–1641', Past and Present, xiv (1958), 45–70.

[48] Stone, Past and Present, loc. cit., pp. 59–65.

[49] Cal. S.P.D. (1627–8), p. 580; (1628–9), p. 5; Mayes, loc. cit., p. 33. Bayning was created Viscount Bayning of Sudbury.

made either to the Crown or to a courtly intermediary. In his careful study of the sale of early Stuart peerages Mr. C. R. Mayes has concluded that 'under the Buckingham régime even the most meritorious deserts were seldom sufficient for reward without supplementary financial or political advantage'.[50] If this view is correct, as it may well be, the crucial issue is whether 'financial advantage' should be interpreted solely in terms of the payment of a purchase price, or whether, for example, the sums amounting to more than £40,000 lent by Bayning in the first three years of Charles I's reign,[51] might be sufficient to secure for him honours which others, who had kept a tighter hold on their purse-strings, would have to purchase in a more conventional manner. The same argument is applicable to Hicks, whose services, though less spectacular, had been more substantial, even if spread out over a longer period of time. In neither case can it be established that the grantees paid for their peerages in cash, and, although this negative evidence certainly cannot be regarded as conclusive, especially in the circumstances attendant upon this type of transaction, it is not unreasonable to assume that the services of Hicks and Bayning as lenders, together with the fact that, as supporters of Buckingham, they were a useful addition to the royalist opposition to the Petition of Right in the House of Lords, may be said at the very least to have marked them out as recipients of honours, possibly at reduced rates of purchase, and perhaps even gratis.

Another form of *quid pro quo* might be the offer of royal intervention to expedite the sluggish administrative processes of government departments. When Sir Baptist Hicks lent £10,000 to Charles I in May 1626, he did so on condition that the arrears of an annuity due to him out of the customs should be paid up. Hicks can hardly be blamed for using the power of his purse to secure this end, the need for which had arisen entirely out of the maladjustments of a financial system which rendered such periodic moratoria on payments of annuities and pensions necessary. The Crown on occasions exploited ruthlessly the opportunities arising out of such situations, as in June 1628, when, as the condition of obtaining the payment of

---

[50] Mayes, loc. cit., p. 30.
[51] Coll. Sign Man. Car. I, vol. vi, no. 36; S.P. Charles I, 42/56, 145/7, 153/17; Docquets, Charles I, bdle. xiii; Exchequer of Receipt, Order Books (Pells), E. 403/2745, fo. 126; E. 403/2746, fo. 195; E. 403/2747, fos. 52(*b*), 53, 161(*b*), 166, 180; E. 403/2748, fo. 151; E. 403/2749, fo. 430; E. 403/2750, fo. 326; *Cal. S.P.D.* (1625–6), p. 557.

the arrears of an annuity, Lady Raleigh found that she had to lend £4,000 to the King.[52]

The granting of exemption from financial and other public burdens in return for loans was a fiscal expedient which was frequently employed in later periods when government financial practice had become more sophisticated.[53] But the early seventeenth century is not lacking in similar examples. In the summer of 1620 Burlamachi lent £10,000 to James I in return for being forgiven the fine of £4,000 which had been imposed upon him for exporting specie, and we have already seen that tariff modifications might sometimes be instituted in favour of particular lenders.[54] Although such exemption was almost invariably confined to particular cases, there is one interesting case of an attempt to generalize the principle. In August 1627 a circular was sent out from the King to various municipalities urging them to lend money towards a project for procuring saltpetre 'without digginge of houses, Cellars, doue houses etc. or procuringe it from beyond the seas at unreasonable rates'. The lenders were to receive a lien on half the profits of the enterprise until such time as they had received full repayment in both principal and interest. In addition, they were to be freed from the attentions of the detested saltpetre men, from having their carts requisitioned for the carriage of saltpetre, and were to be given the opportunity of buying gunpowder cheaply, 'which graces of ours', the royal letter concludes, 'wee hope wilbe equivalent to your layinge downe soe small a somme of money as shalbe required for soe short a tyme, to performe soe greate a service'.[55]

Just as new privileges might be granted to lenders in return for their services, existing privileges might be withdrawn in cases of failure to comply with the royal demands. Threats to withdraw the partially consumed carrot might also be accompanied by a simultaneous brandishing of the royal stick. Privileged corporations, and notably the Corporation of London, were particularly vulnerable to this type of pressure. In April 1610 the then Venetian ambassador

[52] For Hicks, A.P.C. (1625–6), pp. 466–7. The original annuitant had been the Earl of Pembroke, who had assigned his annuity to Hicks in requital of a debt. For Lady Raleigh, A.P.C. (1627–8), pp. 505–6; Coll. Sign Man. Car. I, vol. vii, no. 49. This annuity was for £400 and was 2¼ years in arrears.

[53] See, for example, Hargreaves, op. cit., pp. 6–7.

[54] See above, p. 72.

[55] For Burlamachi, Cal. S.P.D. (1619–23), pp. 101, 115, 173; Exchequer of Receipt, Order Book, E. 403/2739, fo. 67(b); for the saltpetre project, S.P. Charles I, 74/45.

in London wrote in one of his dispatches that 'as the whole government of this City [London] is in the hands of the merchants, they have acquired great power on account of the need which the King and his Ministers have of them in realizing the revenue and the subsidies'.[56] Nevertheless, what had been acquired as a result of lending might be as easily withdrawn as a result of refusing to lend. It would be unreal, as indeed the ambassador suggests, to dissociate the two variant concepts of the 'city' as the municipal government which, inter alia, provided the machinery for raising loans to the Crown, and as the commercial and financial capital of the realm. Aldermen, common councilmen, and wealthy merchants were one and the same, and the municipal government might well hesitate to adopt any course which might prove displeasing to the King, on whose arbitrary action their continued prosperity might well depend. When, in the summer of 1640, the Drapers' Company refused to contribute to a loan to Charles I, Garway, the royalist Lord Mayor, reported that the King was more than unusually displeased, 'consideringe yᵉ lardge privilidges this Companye hath enjoyed from his highness. . . . And if his highnes shal please to question yᵉ company, they cannot be free from some excepcons which may be taken against them.' A no less striking illustration of the difficult position in which a privileged corporation might find itself when confronted by a royal demand for money is provided by a memorandum which was drawn up in 1617, when the raising of a large loan from the East India Company was mooted. The author emphasized the strength of the royal position vis-à-vis the company, claiming that 'Without his Majesty's vsinge his prerogative power, the said Companie and theire stock are at his Majesty's grace and pleasure to require of them what his highnes thinketh meete for his honner and proffit, which, as their case standeth, they nether may nor will deny.' It is difficult to imagine a more brutally eloquent statement of the reality of political force which, more than any other factor, distinguishes government from private borrowing in this period.[57]

Privileged individuals might find themselves in a position as unenviable as that of privileged corporations. In his recent exposure

    [56] Cal. S.P. Ven. (1607–10), p. 475.
    [57] On the Drapers, A. H. Johnson, A History of the Worshipful Company of Drapers of the City of London (Oxford, 1914–22), iii. 146–7; on the East India Company, S.P. James I, 90/54.

of the fiscal skeleton in the cupboard of Caroline administrative reform, Dr. Aylmer has shown how, in 1626-7, it was proposed to raise loans from royal officials who had exacted excessive fees from the public, about forty of whom, it was reckoned, 'may wel lend the Kings Majestie 1000 li. a peece; both in respect of their greate estates; and the grace and favor they receive from his Majestie by his late pardon, other wise the exacting unwarrantable fees from the subject might bring them to the danger of the Lawes'. This interesting and unscrupulous project was not adopted, but in 1639 a more ambitious version of the same idea was tried out.[58]

When all refinements such as the award or withdrawal of privileges or exemptions together with the quasi-blackmail of the last example, are removed, there still remains naked force, the most obvious examples of which in this context are the celebrated Forced Loans on letters of Privy Seal. But there was a strong element of compulsion in very many other loans which were raised by the Crown. A spell in jail might be the most speedy and convenient way to induce a favourable response both from the unfortunate brewer who, in 1615, refused to serve James I with beer on credit,[59] and from those members of the Vintners' Company who refused in 1628 to subscribe to the loan raised from their company.[60] A long walk in the height of the summer of 1617, following the royal progress from Carlisle to London was an expedient admirably designed both to stiffen the joints and loosen the purse-strings of the obdurate Londoner who can hardly have been accustomed to such strenuous and extended exercise.[61] And the official attitude to the stubborn aldermen who refused to co-operate as part of the machinery for raising money through the Corporation of London is admirably summed up in a letter from Sir Kenelm Digby, written on 23 June 1640:

As for my aldermen, methinks he would not be much out that compared them to nuts, they must be cracked before one can have any good of them, and then too at first they appear dry and choky, but bring them to the press, they yield a great deal of fat oil.[62]

[58] G. E. Aylmer, 'Charles I's Commission on Fees, 1627-40', *B.I.H.R.* xxxi (1958), 63-64. I am indebted to Dr. Aylmer for his kind permission to print this extract.

[59] *Cal. S.P.D.* (1611-18), pp. 273-4; *The Letters of John Chamberlain* (ed. N. E. McClure) (Philadelphia, 1939), i. 579.

[60] See below, p. 136. [61] See below, p. 124.

[62] *Cal. S.P.D.* (1640), p. 332.

Indeed, the city fathers were threatened in no uncertain terms on occasions when the council felt them to be dilatory in the financial service of the Crown.[63] They were also susceptible to some extent to more subtle forms of pressure. In the summer of 1640 Charles I threatened to coin £300,000 or £400,000 in brass or copper money if the Corporation refused to meet his demands.[64] Threats of a rather different kind were applied in 1616 to the wealthy Cornish business man and moneylender, Richard Robartes, who was compelled to lend £12,000 gratis to James I on pain of the confiscation of all his property for usury. Such at least is the story recounted by the gleeful Chamberlain, but another writer suggests that Robartes coveted a knighthood, an honour which was shortly to be conferred upon him, and it is possible that both types of inducement were present in this case.[65]

The elements of privilege and pressure, so admirably exemplified in the case of Robartes, were obviously not involved in every case concerned with royal borrowing, though it is highly probable that they were a good deal more prevalent than surviving records, rich though they are in examples, indicate. Nevertheless, these imponderables both provide a final solution to the otherwise mystifying uniformity of royal interest rates and impose an insuperable obstacle to significant generalization about the price which the Crown paid for its borrowings.

[63] For examples, see below, pp. 124–5, 129.
[64] *Cal. S.P.D. (1640)*, pp. 497, 513, 514, 521–2, 535; *Cal. S.P. Ven. (1640–2)*, p. 61.
[65] *Cal. S.P.D. (1611–18)*, pp. 412, 427.

IV

THE CROWN AND THE CUSTOMS FARMERS

1. *The Nature and Purpose of Customs Farming*

THE establishment of the great farm of the customs in 1604 regis-
tered a definite decision on the part of the government that the
greater part of the early Stuart customs revenue was to be vested
in the hands of business men who, in return for an annual rent,
obtained the right to appropriate the customs to themselves.
Although the new impositions and increases of the period were for
the most part administered directly under the Crown and not
farmed out to syndicates of financiers,[1] there can be no doubt that,
despite widespread opposition to the system of farming, early Stuart
governments favoured it sufficiently strongly never to reverse the
decision of 1604. Since the syndicates of customs farmers comprised
the most indispensable single group of lenders to the Crown as well
as important financial intermediaries through whom it approached
the money market, it is important to appreciate the motives which
impelled the government to call them into being and keep them in
existence in the face of bitter and often influential opposition.

The first and most obvious consideration is that of profitability.
Although customs farming was clearly a profitable business to the
farmers themselves, it is not necessarily true that it was less profitable to the Crown than a system of direct administration such as
was within its power and competence to establish would have been.
Numerous estimates, almost all of them equally unreliable, have
survived of the profits made by the various syndicates of customs
farmers at different times,[2] and many contemporaries were not slow
to point the moral that these profits might have gone to the Crown
under an efficient system of direct administration. Such statements
were of obvious utility even to a government which had no intention of doing away with customs farming, for they provided cogent
arguments in favour of screwing up the rents which it obtained

---

[1] On these, see F. C. Dietz, *English Public Finance 1558–1641*, pp. 362–79.
[2] On the difficulties of accurately estimating these profits, see Ashton, *Econ.
Hist. Rev.* 2nd ser. viii (1956), 319, note.

from the farmers at, or sometimes even before, the expiration of their leases. That this was their chief significance is amply demonstrated both by the history of the various leases of the first syndicate of the farmers of the great customs, and by the fate of the elaborate schemes for the replacement of customs farming by direct administration which were put forward by the customs expert, John Harrison, in the reign of Charles I.[3] Whether such schemes could have succeeded in combining maximum fiscal yield with royal control is uncertain. Their success presupposed the government's financial ability to afford an efficient administration of its revenue, and it is one of the fundamental paradoxes of early Stuart financial history that the royal finances were never in a sufficiently favourable position for the Crown to be able to afford to adopt the extensive administrative remedies which, though initially expensive, would have ultimately benefited its finances. As in the sphere of general economic policy, the administrative difficulties of the State were often solved, if only partially and sometimes with disastrous long-term results, by the vesting of public powers in the hands of private individuals. As a measure of administrative decentralization the farming of the customs is thus a parallel in the sphere of financial policy, to the issuing of the various types of patents of monopoly in those of industrial, commercial, and social policy.[4] To appreciate the value of customs farming to the hard-pressed contemporary statesman it is therefore not necessary to take very seriously statements such as the claim which was made in 1606 in answer to parliamentary grievances against the farmers of the currant duties, when it was asserted that 'the same farme yeldeth a far greater Revenue to the Kinge than the Customes did to the late Queene'.[5] In the circumstances of the revived commercial prosperity of the opening years of the seventeenth century, it would have been very shocking if it had not. It is reasonably certain that, when Lord Treasurer Dorset wrote in July 1604 that the King had decided that it was more profitable to farm the customs than to administer them directly, it was the saving of the administrative expenses of collec-

---

[3] See below, pp. 98, 101–2, 103.
[4] On these aspects of policy, see E. Lipson, *The Economic History of England* (London, 1947), iii. 352–86; W. H. Price, *The English Patents of Monopoly* (Cambridge, Mass., 1906), *passim*; M. W. Beresford, 'The Common Informer, the Penal Statutes and Economic Regulation', in *Econ. Hist. Rev.* 2nd ser. x (1957), 221–38.
[5] S.P. James I, 20/26.

tion that he had chiefly in mind.[6] The Crown could not afford to pay its customs officials adequately, a situation which made peculation inevitable, as the reforms of Customer Smythe had clearly demonstrated in the previous reign.[7] Peculation meant a decrease in revenue, and on that account a lessened royal ability to remedy the administrative deficiencies out of which this loss of revenue had arisen. In these circumstances revenue farming presented too easy a way out of the difficulty not to commend itself seriously to the minds of contemporary statesmen who were adopting similar solutions in other spheres of political and economic administration.

But the most widely canvassed argument in support of customs farming was that this system alone gave to the Crown the inestimable advantage of certainty in the revenue, or, as the Venetian ambassador put it, writing in 1604 of the negotiations then in progress over the establishment of the great farm, that in those branches of the revenue which were let to farm the King would know 'exactly how much he has'.[8] It is unnecessary to labour the utility of this fact to a government whose estimates of revenue were frequently wildly inaccurate, nor its particular applicability in the case of that branch of the royal revenue which was most obviously sensitive to fluctuations in commercial prosperity. Ideally, by adopting customs farming the Crown safeguarded itself against a fall in the revenue resulting from short-term commercial depressions, while, conversely, it was, of course, unable to take advantage of any improvement in trade which might occur during the continuance of a lease. That the system did not always work out quite so smoothly as this in practice deterred neither its private advocates nor the government itself. Sometimes departures from the theoretical ideal favoured the Crown, as in 1606, when the farmers of the great customs were forced to take a new lease at a higher rent before their old lease had expired.[9] The case for the change was reinforced by cloudy legal arguments, but these served only to obscure the government's real motive, which was to take advantage of the improvement in trade which had taken place since the granting of the first lease in 1604. Sometimes, however, by the insertion of saving

[6] S.P. James I, 8/134.
[7] On Customer Smythe, see F. C. Dietz, op. cit., pp. 317–19; A. P. Newton, 'The Establishment of Great Farm of the English Customs', in *Roy. Hist. Soc. Trans.* 4th ser. i (1918), 136–40.
[8] *Cal. S.P. Ven. (1603–7)*, p. 192.
[9] See below, p. 90.

clauses in their leases, the farmers were able to detract from the value of the farm to the Crown as a fixed source of revenue. Thus under the terms of their lease which ran from Christmas 1611, the farmers of the great customs were allowed to give short notice of their intention to relinquish the farm in any cases of over-restraint or prohibition of trade on the part either of the King or of any foreign prince.[10]

While these considerations do not disprove the widely held official notion that the system of customs farming gave greater certainty than that of direct administration, they do suggest that such arguments alone may not have been sufficiently cogent to compel the retention of the system, especially in the face of rival schemes which also impugned its profitability. It is necessary, therefore, to look beyond the main claims of the apologists for customs farming for an adequate explanation of the government's predilection for the system. It is not necessary to look farther than the peculiar ability of syndicates of business men to meet the royal demands for loans, and their greater willingness to do so if the retention of their lucrative privileges were made dependent upon the continuance of that ability. In return for loans made in anticipation of their rent, and for payments made on tallies directed on them in the course of an accounting year to total amounts which frequently exceeded by considerable sums the rent due from them, the Crown was prepared to offer to the lenders a farm of the revenue which they undertook to anticipate.[11] The connexion between borrowing and revenue-farming operations becomes all the more obvious when the financial services of the farmers are compared with those of collectors of those branches of the revenue which were not let to farm. It is true that such collectors could, and often did, make advances on their revenue to the government, and that, on occasions, one finds the sum of their advances exceeding the total revenue which they collected during the course of the accounting year.[12] Now each of these functions, the anticipation of revenue, and what amounts to the granting of overdrafts, was obviously the equivalent of the financial services which the farmers rendered to the government.

[10] P.R.O. Close Roll, 11 Jac. I, pt. 22.

[11] For a more detailed account of the technicalities of this system of advances and overdrafts, see Ashton, *Econ. Hist. Rev.* 2nd ser. viii (1956), 311–13.

[12] As in the case of Sir Richard Weston, who was 'in surplusage' by £100 on his account for the pretermitted customs for 1620, and £40 for 1622 (P.R.O. MS. Cal. of Sackville MSS. 7225, 8739).

In what sense, then, may these services be said to have carried sufficient weight for them to be considered as additional and powerful arguments in favour of customs farming as against direct customs administration? The answer to this question is to be found not in differences as to the kind of advances made, but in differences of *degree*, and especially of the size and term of the loans made. Of these two considerations, size is the more important. In the matter of term, it is perfectly true that while the advances of customs collectors appear to have been made almost entirely in anticipation of currently due revenue,[13] those of the farmers were, in the reign of Charles I at least, designed to anticipate not only the current rent but also the rents of future years. While there can be no doubt that this consideration was a major factor in causing the government of Charles I to decide in favour of the retention of customs farming in the face both of hostile criticism and constructive alternative proposals, it can hardly be adduced as a reason for its establishment, since, with very few exceptions, the farmers' advances in the reign of James I were of a short-term nature. It was largely, therefore, the size of the farmers' advances which made the system as such invulnerable to attack. In general if the Crown required regular loans of the magnitude of those which it obtained from the customs farmers, it must pay for them not only in terms of interest at the statutory maximum rate, but also by making it worth while to the lenders by farming out to them the revenues which they anticipated.

Another consideration may have been the fact that, for a time at least, no interest was paid in respect of one category of the royal borrowings from the farmers, their tenure of the farm itself apparently being considered a sufficient reward. It has been seen that one of the most important of their services was to grant overdrafts to the Crown, that is, to make more payments than their rent would bear over the course of an accounting year. It has also been shown that similar functions were performed by some collectors of directly administered revenue, though the size of the overdrafts granted by the latter was far less spectacular in relative as well as absolute terms. Now it was not until the reign of Charles I that the farmers were able to establish that interest should be allowed to them on

---

[13] There are some exceptions to this rule. For instance, on 9 March 1626 George Mynne, the Clerk of the Hanaper, lent £500 on his collection due in May 1627, and, on 28 July 1627 a further £1,000 on his collection due at Michaelmas, 1628 (P.R.O. Exchequer of Receipt, Order Books (Pells), E. 403/2745, fo. 37; E. 403/2747, fo. 150(*b*)).

these overdrafts,[14] and while it is uncertain whether more favourable treatment was, as a general rule, meted out to those collectors
of directly administered branches of the revenue who were from
time to time 'in surplusage' in the reign of James I, such cases were
by no means unknown. For instance, George Willmer, the collector
of the impositions of threepence in the pound on aliens' goods, was
paid interest for an overdraft of £530 incurred upon his account for
the year which ended at Michaelmas 1618.[15]

Nor was it only by overpaying their rents and making loans in
anticipation of them that the customs farmers made themselves
useful to the government. While some of them, such as Sir Francis
Jones and the two Wolstenholmes, were customs experts rather
than top-grade financiers, others such as Sir William Cockayne and
Sir Paul Pindar were among the richest members of the business
community, and as such were obvious targets for individual as well
as syndicated loans. In their private and individual, no less than
their public and corporate, capacity the willingness of these farmers
to lend money was rendered all the greater by the fact that they
were privileged concessionaires. And even among those farmers
who were not prominent as lenders to the Crown other than in their
capacity as members of a syndicate whose main *raison d'être* was
to make loans, there were persons who were able to make themselves useful in other ways, like the elder Wolstenholme and Sir
Abraham Dawes, by sitting as experts in customs causes and on
commissions of trade, as well as by proffering advice on other
problems of taxation; or like Sir Job Harby as an agent for the
purchase of military equipment overseas.[16] Moreover, on at least
one occasion, that of the great loan of £120,000 made in 1607, the
farmers lent money as a syndicate in a financial operation which
was quite distinct from their more normal anticipations of customs
revenue.[17] It was, however, these more regular advances which
constituted their main utility to the government, and to describe
these it will be necessary to give some account of the financial
organization and history of the various syndicates of customs
farmers. For this purpose, only the farm of the great customs and

---

[14] Ashton, *Econ. Hist. Rev.* 2nd ser. viii (1956), 312–13.

[15] Exchequer of Receipt, Order Book (Pells), E. 403/2740, fo. 6(*b*).

[16] *A.P.C. (1618–19)*, pp. 264, 486; *Cal. S.P.D. (1619–23)*, p. 157; *(1635)*,
pp. 11–12, 392, *(1639–40)*, pp. 368, 393; A. Friis, op. cit., p. 412.

[17] Ashton, *Econ. Hist. Rev.* 2nd ser. viii (1956), 315 and note; ibid. 2nd ser.
x (1957), 26.

the most important of the minor farms have been treated in detail, but such evidence as has survived relating to the smaller farms, such as the farms of the duties on seacoal, silks, and tobacco, suggests that here, too, the connexion between revenue farming and government borrowing was very close.

2. The Financial Organization of the Farms

It was observed earlier[18] that the main sources of the farmers' loanable funds were three—the collections of customs revenue, their other cash resources, and the money which they were able to borrow either collectively or individually. In the case of the last practice, borrowing by individual farmers upon their own credit appears to have been the most usual method, although individual farmers sometimes raised money on the collateral security of the bonds of their more wealthy partners.[19]

In the reign of Charles I, and probably earlier, the management of the business of collection was centralized in the hands of one of the farmers, whose task it was to supervise the collection of receipts, to make the stipulated payments of instalments of rent to the Crown, to pay out wages to customs officers, and 'To be earnest with the severall Collectors, Cashiers and receivors from time to time to make speedy payment to him of such money as every of them ought to pay to the end there may be money in cash to serve the great occasions of the farme.'[20] Among these 'great occasions' was the making of advances to the government, towards which current collections of customs revenue might form a part, a fact which provides the occasion for the common charge that the farmers were receiving interest for lending the King his own money.

It was probably the normal practice for the treasurer to be assisted by what served in this period for a professional accountant. That this sometimes had the effect of shedding more confusion than light upon the financial affairs of the great farm is suggested by a contemporary account of the management of that farm in the opening years of Charles I's reign, when the accountant was a certain Mr. Withers, who 'Kept his buisiness in luse papers tyed up in bundells

---

[18] See above, pp. 24–25.

[19] For an example, see Ashton, *Econ. Hist. Rev.* 2nd ser. viii (1956), 321, note.

[20] B.M. Stowe MSS. 326, fos. 79–79(*b*).

carried aboute him in five pocketes of his great breeches having not entred anything in books, for although he was entertayned as an accomptant he never appeared to have any skill therein.'[21]

In turning from the machinery for the collection and account of the receipts of customs revenue to the farmers' use of their resources, both in terms of their personal cash and of their ability to raise money by pledging their credit in the city, it is not easy to determine exactly who was responsible for raising the money which was required for making loans to the government, that is how far such responsibility extended from the principal patentees or directors, whose names are mentioned in the leases, to the lesser investors. Of the personnel of these subsidiary investors in the great farm, Sir Henry Wyndham wrote in June 1606 that there were at least thirty other investors besides the principals.[22] The farms appear to have been divided into shares, of which a controlling interest was held by the principals and the remainder were marketed. Sometimes, as was apparently the case with Pindar in the reign of Charles I, one farmer consolidated and increased his financial power at the expense of the others by buying up many of the shares of the subsidiary investors.[23] The financial organization of the great farm in the later 1630's emerges clearly from a petition to the King made (probably in the late 1630's) by Job Harby, in which he noted that the present principals divided the farm into thirty-two shares, twenty-four of which they retained for themselves, while eight shares went to 'certain under customers who perform no part of the service'. Harby desired the King to see to it that four of these shares should go to him, which would have given him an eighth share in the whole farm.[24] And, of course, these fractional shares might be further subdivided, by which process the financially weaker farmers —the customs experts rather than the financial magnates—might shift some of the financial burden from themselves to their richer fellows or to the investing public in general. John Harrison tells how a quarter share in the reorganized great farm of 1640 was divided between himself and Pindar, each having an eighth share of the

---

[21] B.M. Stowe MSS. 326, fos. 81–81(b).

[22] S.P. James I, 322/23.

[23] Stowe MSS. 326, fos. 81–81(b).

[24] Cal. S.P.D. Addenda (1625–49), p. 568. There is also evidence that the farm was divided into thirty-two 'parts' in the early 1620's (H. of Lords Journals, iii (1620–8), 318, 351–2, 354 et seq. I am indebted to Professor R. H. Tawney for drawing my attention to this source of information).

whole farm, and how he later sold a half of his holding, that is, a sixteenth share of the whole farm to a certain Mr. Toomes.[25] There seems in fact to have been hardly any limit to the fractional subdivision of shares. Lionel Cranfield, for instance, held a forty-eighth share in the great farm of 1604, and five years later he increased his holding of this stock by purchasing from Thomas Ivatt one-half of the latter's thirty-second share.[26] Sir Thomas May paid £300 for a twenty-fourth share in the second lease of the farm of the duties on French and Rhenish wine to be made in the reign of James I. Soon afterwards he assigned this share to Alderman Bennet, who sold half of it and retained the other half.[27] In such circumstances the opportunity for speculation in shares was considerable and speculative dealings were probably rife. Thus in December 1604 Cranfield bought a sixth of an eighth share in the silk farm from Samuel Hare and Richard Venn for £103. 6s. 8d. and was able to sell it ten months later at a profit of £201. 13s. 4d., 'for which Almighty God be praised'.[28]

Although it is clear that subsidiary investors in farming syndicates were expected to contribute proportionately to all normal charges such as the payment of entry fines, it is uncertain whether this liability extended to the provision of loanable funds, when the Crown demanded an advance from the farmers and the required sum was not available from customs receipts. While there is no obvious reason why the provision of such funds should not be a charge on the subsidiary investors as well as on the principals, the negative nature of the evidence precludes certainty in this matter.

3. *The Operations of the Farmers of the Great Customs*

After much competitive bidding the first lease of the great farm was made out to run for seven years from 24 December 1604, at an annual rent of £112,400.[29] The successful bidders were Francis

---

[25] Stowe MSS. 326, fo. 67.

[26] *Hist. MSS. Comm., Sackville MSS.* i. 101; for Cranfield's farming speculations, see R. H. Tawney, *Business and Politics under James I*, pp. 95–109.

[27] P.R.O. E. 126/3/78.

[28] *Hist. MSS. Comm., Sackville MSS.* i. 69.

[29] Close Roll, 2 Jac. I, pt. 18; S.P. James I, 12/51, 54; Exchequer, Declared Accounts, E. 351/609. For details of the competition for this lease, see A. P. Newton, *Roy. Hist. Trans.* loc. cit., pp. 149–50.

TABLE I

Credit Operations of the Jones–Salter–Garway Syndicate (1604–21)[a]

Year (Christmas to Christmas)	Rent (£)	Advance payments of current rent charged with interest[b] (£)	Advance payments of rent of subsequent year[c] (£)	Overdrafts on current account (£)
1604–5	112,400	Nil	Nil	Nil
1605–6	118,400[d]	Nil	16,000	1,525
1606–7	120,000	4,000	4,000	Nil
1607–8	120,000	Nil	Nil	4,470
1608–9	120,000	45,754	Nil	Nil
1609–10	120,000	18,817	2,000	Nil
1610–11	120,626[e]	2,000	Nil	Nil
1611–12	136,226	Nil	Nil	Nil
1612–13	136,226	Nil	Nil	Nil
1613–14	136,226	Nil	Nil	18,000[f]
1614–15	140,000	Nil	Nil	90,071
1615–16	140,000	Nil	Nil	34,114
1616–17	140,000	Nil	Nil	19,004
1617–18	140,000	21,500	Nil	27,488
1618–19	140,000	40,078	Nil	18,100
1619–20	140,000	6,000	Nil	18,000
1620–1	140,000	2,000	Nil	Nil[g]

[a] Unless otherwise stated, details from the declared accounts of the farmers (P.R.O. E. 351/609–24; A.O. 1/594/2–4; A.O. 1/596/11). The figures in this and subsequent tables do not include shillings and pence.

[b] Details from miscellaneous entries in Exchequer of Receipt, Receipt and Order Books (Pells).

[c] All advance payments of future rent bore interest. This applies to all subsequent tables also.

[d] £6,000 surcharge added to rent.

[e] £626. 10s. 2d. surcharge added to rent.

[f] These arrears were not technically an overdraft, since they were not carried over as a charge on the next year's account, but paid direct to the farmers from the Exchequer.

[g] When they relinquished their lease at Michaelmas 1621, the farmers had not fully paid up their rent for 1620–1; the deficiency of £2,369. 7s. 0¼d. was paid by them into the Exchequer in October 1623.

Jones, Nicholas Salter, and William Garway. Jones was first and foremost a customs expert, and although he is found engaging in a few speculative ventures in the reign of James I,[30] there can be no doubt that customs farming was both the main cause of his rise in wealth and by far his main economic interest, though he was later to launch himself into municipal politics with some enthusiasm, becoming Lord Mayor in 1620, the year before he went bankrupt.[31] Salter was a man of a quite different stamp and had been prominently engaged in the Levant trade long before he took up customs farming.[32] Goodman's gibe about the third member of the triumvirate, William Garway, the founder of a dynasty of customs farmers, that he was 'known to be a very poor man when he entered upon the customs, yet left great treasures behind him', is a rather misleading half-truth. It is indeed true that Garway made a fortune out of customs farming, and that his commercial interests, especially in the Levant trade, expanded considerably after 1604, due probably to the wealth which he derived from this source. But he was by no means a nonentity in the business world before the establishment of the great farm.[33]

Apart from the very large loan of £120,000, which was not made in the normal way of anticipation of rents and which has been treated elsewhere,[34] the credit operations of the farmers were relatively modest down to 1613. The rent was rarely overdrawn, and advances over and above the stipulated instalments of current rent were not noticeably large, though during this period they made more advances of future rent than were made during the rest of the reign. Perhaps the most important feature of the period down to

[30] For example, investment in a company formed to discover the North-West Passage, and the taking of shares in a syndicate of speculators in logwood (*Cal. S.P. E. Indies (1513–1616)*, p. 240; *Hist. MSS. Comm., Sackville MSS.* i. 150).

[31] A. B. Beaven, *The Aldermen of the City of London* (London, 1908, 1913), i. 12; G. E. Cokayne, *Some Account of the Lord Mayors and Sheriffs of City of London during the First Quarter of the Seventeenth Century* (London, 1897), p. 90; *Cal. S.P.D. (1619–23)*, p. 308; P.R.O. MS. Cal. of Sackville MSS. 508.

[32] *Hist. MSS. Comm., Salisbury MSS.* x. 216; *Select Charters of Trading Companies* (ed. C. T. Carr) (Selden Society) (London, 1913), p. 31; A. C. Wood, *History of the Levant Company* (Oxford, 1935), p. 24.

[33] G. Goodman, *The Court of King James the First* (ed. J. Brewer) (London, 1839), i. 305; *Cal. S.P. E. Indies (1513–1616)*, pp. 100, 117; *A.P.C. (1616–17)*, p. 343; *(1618–19)*, pp. 132, 271–2; Friis, op. cit., pp. 177–8.

[34] See above, p. 84.

Christmas 1614 was the successive enhancement of the rent. In the case of the first increase obtained from Christmas 1606 onwards, the government made use of bids made by a rival syndicate, headed by the farmer of the duties on sweet wines, Sir John Swinnerton, who had hoped to obtain the first lease in 1604, and, after his failure to do so, never let any opportunity slip of discrediting the successful syndicate. With the aid of his offer, the government was able to obtain an increased rent of £120,000 from the reigning farmers despite the fact that their lease still had several years to run.[35] On its expiration at Christmas 1611 a further increase followed. In face of fierce competition from the indefatigable Swinnerton, backed by the powerful Earl of Northampton, there was fierce bargaining and counter-bargaining, which lasted until October 1612, when a new lease was finally made out to the old syndicate for three years to run retrospectively from Christmas 1611 at the greatly augmented rent of £136,226. 10s. 2d.[36] Disgruntled at this increase and at the new and higher rent which they had been forced to pay for the farm of the duties on French and Rhenish wines, in which they had recently acquired an interest, the farmers—if Cranfield's account is to be trusted—planned to effect a reduction of £10,000 when the lease fell in at the end of 1614. But once again competition in the form of rival bids, this time from a ghost syndicate created by Cranfield with the deliberate purpose not of taking over the farm but of enhancing the rent of the existing farmers forced the rent up rather than down, and for the next seven years the great farm was held at a rent of £140,000 per annum.[37]

From about this time it is possible to discern an expansion of the credit operations of the farmers. It is clear that in one way or another the government was able to bring pressure to bear upon them to overpay their rents by substantial, and in the case of the year 1614–15, spectacular amounts, and that, since such overdrafts were free of interest, this was a very cheap way of borrowing. From the farmers' point of view the obvious way out of this difficulty was

---

[35] P.R.O. A.O. 1/594/3; *Hist. MSS. Comm., Sackville MSS.* i. 285, 291; *The Letters of John Chamberlain* (ed. N. E. McClure) (Philadelphia, 1939), i. 243.

[36] Close Roll, 11 Jac. I, pt. 22; E. 351/613–14; S.P. James I, 70/49, 55, 62, 63; B.M. Harleian MSS. 1878, fos. 146–146(*b*); *Hist. MSS. Comm., Sackville MSS.* i. 283–4, 285. The lease was not finally sealed until 16 April 1613.

[37] Patent Roll, 12 Jac. I, pt. 24; E. 351/616; A.O. 1/596/11; S.P. James I, Grant Book, p. 134 (S.P. 14/141); MS. Cal. of Sackville MSS. M. 395–6.

via insistence that overdrafts be charged with interest, and either
that all payments of current rent over and above the stipulated
instalments of rent should also be charged with interest for the
accounting year during which they were made, or that all such
additional payments should be assigned upon the rents of subsequent years and should bear interest from the dates at which they
were made until those on which they were repaid by defalcation
from the rent. Their inability for a long time to achieve any of these
aims can probably be attributed to their consciousness of the precarious nature of their position and their fear of being supplanted.
From 1618 onwards, however, there appears to have been a definite
improvement in their position. It is true that the customs farmers
had to wait until the next reign before the point about interest on
overdrafts was conceded by the Crown, but by reverting to what
was in a sense the practice which they had employed during the
years 1604–11, they were able to maintain some sort of a check on
the royal ability to take advantage of this cheap method of borrowing. In the first place, by insisting that all payments over and above
the instalments of rent stipulated in their contract should be
charged with interest, they were able to secure the payment of
interest, at least for the accounting year in which such advances
were made, after which time, of course, they were carried over to
the rent of the subsequent year as an interest-free overdraft. The
accounts suggest that, despite a temporary aberration in 1617–18,
they aimed at maintaining their annual overdrafts at the £18,000 or
£19,000 mark, in which circumstances it is reasonable to assume
that the exaction of interest on all payments other than stipulated
instalments of rent was used by them as a means of achieving this
end. From Christmas 1617 the charging of interest on such advances
became a regularly recurring feature of their financial operations,
reaching its peak in the year 1618–19, when the Crown directed
tallies to the amount of £113,940 upon them, of which sum £40,078
was charged by them with interest.[38] The fact that they finished the
last year of their lease in arrears rather than in 'surplusage' is probably indicative of difficulties which they experienced in the depression, during which Jones went bankrupt, as well as of the fact that
they would be more eager to underpay rather than to overpay their

[38] These tallies were for payments of rent other than those regular assignments which were made at stipulated intervals for disbursing departments such
as the Household and the Wardrobe.

rent since the reversion of their lease was granted to a new syndicate.[39]

In this analysis stress has been laid upon the devices which were
employed by the farmers to curb the royal tendency to run into
huge annual arrears. It is, however, quite possible that, from
1618 onwards, the Crown itself had less need for such overdrafts,
and that the reduction in their size reflects in some measure the
general improvement in all departments of the royal finances which
resulted from the reforming activities of the Treasury Commissioners. For in so far as the expenses of government departments
were reduced, the royal need to borrow would be correspondingly
diminished.

The only element of continuity between the personnel of the old
farming syndicate and that of the new group which took over at
Christmas 1621 was that of heredity. Jones's bankruptcy had precluded him from further participation, Salter either retired or was
excluded,[40] and Sir William Garway gave way to his son, Henry. Of
the younger Garway, more is known about his interests and wealth
in the 1630's and early 1640's than at the time of his accession to the
great farm, for his royalist activities during his mayoralty in 1639–
40 and after have engaged the attention of political historians, while
his great prominence in the Levant, East India, and Muscovy trades
distinguish him as a notable member of the business world in the
years of Charles I's personal government. In 1621 he was a less outstanding economic figure, and it seems likely that his experience as
a petty farmer and as collector of the new impositions were, together with the accident of heredity, at least as important qualifications for his entry to the farm as his wealth and standing in the city
at that time.[41]

This is emphatically not true, however, of the second member of
the new syndicate, Morris Abbot, the brother of the Archbishop of
Canterbury, and one of the outstanding merchants of the period.
Abbot's interests in the East India and Levant trades were very
extensive, and he had made a personal voyage to the Orient in 1615,

---

[39] The fact that the new lease was not granted until November 1621 does
not materially affect the argument.

[40] Salter retained an interest in the farm of French and Rhenish wines.

[41] D.N.B.; Beaven, op. cit. ii. 60; R. R. Sharpe, London and the Kingdom
(London, 1894), ii. 124–6, 130–1; M. C. Wren, 'The Disputed Elections in
London in 1641', in Eng. Hist. Rev. lxiv (1949), 40–41; Cal. S.P.D. (1641–3),
p. 99.

while in 1620 he had been sent to Holland in an attempt to settle
by negotiation the outstanding questions at issue between the English and Dutch East India Companies. Although these trades were
his chief, they were by no means his only, commercial interests. To
them should be added participation in a number of transatlantic
trading ventures and regular commerce of uncertain proportions
with France, Italy, and Russia. Abbot represents, perhaps as well as
any other great merchant who could be named, the nearest early
seventeenth-century equivalent to the merchant princes of other
lands and earlier periods, when even though the totality of commercial wealth was smaller, it was less widely diffused, and
the individual fortunes of a relatively small number of magnates
were correspondingly more spectacular. It was in his own right as
one of the richest and most influential merchants of his day that
Abbot sat—long before he became a customs farmer—on a number
of important commissions relating to trade and taxation, and he
was later to crown an outstandingly successful career by participation in both national and municipal politics, in the former case as
a member of the parliaments of 1621 and 1624, while his municipal
career culminated in 1638–9, long after he had relinquished his
interest in customs farming, in the office of Lord Mayor.[42]

Neither Sir John Wolstenholme nor Abraham Jacob, the other
two principals in the reconstituted great farm of 1621, were men of
anything approaching Abbot's wealth. Yet both of them, and
especially Wolstenholme, left a more enduring mark upon the
direction and organization of the farm, and it is tempting to conclude that Abbot's role was that of sleeping partner, while his more
experienced but less opulent colleagues provided the managerial
expertise. For although there is evidence that both Wolstenholme
and Jacob had participated in colonial and East India trade, and
Jacob had been a member of a syndicate which had been formed
to farm the pre-emption of tobacco in 1619, the primary qualification of each was the experience in customs affairs which they had
gained as collectors of several branches of directly administered
customs revenue. Wolstenholme, indeed, had been brought up in
the customs service, his father having been a Tudor customs official.
Like the Garways, the Wolstenholmes represent one of the great

    [42] D.N.B.; Beaven, op. cit. ii. 60; Friis, op. cit., pp. 222, 353, 404; Cal. S.P.D.
(1580–1625), p. 498; A.P.C. (1615–16), pp. 272, 366; (1619–21), pp. 102–3,
181–2.

customs families of the period, and Wolstenholme's interest was later to be transmitted to his son.[43]

The new lease was to run for seven years at a rent of £160,000, most of the increase being due to the absorption by the great farm of the farm of the duties on silks and other similar materials which had been let for the past two years at £16,000 per annum. But even the small net increase in the rent of the great farm is surprising in view of the depressed state of trade, and it may well be that the offer of a rent of £159,000 by a rival syndicate headed by Sir Arthur

TABLE II

Credit Operations of the Abbot–Garway–Wolstenholme–Jacob Syndicate (1621–5)[a]

Year (Christmas to Christmas)	Rent (£)	Advance payments of current rent charged with interest (£)	Advance payments of rent of sub- sequent year (£)	Overdrafts on current account (£)
1621–2	160,000	10,000	Nil	200
1622–3	160,000	38,380	11,760[b]	2,262
1623–4	160,000	29,435	Nil	188
1624–5	160,000	20,000	Nil	1,842[c]

a Details from E. 351/626–9.
b P.R.O. Exchequer of Receipt, Order Book (Pells), E. 403/2743, fo. 90(b).
c The farmers were repaid this sum by their successors who carried it as a defalcation from the first year's rent of their farm (E. 351/630).

Ingram was little more than a ruse of Cranfield's, and that the new Lord Treasurer was using the services of his old crony and business associate as a means of artificially inflating the offer of the successful syndicate. Cranfield, however, did concede that the new lease might be called in either by the farmers or by the Crown when it had run for three years, a provision which was based on his expectation that by the end of three years trade would have revived sufficiently to permit of a further enhancement of the rent. Cranfield's gamble was, however, conspicuously unsuccessful.[44]

43 *D.N.B.*; *Cal. S.P.D. (1603–10)*, pp. 329, 366, 449; *(1619–23)*, p. 91; *Cal. S.P. E. Indies (1513–1616)*, pp. 239–40; *P.R.O. Lists and Indexes*, ii. 22–23, 26.
44 P.R.O. E. 351/626; MS. Cal. of Sackville MSS. 7194, 7239; Goodman, op. cit. ii. 212–13; Dietz, op. cit., p. 334, note.

Although the early 1620's were a period of quite heavy government borrowing, this fact is not reflected in the credit operations of
the new syndicate. The overdrafts, still free of interest, were kept
down to manageable levels, well below those of 1613–20, and in
each year the farmers charged with interest a number of the payments which they made into the Exchequer or to assignees. Such
payments were in excess of stipulated instalments of rent, though in
the autumn of 1623 they made one advance of rent due in the
following year, this being connected with the repayment of sums
borrowed by Prince Charles when in Spain. This money had been
provided by the sale of bills on one Alexander Stafford, who acted
as drawee in London. The farmers provided Stafford with the sums
required, and in return they deducted £21,177 from their second
half-yearly payment for 1622–3, and the remaining £11,760 from
the first half-yearly payment of the rent of the following year.[45]

One of the reasons why the syndicate was not prolific in the
matter of loans may have been its resentment at the fact that, for
a period of commercial depression, the farm was over-rented. At
any rate the Crown was unable to avoid a decrease in rent in 1625
when the farmers relinquished their lease in accordance with the
agreement of 1621. They are said to have offered £148,000 per
annum for a new lease, but once again a bid from a new syndicate
succeeded in raising their offer to £150,000. Despite the fact that
both syndicates were willing to pay this sum, the Crown, perhaps
because of its experience of the unresponsive attitude of the older
group to its demand for loans in the early 1620's, and, as one contemporary alleges, because the rival syndicate was backed at Court
by the all-powerful Buckingham, granted the farm to the latter
syndicate for five years from Christmas 1625 at an annual rent of
£150,000.[46]

Wolstenholme and Jacob deserted their former colleagues to join
the new syndicate, which thus obtained the essential services of
'men of experience in customs affaires to manage so waighty a
service'.[47] The first of the other two farmers was the celebrated, or,
as many of his contemporaries would have preferred to describe

[45] E. 403/2743, fo. 90(b). In addition, they received interest on these
advances.
[46] P.R.O. E. 351/630; B.M. Stowe MSS. 326, fos. 58–59, 79(b)–80(b);
A.P.C. (1625–6), pp. 412–13.
[47] Sir Abraham Jacob died shortly afterwards and was succeeded by his son
John.

him, notorious, Sir William Cockayne. Cockayne, however, was not destined to play so important or disastrous a role in royal finance as he had done in the English cloth export trade in the previous decade, for he died in the next year, and was succeeded by his son Charles.[48]

But by far the most important member of the new syndicate was the remarkable Sir Paul Pindar. In the later Elizabethan and early Jacobean period Pindar had gained much business experience in Italy and the Levant. He lived in Italy for about fifteen years, where he acquired 'a very plentiful estate' by trading on his own account and by acting as a financial agent for others, including, so it was said, Robert Cecil. His experience of Italian financial institutions was later to bear fruit in an interesting proposal for an English national bank.[49] From 1609 he became involved in the diplomacy of foreign trade, acting as the consul of the English merchants at Aleppo, and, from 1611, as the Levant Company's ambassador to Turkey. When he finally returned to England for good in 1620, he was already an immensely rich man with a fortune to invest, and, despite the knighthood which was conferred upon him in that year, a disinclination to retire from business to the obscure pleasures of the life of a country gentleman. The years of depression which followed his return were not the most favourable time to launch himself upon a business world from which he had been isolated almost since childhood, but from about the beginning of Charles's reign he appears as one of the most outstanding figures in the city. Customs farming, which he completely dominated for by far the greater part of the period down to 1641, was only one, albeit the most important, of his many economic interests. He was one of the two projectors who together achieved the economic miracle whereby that greatest of royal white elephants, the alum farm, was at last made to show a profit. In addition, he was a money-lender on a truly grand scale. His individual loans to the Crown, which are treated elsewhere,[50] were the greatest advances of their type in the 1630's, and among the more notable of his private transactions were financial support for Courteen's East India expedition in 1635 to the tune of £36,000 and, in the following year, a loan of £18,620 to the Naval Treasurer, Sir William Russell, for payment of seamen's wages. The contrast between Pindar and Morris Abbot,

[48] For Cockayne, see Friis, op. cit., *passim*.
[49] See below, p. 189.   [50] See below, pp. 175–6.

the wealthiest member of the previous syndicate, is illuminating. Abbot's interest appears to have been that of an investor pure and simple; Pindar's that of a managing director who aspired to use his

TABLE III

Credit Operations of the Pindar–Wolstenholme–Jacob Syndicate (1625–38) and of the Goring–Crispe–Jacob–Nulls Syndicate (1638–9)[a]

Year (Christmas to Christmas)	Rent (£)	Advance payments of current rent charged with interest (£)	Advance payments of rent of sub-sequent year (£)	Advance payments of rent further into the future (£)	Overdrafts on current account (£)
1625–6	150,000	24,000	Nil	Nil	4,993
1626–7	150,000	Nil	20,000	Nil	10,057
1627–8	150,000	25,996	7,816[b]	Nil	3,305
1628–9	140,000	Nil	4,500	Nil	13,447
1629–30	150,000	Nil	27,000	Nil	12,669
1630–1	150,000	Nil	30,000	Nil	23,917
1631–2	150,000	5,000	57,200	Nil	35,589
1632–3	150,000	1,230	67,569	6,000	38,122
1633–4	150,000	30,000	25,000	7,000	53,067
1634–5	150,000	Nil	27,000	38,500	20,291
1635–6	150,000	28,814	20,000	30,000	33,046
1636–7	150,000	Nil	20,000	30,000	36,873
1637–8	150,000	1,614	31,000	Nil	31,244
1638–9	172,500	Nil	30,000	Nil	16,600

[a] Details from declared accounts, E. 351/630–42; A.O. 3/297. Details of interest-bearing advances on current rent from ibid. and miscellaneous entries in Exchequer Receipt and Order Books. The declared accounts do not always provide full information about the advance payments of future rents. Where necessary, therefore, this information has been supplemented by the accounts of anticipations of future revenue, which were issued at very frequent intervals during the reign of Charles I (S.P. Charles I, *passim*). All cases where it is doubtful whether a charge on future revenue represents an advance *payment* or merely a prior charge not payable until the revenue on which it was assigned had matured have been excluded.

[b] This sum represents the total of all advances for which there is definite evidence. But the charge of £4,956 for interest, which appears in the account for the next year (E. 351/633) suggests that this total may well be short of the full sum advanced on future rents in 1627–8.

wealth not simply as a means of deriving an income, but also to increase his economic control and assume a directive power which was little short of complete predominance. To this end he bought up many of the shares of subsidiary partners in the farm with the idea of acquiring a controlling interest.[51]

In 1628 Charles Cockayne was replaced by Abraham Dawes, another customs expert, and, with this exception, the personnel of the farmers remained unchanged down to 1638. The first lease, reduced in the meantime from five to three years, expired in 1628, and from then onwards until 1632 leases were renewed annually, after which time there was a return to leases for terms of three years.[52] Professor Dietz's explanation of the recourse to annual leases in terms of the farmers' timidity in the face of 'war conditions and political disturbances at home' is not very convincing,[53] and there are a number of more plausible alternative explanations for these fluctuations in policy. The period of annual leases coincides with one of Harrison's most determined attempts to persuade the Crown to abrogate the system of customs farming and to replace it by the form of direct administration which he had devised, and which, he claimed, would possess all the advantages of revenue farming and none of its disadvantages. The renewal of leases annually suggests that the Crown was at least toying with the idea. But Harrison's scheme was frustrated, partly, as it was claimed by one contemporary, by the liberal use of backstairs influence with Lord Treasurer Portland, during whose term of office, 'there was no means to divert this revenue . . . out of the ould way of farming, as being against the interests of that great man and of the farmers, his creatures'.[54] Whatever the truth of these charges, such backstairs influence as may have been exerted was supplemented by the farmers' adoption of a new lending policy which virtually made certain that their lease would be renewed annually. Overdrafts, the payment of interest on which was by now clearly established,

[51] D.N.B.; A Brief Narrative of the Cases of Sir William Courteen and Sir Paul Pindar (1679); T. Carew, Hinc Illae Lacrimae, or an Epitome of the Life and Death of Sir William Courteen and Sir Paul Pindar; Cal. S.P.D. (1601–3), p. 166; (1625–6), p. 546; (1627–8), p. 65; (1629–31), p. 291; (1635–6), p. 32; (1637), p. 500; A.P.C. (1627–8), pp. 364–5; B.M. Lansdowne MSS. 108, No. 90; Stowe MSS. 326, fo. 81(b); M. Epstein, The English Levant Company (London, 1908), p. 213; A. C. Wood, op. cit., pp. 42, 80–81, 84, 87, 247; A. Friis, op. cit., p. 417; W. H. Price, op. cit., pp. 96–100; R. B. Turton, The Alum Farm (Whitby, 1938), pp. 154–74.

[52] E. 351/630–42.

[53] Dietz, op. cit., p. 335. The period of annual leases lasted from 1628 to 1632, but war ended in 1630. And Dietz does not specify either the nature of the 'political disturbances' or the way in which they affected the farm.

[54] Stowe MSS. 326, fos. 89–89(b).

became more substantial over these years, and the farmers were in addition prepared regularly to assign a proportion of their advances upon the rent of the subsequent year. The statement of another contemporary writer on the subject that, 'by reason of anticipations of rentes and many before hand paymentes and surplusages or over-paymentes of rentes to be allowed out of following years, every foregoing farme depended upon the succeeding farme', puts the situation in a nutshell.[55]

The return to three-yearly leases from Christmas 1632 saw a corresponding change in the lending policy of the syndicate. Rather than draw in their horns and revert to short-term advances of current rent and more modest overdrafts they adopted a more realistic view of the situation, responding to the royal concession by expanding their lending operations still further by being progressively more prepared to anticipate the rent not only of the subsequent year, but also of the year following that. The large increase in the amount of such advances in 1634–5, the final year of the first three-yearly lease, is particularly noticeable. It is difficult not to see the directing force of Pindar behind this sagacious policy, which bore fruit in a further lease for another three years.

This expansion of the farmers' lending operations down to 1638 fits in perfectly with what is known of the general conduct of the royal finances in the period of personal government. It was shown earlier[56] that the tendency to cumulative hypothecation was one of the most important features of the financial policy of this period, and the credit operations of the farmers form an integral part of this tendency. They also reflect the growth of royal dependence upon the farmers in a period when many of the other sources of loanable funds were for various reasons drying up. Disputes with the Corporation of London made borrowing from this source difficult,[57] while many of the great individual lenders of the Jacobean and early Caroline periods, such as Hicks, Bayning, and Vanlore, were now dead, and the greatest of them all, Philip Burlamachi, whose lending activities had greatly declined since the mid-1620's, went bankrupt in 1633.[58] That adequate replacements were not at hand can probably be attributed to the decline in the royal credit.[59]

[55] Ibid., fo. 82.   [56] See above, pp. 41–45.
[57] See below, pp. 145–9, 152–3.
[58] A. V. Judges, 'Philip Burlamachi: A Financier of the Thirty Years War', in *Economica*, vi (1926), 299–300; Ashton, in *B.I.H.R.* xxx (1957), 168–70.
[59] See below, pp. 173–5.

Despite their heightened importance as lenders, Pindar and his associates were to receive a rude shock in July 1637, when they were informed that the King desired them to join in partnership with the courtier, Lord Goring, Sir Nicholas Crispe, and others. The next few months were to see a prolonged process of bargaining and negotiation, to parallel which it is necessary to go back to the days when the great farm had first been put on the market, and the early years of its history when Swinnerton and others had bid for the reversion of the lease. Difficulties probably arose from the beginning through Goring's insistence that the farmers should cease to exact interest on their loans for the whole of the ninety days allowed to them after Christmas till the closure of their account—an eminently reasonable proposal which the farmers accepted, though doubtless with an ill grace. A more important cause of disagreement was Goring's second proposal that a regular new year's gift should be bestowed upon the King. In October 1637 a new distraction appeared upon the scene in the form of yet another rival syndicate, headed by Henry Garway, the customs farmer of the early 1620's, and backed by the Earl of Dorset. This is probably the group which is recorded as making an offer to farm both the great and petty customs for a total increase of £30,000, the whole of which increase was to be paid in advance as an interest-free loan. The offer was not accepted, but neither was it successful in reconciling Goring and Pindar, and the latter is reported to have said that 'he could finde in his part to give 10,000 per annum more, soe he might chuse his owne partners'.[60] But this was just what he was not to be allowed to do, and the final break came in November. The most important issue now at stake was the method to be employed by the farmers in raising money for the service of the farm. The hotly contested discussion as to whether this money should be borrowed on the joint bond of the syndicate or on the security of the individual farmers was more than a mere dispute about esoteric matters of financial technique which provided Pindar with an excuse to break off negotiations. Pindar favoured the latter expedient for the reason that borrowing upon joint bond meant closer financial entanglement with Goring, whose judgement he clearly distrusted. Negotiations reached a deadlock on this issue despite Dawes's attempt to compromise with 'a proposition for the accomodation there of by give-

---

[60] Presumably £10,000 above the £20,000 increase which his syndicate had already offered.

ing and takeing of bondes one of another in such an abstruse way expressed as it could not be well understood what he meant there by'. Dawes's lucidity of exposition may have been at fault, but despite the apparent complexity of his proposals, they probably amounted to no more than a suggestion that individuals who entered into such joint bonds should counter-secure their partners by entering into additional bonds with them. Whatever the merits of the scheme, it failed to convince Pindar, and he and Wolstenholme withdrew from the proposed coalition, leaving Dawes and Jacob to join Goring's new syndicate, which thus acquired the services of two customs experts.[61]

Pindar, however, had yet another card up his sleeve. The lease was not due to expire until Christmas 1638, and even if he could not secure the reversion in conjunction with partners of his own choosing, he might at least play dog in the manger to Goring's ambitions. Hence we observe the strange and unedifying spectacle of the outstanding customs farmer of the Caroline period, when once deprived of the opportunity of directing the farm according to his own desire, joining forces with John Harrison in support of the latter's latest scheme for abrogating the system of farming. This unnatural alliance was short-lived, however, and Pindar withdrew on the grounds that his new-found disinterestedness in the efficient direct management of the customs might be interpreted as being motivated by envy and malice towards Goring and his partners. Despite his protestations to the contrary, such an interpretation would not be very wide of the mark, and it is probable that the lesser opportunities for profit presented by Harrison's scheme were the main reason for Pindar's lukewarm attitude. Harrison, however, continued to persevere with his proposals, and by February 1638 had obtained the backing of the Lord Chamberlain, the Earl of Pembroke, for his project. Influence at Court was essential if the plan were to succeed, but although this influence secured for Harrison a hearing from the King, Charles was unconvinced, and the plan was rejected on the grounds that it offered him 'noe more in certayntie than what he had contracted for with the new Contractors'. If this was the King's real reason for refusal, his arguments were threadbare in the extreme, for it was only the surplus over and above the already agreed rent which was uncertain, since Harrison's scheme offered the Crown certainty up to this point, and an

[61] Stowe MSS. 326, fos. 35(b)–39; S.P. Charles I, 369/48.

additional, though uncertain, surplus above it. Probably the connexion between customs farming and government borrowing was
the more important consideration, for while Harrison's proposal
contained provision for advances of rent, it made no mention of
overdrafts. Seeing that the cause was lost, Pembroke now made a
bid for the farm himself with the idea of drawing up the offer of
Goring and his partners, to whom the new lease from Christmas
1638 eventually went at an increased rent of £172,500.[62]

Despite the defection of Pindar, the new syndicate appeared to
possess all the ingredients which were required for success in the
business of customs farming. Expertise in customs administration
was provided by Dawes and Jacob; business experience and substantial wealth by Crispe, Sir Job Harby, and perhaps by Sir John
Nulls, about whom little is known, but who appears to have been
one of Harby's business associates; and influence at Court by
Goring, who had already had considerable experience in the exploitation of such influence to the end of securing lucrative economic concessions from the Crown.[63] If Harrison is to be believed,
the Pindar syndicate was safe in its tenure of the farm so long as
Portland was Lord Treasurer, but it was Goring's influence over his
successor, Juxon, that was the prime factor in ousting Pindar from
control.[64] Even allowing for Harrison's dislike of Juxon, whose
financial probity he was prepared to impugn,[65] the picture which he
paints offers a coherent and plausible explanation of the history of
the great farm in the 1630's. It is a picture which is familiar enough
to students of early Stuart economic history, and provides yet
another illustration of the degree to which success in so many
branches of economic life was dependent upon fortuitous factors,
such as the varying degree of influence which different parties were
able to bring to bear at Court.

Of Goring's other partners, Sir Nicholas Crispe was later to be
described by Clarendon as 'a citizen of good wealth, great trade
and an active spirited man'. Monopolist, shipowner, large-scale

[62] Stowe MSS. 326, fos. 39–52(*b*), 63(*b*)–66; P.R.O. A.O. 3/297, fo. 1.

[63] Notably licences to export butter and to make gold and silver thread, and
the pre-emption of tobacco. For his interest in the regulation of the tobacco
trade, see M. W. Beresford, 'The Beginning of Retail Tobacco Licences, 1632–
41', in *Yorkshire Bulletin of Economic and Social Research*, vii (1955), 135–43.

[64] Stowe MSS. 326, fos. 62(*b*)–63. He writes that Goring had 'obtayned the
power of disposing all thinges in this great office by placing therein his creature
the Bishop of London'.

[65] See his interesting allegations in ibid., fos. 62–62(*b*).

dealer in East Indian commodities, and member of the Merchant Adventurers' Company, Crispe is, however, chiefly remembered by posterity for his foundation and domination of the new Guinea Company in the 1630's, a project which, after making an unpromising start, was at last beginning to show a substantial profit. When Crispe fled from London to join the King at the beginning of the Civil War, the Long Parliament confiscated £5,000 worth of bullion which he had deposited in the Mint, as well as sequestering his stock in the Guinea Company.[66] Sir Job Harby was also a man of widespread economic interests, which included the Russia trade, through which he had obtained a number of naval contracts for the supply—on at least one occasion on credit—of cordage. In the mid-1630's he was shedding his considerable investments in the East India trade, perhaps as a prelude to his greater involvement in government finance. He was also a farmer of the pre-emption of tin, but his interests in that commodity extended beyond his holding in this lucrative royal concession to the export of tin in conjunction with other items of merchandise in considerable quantities to Mediterranean lands.[67]

The credit operations of the farmers of the great customs in the reign of Charles I provide a perfect example of the connexion between loans and economic privileges which was worked out in the previous chapter. It was primarily their indispensability as lenders which persuaded the Crown to reject the elaborate and well-thought-out proposals of John Harrison. It was the royal concession on the point of interest on overdrafts which induced the farmers to expand this side of their credit operations. And it was the supersession of annual by triennial renewals of leases which elicited a further response in the form of their willingness to anticipate rent even further into the future. Moreover, in considering the reasons

[66] D.N.B.; Clarendon, History of the Great Rebellion (ed. W. D. Macray) (Oxford, 1888), iii. 41–42; Cal. S.P. E. Indies and Persia (1630–4), pp. 268, 412, 414–15, 418, 429, 473, 497, 593, 596; Biographia Brittanica (ed. A. Kippis) (London, 1778–93), iii. 1522, 1525; Select Charters of Trading Companies (ed. C. T. Carr) (Selden Society, London, 1913), xliv–xlv; W. R. Scott, op. cit. i. 200–1; ii. 14–15; J. and J. B. Burke, The Extinct and Dormant Baronetcies of England (London, 1838), p. 141.
[67] A.P.C. (1623–5), pp. 153–4; Cal. S.P.D. (1629–31), pp. 19, 100, 136; (1634–5), p. 586; (1635–6), p. 347; (1636–7), p. 376; (1637–8), p. 83; (1638–9), p. 127; Cal. S.P. E. Indies (1617–21), p. 229; Cal. of Court Minutes of East India Company (1635–9) (ed. W. Foster), pp. 10, 73; G. R. Lewis, The Stannaries: A Study of the English Tin Miner (Cambridge, Mass., 1907), p. 52.

for the marked and progressive changes in the character of the farmers' advances in this reign, it is notable that the revival of trade after the end of the war in 1630 was not reflected in the rent of the farm, which, with the exception of one reduction to £140,000 in 1628–9, remained at £150,000 until the end of 1638. Although during the period of annual renewal of leases from 1628 to 1632, the farmers' advances of subsequent rent and the size of their over-drafts—in each case markedly higher than those of the early 1620's —made it difficult for the Crown to replace them, they at least did not directly impede it from taking advantage of the improved yield of the customs revenue by raising their rent. The royal failure to do this suggests that this was also part of the price which the Crown chose to pay for the expansion of the credit operations of the farmers, an inference which is strengthened by an examination of the loans which were made by Goring's new syndicate after 1638. For, in raising the rent of the farm to £172,500, the Crown suc-ceeded only in losing on the swings what it had gained on the roundabouts, and the most marked features of the operations of Goring's short-lived syndicate were a reversion to shorter-term lending and a substantial drop in the size of the overdraft.[68] There can be no doubt that the Crown had no intention that there should be a reduction in the overdraft, even proportionately to the increase in rent, especially in 1639, when its demand for loans was greatly increased.

The royal dissatisfaction at the performance of the new farmers was further increased by their inability to make adequate advances in the summer of 1640, when Charles was at his wits' end to find ready money. To meet this desperate situation a plan was devised whereby the indispensable Sir Paul Pindar, who had further demon-strated his worth by massive personal loans to the King in 1638–9,[69] should rejoin the farm, in conjunction with John Harrison, who, despite his opposition to customs farming, had obtained consider-able experience as a farmer of the petty customs over the past few years. Pindar showed a reluctance to take up customs farming again, which is not unnatural in view of his experiences in 1637–8 and the obviously desperate state of the royal finances in 1640.

---

[68] The falling off of the Pindar syndicate's advances in 1637–8 is, of course, attributable to the fact that the new lease from Christmas 1638 had by now definitely been acquired by Goring's company. In these circumstances it is perhaps surprising that any advances whatever were made in this year in anti-cipation of future rent.   [69] See below, pp. 175–6.

However, the retirement of the obnoxious Goring made the proposition somewhat less unattractive, while an interview with the King,
who pleaded prophetically that Scottish treachery 'had brought him
into so sad condition as that his crowne lay at the stake, and therefore desired for godes sake to help him with langage of such expres-
sion as inforced Sir Paule to weepe', reinforced the now rapidly
waning inducements of private profit by sentiments of public duty.
Cottington employed similar methods of persuasion with Harrison,
and in the summer of 1640 both the great farm and the petty farm
of wines and currants were let to Crispe, Harby, Nulls, Jacob,
Dawes, Pindar, and Harrison from Christmas 1640 and Lady Day
1641 respectively. The coalition of old and new farmers was virtually completed with the accession of the younger John Wolstenholme, whose father had died in the interim period since he had left
the farm in 1638.[70]

Since the final advances of the members of the new syndicate
were made in their joint capacity as great and petty farmers, it will
be convenient to precede the account of the last days of the early
Stuart customs farms by a short description of the development of
the three chief petty farms down to this time.

4. *The Operations of the Farmers of the Duties on Wines and Currants*

The three customs farms which were leased with the great farm
in 1640 were the petty farms of the duties on French and Rhenish
wines, sweet wines, and currants. The arrangements of 1640, however, simply mark the culmination of a process of consolidation
which had been apparent from the beginning of the period. This
process took two forms, of which the first was the tendency towards
greater integration of the three petty farms, culminating in the
establishment of one consolidated petty farm in 1632, and the
second, greater integration as between the personnel of the great
and petty farms, culminating, as we have seen, in 1640 in the leasing
of both great and petty farms to the same syndicate.

Apart from the ambitions of the more powerful farmers like Sir
William and Henry Garway, Salter, and Pindar, who desired to
obtain greater control over the whole farming system by means of
interlocking directorates, the main reason for these developments

[70] Stowe MSS. 326, fos. 66(*b*)–67, 71–71(*b*), 75–75(*b*), 89(*b*)–90, 100.

lay in the obvious utility of an integrated farming system for purposes of government borrowing. The more integrated the farms, the more powerful the farmers; the more powerful the farmers, the greater the possibility of obtaining substantial advances from them; and the greater the number of privileges which they obtained, the more willing they would be to make such advances. In fact, the same arguments which applied to the formation of a consolidated great farm in 1604 were equally applicable both to the consolidation of the main petty farms and to their closer integration with the great farm.

Both processes can be seen at work throughout the period. During the first period of the great farm's existence, when it was in the hands of the Jones–Garway–Salter syndicate, Garway and Salter acquired directive interests in the currant and French wine farms, the former in 1613 and the latter in 1607.[71] By these moves two of the petty farms were brought under more unified management[72] and into a closer connexion with the great farm. But for a long time the main stumbling block to further consolidation lay in the formidable person of Sir John Swinnerton. The early history of Jacobean customs farming was, in fact, dominated by the feud between Swinnerton and the Garway–Salter group. Swinnerton, with considerable experience of customs farming already behind him, had formed a syndicate which had been a strong competitor for the first lease of the great farm in 1604, and, if his bid had succeeded, the process of consolidation might well have moved even faster, for he had already held the lease of the farm of French and Rhenish wines since 1599. Both before and after his failure to obtain the great farm in 1604, he lost no opportunity to further his ambitions by canvassing powerful interests at Court, by entertaining the King and Queen sumptuously in July 1607, and by making a number of loans to James I.[73] The results of his efforts hardly repaid his trouble and expense, for he failed to supplant the Jones–Garway–Salter

[71] Close Roll, 4 Jac. I, pts. 38, 39; Grant Book James I, p. 125 (S.P. 14/141). Garway and Salter had obtained the reversion of the lease of the French and Rhenish wine farm in 1606 from Sir William Godolphin and Joseph Earth, for whom it had been obtained by the Earl of Devonshire. The rent was £13,662. 10s. and the previous farmer, Sir John Swinnerton, had paid £15,000.

[72] Another member of both syndicates was Wolstenholme, who was closely associated with Garway and Salter.

[73] P.R.O. Exchequer of Receipt, Order Books (Pells), E. 403/2724, fo. 212(b); E. 403/2726, fo. 2; E. 403/2730, fos. 96(b), 130(b), 138(b); Cokayne, op. cit., p. 55. Swinnerton lent at least £17,000 between 1604 and 1615.

group in the great farm, and, moreover, on the expiration of his lease of the farm of French and Rhenish wines in 1607, was forced to relinquish it to a syndicate of which the hated Garway and Salter were prominent members.[74] The sweet-wine farm, which he obtained in 1612, was little more than a sop to his frustrated ambitions, but his tenure of it, and, following his death in 1616, that of his widow, effectively blocked further consolidation until the lease expired in 1623.

Before this happened, changes had taken place in the great farm itself, for Abbot, Abraham Jacob, Wolstenholme, and Henry Garway succeeded William Garway, Jones, and Salter in 1621. Of the members of the new syndicate, Jacob and Wolstenholme were both to become farmers of the duties on sweet wines; Henry Garway was a member of the syndicates of currant and French and Rhenish wine farmers, while the latter's brother, William Garway the younger, though never a farmer of the great customs, was a member of all three syndicates of petty farmers. Although some members of these syndicates (like Salter, who had been deprived of his directorate in the great farm in 1621 but retained an interest in the French and Rhenish wine farms, Samuel Hare, John Mayle, and Richard Croshaw) were members of only one syndicate, and although some members of the great farm, such as Abbot, confined their interests to that farm, the early 1620's may be said to have seen further progress in the matter of greater syndication both as between the great and petty farms and as between the three petty farms themselves. In addition to this, the silk farm had been absorbed into the great farm in 1621, but, above all, the great barrier to further consolidation, Lady Swinnerton's hold on the sweet-wine farm, had at last been broken down.[75]

Down to this time the credit operations of the petty farmers had mostly been in the nature of short-term advances over and above stipulated instalments of current rent, though there are a few examples of longer-term advances.[76] The farmers' declared accounts for this period have not survived, but it is certain that some overdrafts were also granted. From 1626 the situation changed

---

[74] Close Roll, 4 Jac. I, pts. 38, 39.

[75] S.P. James I, Docquets, bk. xi; *Cal. S.P.D. (1619–23)*, p. 101.

[76] For a detailed account of these advances and full supporting evidence for the analysis which follows, see my unpublished Ph.D. thesis, 'Government Borrowing under the First Two Stuarts (1603–1642)' (U. of London, 1953), pp. 333–44.

abruptly, for in that year a loan of £20,000 from the aldermen of London was secured upon the rents of each of the petty farms down to 1628. Since in the meantime the Crown's need for other loans from the farmers did not cease, many of these advances had necessarily to be secured on the rents of years other than those in which they were made, and the pattern of regular longer-term advances which was observed in the case of the great farm now begins to be reproduced on a smaller scale in that of the petty farms also. Moreover, it was from about this time that the petty farmers began to make advances as a combined syndicate, even though these advances were made on the security of the rents of notionally separate farms. The first of such advances was a loan of £6,000 early in 1627, and a further £20,000 followed in September of that year. Thus, although the official existence of a consolidated petty farm dates from 1632, such an arrangement had a *de facto* existence, at least in connexion with government borrowing, long before that date. In this process of consolidation the royal demand for loans had played as important a role as the ambitions of the farmers themselves.

By 1632, when the consolidated petty farm became a legal as well as an economic fact, and was let at an annual rent of £60,000, the parallel process of integration with the great farm had also proceeded apace. Two of the members of the petty-farming syndicate, Pindar and Wolstenholme were also farmers of the great customs, while a third, Thomas Dawes, was a relative of the great farmer Abraham Dawes.[77] In these circumstances it is hardly surprising that the change in the personnel of the great farmers from Christmas 1638, was accompanied by a parallel change in the petty farm, which was to become operative on the expiration of the lease in 1639. Dawes, like his relative in the great farm, remained in the new syndicate, but Wolstenholme and Pindar, the retiring great farmers, were replaced in the petty farms also. Two of their successors, Robert Jacob and Samuel Crispe, were related to prominent members of Goring's syndicate of farmers of the great customs, while the other petty farmers, John St. Amand, William Ashwell, and Henry Boothby were probably men whose chief claim to consideration was their association with Goring, Harby, or Sir Nicholas Crispe.[78]

[77] The other member of the syndicate was John Harrison.
[78] P.R.O. A.O. 3/297, fo. 11.

The similarity with the great farm is no less striking in the matter of credit operations than it is in that of personnel. Due to the fact that most of the petty farmers' declared accounts have survived

TABLE IV

Credit Operations of the Petty Farmers of Wine and Currants (1633–40)

Year (25 March to 25 March)	Rent (£)	Advance payments of current rent charged with interest (£)	Advance payments of rent of subsequent year (£)	Advance payments of rent further into the future (£)	Overdrafts on current account[a] (£)
1633–4	60,000	?	11,500[b]	Nil	984[c]
1634–5	60,000	?	10,000[d]	Nil	2,298
1635–6	60,000	?	15,000?[e]	Nil	4,590
1636–7	60,000	?	20,000[f]	Nil	9,916
1637–8	60,000	20,000[g]	28,000[h]	10,000[i]	12,552
1638–9	60,000	10,000[j]	40,000[k]	20,000[l]	10,394
1639–40	72,500	10,000[m]	Nil[n]	Nil	23,509

[a] Details from P.R.O. Declared Accounts, E. 351/673–7; and for 1639–40, A.O. 3/297.

[b] S.P. Charles I, 263/36.

[c] No account has survived for 1633–4. The figure is derived from the account for 1634–5, to which the overdraft was carried over (E. 351/673).

[d] S.P. Charles I, 290/44.

[e] The declared account for 1636–7 gives evidence that advances were made in 1635–6 on the rent of the subsequent year, but the amount advanced is not specified (E. 351/675). It seems probable from the list of sums assigned by tallies and paid into the Exchequer that this was £15,000.

[f] E. 351/676; S.P. Charles I, 371/101.

[g] E. 351/676.

[h] E. 351/677.

[i] A.O. 3/297; S.P. Charles I, 410/108.

[j] E. 351/677.

[k] A.O. 3/297.

[l] Ibid.; S.P. Charles I, 450/30.

[m] A.O. 3/297.

[n] Ibid.

from Lady Day 1634, it has been fairly easy to reconstruct a tabular representation of these operations.

It is clear that the petty farmers, like their greater counterparts, were becoming prominent as longer-term lenders in the 1630's, a process which has been shown to have extended back into the later 1620's, before the establishment of the consolidated petty farm.

Apart from this, short-term lending by allowing the Crown to over-draw its current account became more and more prominent over these years, and, as in the case of the great farm, such overdrafts were charged with interest. Moreover, except in the matter of the size of the overdraft, which shows an increase which is more than proportionate to the increase in rent in 1639–40, the replacement of the old syndicate by the new in 1639, as a result of the machinations of Goring, had precisely the same results as the parallel develop-ments in the great farm—that is, a drying up of longer-term ad-vances. That the royal dissatisfaction with the customs farmers extended to the petty as well as to the great farmers is hardly sur-prising, for it has been shown that the very minor differences of personnel as between great and petty farmers in the late 1630's mask a fundamental identity of interest, directive power, and policy. In these circumstances the merging of the personnel of both great and petty farmers in 1640, like the consolidation of the three petty farms in 1632, was little more than an official recognition of what had long been an accomplished fact.

5. *The Last Days of the Early Stuart Customs Farms*

At no time during the period was the connexion between customs farming and government borrowing closer than in 1640, and Pindar and the reconstituted syndicate of great and petty farmers were under no illusions about the financial services which would be immediately required of them. Although the precise amounts which they lent at this time cannot be certainly determined, they were very considerable. It seems probable that the statement that they advanced more than £250,000 which is usually rather uncritically accepted by authorities,[79] is an exaggeration, based upon a misread-ing of the evidence. It can clearly be established that they advanced £84,500 in cash on the rents of the great farm falling due between 1641 and 1643, and £20,000 on those of the petty farm for 1641–2. In addition, tallies to the value of £112,470. 6s. 7d. were directed upon the rents of the great farm, and £36,272. 6s. 10d. on those of the petty farm, falling due between 1641 and 1644, and although it is clear that some of these tallies were never honoured, others, and notably the sums due to merchants for bullion taken from the Tower

---

[79] e.g. by Dietz, op. cit., pp. 285, 337.

in 1640, were. Thus the sums lent by the farmers in 1640 certainly amounted to considerably more than £104,000, though probably to considerably less than £253,000, and much of the latter sum, which at the Restoration was reckoned to be the principal sum owing to them, was certainly still due by them to the unsatisfied assignees of 1640.[80] During what remained of the reign of Charles I a number of projects to repay the farmers were mooted,[81] but all fell through, and none of the farmers were so fortunate as Sir Nicholas Crispe, who on joining the King at Oxford in the autumn of 1643, was repaid £12,000 of the principal sum of £15,000 due to him.[82] Long after the defeat and execution of the King, other measures were proposed in 1653, but these were no more than a rather futile attempt to wring blood out of a stone, for the condition that the ex-farmers should 'double'—that is, make an equivalent advance before receiving later satisfaction for both sums—was obviously too onerous for the now penurious survivors of the syndicate, who had to wait until after the Restoration before a start was made with the repayment of their debt.[83]

But the problem of the repayment of their advances was only one of many troubles with which the farmers were beset during the period between the calling of the Long Parliament and the accession of Charles II. The now powerful parliamentary party was naturally hostile to those who had collected customs duties which had never been granted to the Crown in parliament, and an all-out attack on the farmers soon developed. Charles I at first assured Pindar and his colleagues that he would stand by them, but, as in the parallel and more famous case of Strafford, he soon gave way before the storm. A Bill was prepared in 1641 for the confiscation of the farmers' estates, but parliament ultimately allowed them to compound for their delinquency by payment of a fine of £150,000, an enormous burden, when one considers the massive advances which they had recently made.[84] The customs farmers were thus

---

[80] Stowe MSS. 326, fos. 71–72, 75–76, 90–90(b), 100; A.O. 3/297, fo. 43; S.P. Charles I, 498/8; Cal. S.P.D. (1641–3), p. 491.

[81] Stowe MSS. 326, fos. 72(b)–73, 76(b)–77, 85, 93(b)–95, 100; Cal. S.P.D. (1641–3), pp. 67, 365.   [82] Cal. S.P.D. (1641–3), p. 491.

[83] Stowe MSS. 326, fos. 85(b), 100(b)–102; Cal. of Treasury Books (1660–7), pp. xix–xx, 506, 628.

[84] H. of Commons Journals, ii (1640–2), 154–7, 169; Sir Ralph Verney, Notes of Proceedings in the Long Parliament (Camden Soc., ed. J. Bruce) (London, 1845), pp. 78–81; Cal. S.P.D. (1641–3), p. 278; B.M. Harleian MSS. 1769, fo. 205(b); Stowe MSS. 326, fos. 72–72(b), 91–93(b).

among the first to experience the ruthless treatment that parliament was prepared to mete out to those whose fortunes were bound up with those of the old régime, and their history during the next two decades, unable to obtain repayment of their advances of 1640, and hotly pursued by their creditors, from whom they had borrowed to obtain the money to make these advances and to pay their shares of the fine of 1641, makes doleful reading. Whatever the merits of the parliamentary case against men like Pindar, Crispe, and Harby, it is difficult not to have some sympathy with Harrison, who ruefully observed that no punishment need ever have been inflicted upon himself or his partners if the King had only adopted his proposals for the abrogation of customs farming. 'And then', he concludes, 'what further benefit would thereby have accrewed and what damage to the crown would have bene prevented, let the understanding man consider and iudge.'[85]

[85] Stowe MSS. 326, fos. 68(*b*)–69.

V

THE CORPORATION OF LONDON AS A LOAN CONTRACTOR (1603–26)

THE adherence of London to the parliamentary cause was probably the most important single factor in the defeat of the Crown in the Great Rebellion. Even in the period immediately before the outbreak of hostilities the support of the city was not obtained without a struggle in which a powerful and influential minority of royalist aldermen was defeated. Nevertheless, in 1640 the overwhelming majority of politically conscious Londoners welcomed the calling of the Long Parliament as a check to the pretensions of the Crown and the end of the rule of 'Thorough'. The reasons for the alienation of the sentiments of that great majority of business men who were, unlike the monopolists and customs farmers, not the beneficiaries of the established system lie largely outside the scope of this study. But among the most neglected causes of London's opposition to the Crown are those which relate to finance. In this context the perennial dislike of business men for new taxes is relatively unimportant, for it is a commonplace that during the Civil War the citizens were prepared to assume, on behalf of a more popular cause, financial burdens which completely dwarfed those which had been imposed by the old régime. More significant is the cavalier treatment which the Crown meted out to its creditors, and more especially, to those most unwilling lenders who had made more or less compulsory contributions through the medium of the Corporation of London. The general significance of the royal use of the Corporation in connexion with its need to adapt the money market to meet its financial needs was treated in the opening chapter.[1] The present chapter serves both to provide detailed exemplification of the royal financial expedients which were outlined earlier, and to throw some light upon a by no means unimportant factor in the support of the capital for the parliamentary cause.

The significance of the Corporation of London in connexion with government borrowing is quite different from that of the customs

---

[1] See above, pp. 26–30.

farmers. Borrowing from the latter was a regular, from the former an occasional, expedient, corresponding usually with peak periods of deficit borrowing to pay off debts or to bridge deficits. The totality of the loans raised from the farmers was much greater than those raised through the Corporation, but with the exception of the abnormal case of their loan of £120,000 of 1607, the size of their individual advances tended to be smaller. The farmers were willing lenders, for they were well aware of the fact that the retention of their concessions, which they had no desire to lose, was conditional upon their making regular and frequent advances; the lenders who provided money through the medium of the Corporation of London did so because they had little or no choice in the matter. The farmers were the spoilt children of government borrowing, whose loans were made on the safest of securities and their bankruptcy in the 1640's was due to a change of régime and not to a change of heart on the part of the old régime; the contributors to loans raised through the Corporation had experienced little but bad faith from the royal borrower, and doubtless felt that the new era which opened in 1640 was the beginning of better times, when parliament would at last assume its proper functions, and taxes whose burden was distributed over the whole country would to some extent replace semi-forced loans, or would, at least, offer an earnest of prompt repayment of such loans. They were soon to be disillusioned.

It is, however, with the prior process of their financial disenchantment with the early Stuart rather than with the parliamentary régime that this work is concerned. This process was a gradual one and to see it at work it is necessary to examine in some detail the loans which were raised through the Corporation of London by James I and Charles I.

1. The Loan of 1604

Among the debts which James I inherited from his predecessor was a loan of £60,000 which had been raised in January 1599 through the Corporation of London. It is in some measure an index of the favourable attitude of the citizens to the new king that, before this loan was completely repaid in 1608,[2] two further loans, the first of them free of interest, had been raised through this body. Nego-

---

[2] For the repayment of this loan see Ashton, 'Government Borrowing under the First Two Stuarts (1603–1642)' (unpublished Ph.D. thesis), pp. 367–72.

tiations for the first of these loans began on 22 August 1604, when the Privy Council wrote to the Common Council of London requesting a loan of £20,000. Parliament had shown no willingness to meet the royal financial needs, doubtless remembering that two-thirds of the subsidies which had been voted in 1601 remained to be collected. In this they hardly did James justice, conveniently ignoring the fact that the estimated yield of about £300,000 on the remainder of the subsidies had to cover an inherited debt of about £400,000 and that the expenses towards which parliament had voted the subsidies did not cease automatically with the death of Elizabeth. James's response was swift, for, by disclaiming any intention that the Commons should burden themselves by granting a supply, he cut short any parliamentary discussion which might have ensued on the subject of the royal financial necessity.[3]

Towards the Crown's needs, a loan of £20,000 was a very small drop in the ocean, but it was at least something. But the Common Council's response to the government's request was not immediately encouraging. First of all it asked for a reduction, and it was conceded that the required sum be reduced to £15,000. Secondly, it requested that foreigners and free denizens who were resident in the city should not be excused from making their contributions to the loan. This may well have been a move in the Corporation's battle to compel foreigners to become free of the city, for if it could be brought home to the government that loans could be raised with greater facility if foreigners were brought within the jurisdiction of the Corporation, it might be induced to add its own pressure to secure this end.[4] This attempt to secure a *quid pro quo* for financial services was not successful on this occasion, and the issues which it raised were in a sense by-passed by the decision to raise the money from the Livery Companies, on whom the onus of assessment was now placed. Each of the companies was to receive a royal letter of Privy Seal as its security, and was to pay in its contribution to a collector whom the Corporation had specially appointed for the purpose. The Corporation's function was thus that of loan contractor, and was confined to the assessment of and collection of moneys from the companies, which, in turn, were secured directly by the Crown.[5]

---

[3] Gardiner, *History*, i. 186–7.

[4] I am indebted to Mr. T. F. Reddaway for this suggestion.

[5] C. of L.R.O. Journal of Court of Common Council (hereafter cited as Journal), xxvi, fos. 241(*b*), 243–243(*b*).

Of the fifty-five companies rated towards this loan the twelve great Livery Companies, of which the Merchant Taylors were rated highest at £1,350 and the Ironmongers lowest at £660, had to bear more than four-fifths of the total assessed sum of £15,127.[6] The Common Council had undoubtedly made this over-assessment in the expectation that it would have to concede pleas for reduction by some of the companies, and since such reductions amounted in all to £202. 10s., the total sum paid into the Exchequer fell short of the required £15,000 by £75. 10s. A wide choice of methods of raising their quotas was open to the companies. However, formal borrowing, as opposed to compulsory assessment of members who could be repaid at a later date without interest, was to be avoided as far as possible, for, since the companies received no interest from the Crown, this expedient would involve them in a heavy loss on the transactions, except in circumstances where, as in the case of the Drapers' and Carpenters' Companies, office-holders of the company were prepared to lend money gratis. And in each of these two cases such borrowing was adopted to help to make up a deficiency in an assessment of members which had fallen short of the required total. The Mercers, who borrowed the whole of their quota of £1,200 from Sir William Craven, a prominent member of the Merchant Taylors Company, were probably less fortunate. In these circumstances it is hardly surprising that most of those companies for whose activities documentary evidence has survived preferred to raise their quotas by a general assessment of their members, or sometimes of the richer brethren only, assessments which were in some cases supplemented by borrowing from individuals or from the corporate funds of the company concerned. In the case of the Fishmongers, a large number of the assessed contributors themselves borrowed out of the company's funds, while in two other cases, those of the Goldsmiths and the Coopers, the whole of the quota was supplied not by assessment, but out of the company's common chest.[7]

[6] Journal, xxvi, fo. 243(b). The ratings of the other major companies were: Grocers (£1,275), Haberdashers (£1,230), Goldsmiths (£1,200), Mercers (£1,200), Drapers (£1,152), Clothworkers (£1,050), Skinners (£900), Fishmongers (£847. 10s.), Vintners (£780), Salters (£712. 10s.).

[7] London Guildhall, Fishmongers' Company, Court Ledger, i. (1592–1610), fos. 397–8; Whitebakers' Company, Audit Book (1581–1625), fos. 144, 146(b); Brewers' Company, Court Minute Book (1604–12), no foliation; Carpenters' Company Court Book (1600–18), fos. 76(b), 79, 81; Wardens' Accounts (1592–1622), fo. 193; Coopers' Company, Court Minute Book (1597–1627), fos. 54(b)–

Delays in paying in the money by the stipulated date of 15 September were largely due to the fact that many of the companies questioned their assessment, a fact which prompted a subsequent municipal inquiry into the whole problem of company assessments towards such charges and towards the provision of municipal corn supply.[8] In a letter from the Lord Mayor, Sir Thomas Bennet, to Lord Cranborne, written in October 1604, probably to excuse the delay in paying the money into the Exchequer, the writer explained that the loan had been levied upon the companies with the idea that the masters and wardens of these bodies were better placed than the Common Council to know the wealth of individual citizens. He went on to plead that he had upbraided the officials of many of the companies on the grounds that it had been intended that no one should contribute who had not been assessed at £4 or £5 at least towards the last subsidy.[9]

Although repayment was due on 24 March 1606, James was unable to give satisfaction on that date, and, despite the fact that most of the companies were repaid in December, the repayment operation was not completed until 24 March 1608, on which day the royal debt to the Goldsmiths and Merchant Taylors was finally discharged.[10]

2. The Loan of 1608

In February 1608 the government began negotiations for a further loan of £70,000, the purpose of which seems to have been to pay off a number of bills currently due on the half-year's ordinary account. Although the evidence relating to this loan is not extensive, it is highly probable that, as in the loan of 1604, the role of the city

55, 56; Merchant Taylors' Hall, Court Book, v, fos. 137, 143–4, 198; Grocers' Hall, Orders of Court of Assistants (1591–1616), fos. 355, 357–62; Haberdashers' Office, Court of Assistants' Minutes (1582/3–1652), fo. 141(b); Goldsmiths' Hall, Wardens' Accounts and Court Minutes (1599–1604), fo. 366; J. J. Lambert (ed.), *Records of the Skinners of London: Edward I to James I* (1934), pp. 292–4; A. H. Johnson, *A History of the Worshipful Company of Drapers of the City of London* (Oxford, 1914–22), iii. 69 and note. In the case of the Goldsmiths, an assessment was made and those assessed were to enter into bonds to pay in the money on 24 March 1606, so that the company's funds might be reimbursed if the loan had not been repaid by that date. In the case of the Mercers, the loan from Craven was repaid by an assessment of members, who were paid interest at 8½ per cent. per annum.

[8] Journal, xxvi, fo. 265(b).
[9] *Hist. MSS. Comm., Salisbury MSS.* xvi. 340–1, 431.
[10] Exchequer of Receipt, Issue Books, E. 403/1703–4, no foliation.

Chamber was unimportant, for the lenders again paid their contributions direct to specially appointed treasurers, who then paid the money into the Exchequer, while for repayment, which was made promptly in June 1609, with interest at the statutory maximum rate of 10 per cent., the reverse procedure obtained. The bulk of the money appears to have been raised by collections made in the wards, and was paid into the Exchequer before the end of June 1608. Some four hundred citizens contributed £63,000 and twenty-four of their number acted as trustees for the lenders as a whole, receiving a royal bond in £100,000 as security. Of the £63,000, the Lord Mayor himself provided £300 in order, as he claimed, to set an example to the other citizens, but that his action was not completely successful may be seen from the fact that it had originally been hoped to raise £64,000 in the wards, but the additional £1,000 was 'retracted by divers persons that promised to be lenders'. The remaining £6,000 of the originally requested £70,000 was provided in equal contributions by Sir Stephen Soame, the wealthy Eastland and Levant merchant, and Sir Thomas Middleton, each of whom received a separate bond from the King. Thus in all £69,000 was provided.[11]

3. *The Loan of 1610*

The next royal request for a loan came in April 1610, when the Crown demanded £100,000 from the Corporation. By this time royal negotiations with parliament on the matter of the Great Contract had already taken an unpromising turn, and the supply of £600,000 which Lord Treasurer Salisbury had requested in February was not forthcoming for the reason that the parliamentary offer of £100,000 as an annual 'support' in return for the abolition of the obnoxious feudal burdens was not acceptable to the Crown. In these circumstances ready money was urgently needed, and of all the financial expedients available the government preferred that of a loan through the Corporation, although a general Forced Loan from the country at large had been considered. A very large loan would certainly strengthen the royal bargaining power, if only

---

[11] *Cal. S.P.D. (1603–10)*, p. 415; *Cal. S.P. Ven. (1607–10)*, pp. 92, 104; S.P. James I, 34/20, 45/116; Exchequer of Receipt, Issue Book, E. 403/1707, no foliation; Order Book, E. 403/2728, fo. 184; Remembrancia, ii. 310; Repertory of Court of Aldermen (hereafter cited as Repertory), xxviii, fo. 280(*b*); ibid., xxix, fos. 42(*b*), 46, 124(*b*); Ashton, *Econ. Hist. Rev.* 2nd ser. x (1957), 25.

because it would relieve the King of the necessity of precipitously accepting parliament's offer for the composition for feudal burdens in order to obtain an immediate supply. Indeed it is possible that the very success of the loan materially strengthened the royal intransigence, and therefore contributed to the failure of the Great Contract by allowing James to put forward his own price for the desired changes in June 1610, a price which parliament was quite unwilling to pay.[12]

At first, however, the city authorities had boggled at the royal request for a loan of £100,000, a considerably greater sum than any lent before by the Corporation, and they had attempted to obtain a reduction. The Privy Council was assured that the 'undertaking of a greater somme than ever the Cyttie lent to a King proceeded out of aboundance of love which might be more now than ever was, but not out of aboundance of riches or meanes being lesse nowe than some former tymes might have produced'. Their touching plea of poverty was rejected by the Council, whose only concession was that the loan might be paid in monthly instalments of £25,000.[13]

The loan was to be repaid in one year with interest at 10 per cent., and the lenders were to receive as security not only a royal bond in penalty of £150,000 made out to them jointly, but also assignments on the customs revenue, backed up by the bonds of the collectors and farmers concerned. It may be that this plethora of obligations was due to the unprecedented size of the loan and the reluctance of the municipal authorities to provide so formidable a sum. Another consideration may have been the exalted nature of the lenders, for the money was raised from the aldermen alone. Indeed, a number of factors suggested that it might be advisable for the city governors to avoid 'any generall Levy by Companies or to have many particuler men used herein'. Among them was the fact that a general levy through the wards had been the method adopted in the last loan, which had been repaid only in the previous year, while recourse to the Livery Companies was probably inadvisable when these bodies were still chafing at having to foot the bill for the Ulster Plantation.

---

[12] *Cal. S.P. Ven. (1607–10)*, p. 481; *Hist. MSS. Comm., Downshire MSS.* ii. 285, 286; *Chamberlain's Letters* (ed. N. E. McClure), i. 298; Repertory, xxvii, fos. 207–207(*b*); Gardiner, *History*, ii. 63–84; Dietz, op. cit., pp. 133–7. Dietz's failure to appreciate the general significance of this loan is due to the fact that he dated it wrongly as taking place after the dissolution of parliament (ibid., p. 148).

[13] Repertory, xxix, fos. 208(*b*)–209(*b*).

Once the aldermen had decided that the money must be raised 'without troubling the comonors of the Citty thereabout', there remained no alternative but to raise it themselves, for which purpose they divided themselves into nine groups, each of which was charged with the provision of an equal portion of the £100,000. Responsibility for a portion of the loan became in effect an *ex officio* burden which automatically accompanied the assumption of the dignity of alderman for so long as the lenders remained unsatisfied, and the three citizens who succeeded to the aldermanry during this time were obliged to reimburse the executors of their predecessors, and thus to assume the same financial responsibilities as their colleagues.[14]

In the case of this loan, as in that of its predecessors, there was no question of the Corporation's lending its credit to the Crown or of its performing any important function other than that of loan contractor. The lenders were overwhelmed by a number of different types of what proved to be uniformly worthless securities, but although some of these obligations were deposited in the Chamber for safe keeping, they were royal obligations to the aldermen themselves and not royal counter-security to the Corporation, as would have been the case if the latter had been acting as loan guarantor. Apart from serving as a place of safe deposit for these obligations, the role of the city Chamber was restricted to the making of occasional disbursements to cover such incidental expenses as were incurred in the drawing up of the bonds, for which services it was ultimately reimbursed by the Crown.[15]

Although royal interest-payments were made punctually, the connexion between this loan and the negotiations over the Great Contract, the failure of the latter, and with it the dashing of the royal hopes of a parliamentary supply, made prompt repayment of the principal impossible, for every revenue, pledged or otherwise, was needed to meet the ordinary expenses of the Crown. The aldermen had perforce to concede two prolongations—though not without serious opposition from some of their number—before the loan was finally repaid in four instalments between May 1613 and March 1614.[16] In these circumstances it is perhaps surprising to find that

[14] Close Roll, 11 Jac. I, pt. 21; Docquets, James I, bk. x; MS. Cal. of Sackville MSS. M. 98; Repertory, xxix, fo. 207(*b*); ibid., xxx, fos. 103(*b*), 108(*b*), 296(*b*)–7(*b*); *Chamberlain's Letters*, i. 298.

[15] Repertory, xxix, fos. 225, 304(*b*); ibid., xxx, fo. 240.

[16] S.P. James I, 63/60; E. 403/2730, fo. 184; E. 403/2731, fos. 172(*b*),

six of the aldermen were prepared to lend a further £2,000 apiece to the King in July and August 1613, these loans being repaid promptly when they fell due six months later.[17]

Nevertheless, there is some indication that the King's delay in repaying the loan of 1610 was reflected in the deterioration of the royal credit in the city, which, in June 1614, preferred to offer a free gift of £10,000 rather than comply with the royal request for a further loan of £100,000.[18] The background to this request is once again to be found in the failure of royal negotiations with parliament, for the Addled Parliament had been dissolved earlier in June without granting a supply. It is not impossible that the city's annoyance at the dissolution may have influenced its attitude to this new royal demand. Certainly previous dissatisfaction with royal policies had resulted in the city's election to parliament of Nicholas Fuller and its rejection of Sir Henry Montague, the candidate who was most favoured by the Crown.[19] However, it would probably be unwise to place great reliance upon an interpretation of events which identifies the Corporation closely with political faction at this early date. Not even the unpopular policies of Charles I could wean some of the aldermen, who were elected for life, from their support for the Crown, though it is true that the Common Councilmen, who had to submit themselves to annual election, were less impervious to currents of popular feeling. It is therefore probable that any political motives which may have influenced the Corporation's action in substituting a small gift for a large loan in 1614 were secondary to economic factors such as the deterioration in the royal credit following the treatment of the lenders of 1610. Moreover the Corporation's attitude may well have been reinforced by the possibility that the royal demand may have coincided with a period of temporary financial stringency in the city partly as a result of the ominous royal negotiations with Alderman Cockayne on the subject of the latter's cloth-finishing project. The case for the existence of such stringency is reinforced by the fact that half the gift of £10,000

196(*b*), 223, 247(*b*); E. 403/2732, fos. 150–150(*b*); E. 403/2734, fo. 17(*b*); MS. Cal. of Sackville MSS. M. 178; B.M. Lansdowne MSS. 165, fo. 196; Repertory, xxx, fos. 108(*b*), 296(*b*); ibid., xxxi, pt. i, fo. 70(*b*); Remembrancia, iii. 58.

[17] E. 403/2733, fo. 84(*b*); *Chamberlain's Letters*, i. 457, 469–70. The aldermen were Sir Stephen Soame, Sir Sebastian Harvey, William Cockayne, Sir Thomas Bennet, Sir John Jolles, and Sir William Craven.

[18] Remembrancia, iii. 152; *Chamberlain's Letters*, i. 546.

[19] Gardiner, *History*, ii. 230; T. L. Moir, *The Addled Parliament of 1614* (Oxford, 1958), pp. 41–42.

which was made in 1614 had to be provided out of the city Chamber, the remainder coming from the Livery Companies.[20]

The Corporation's substitution of a gift for a loan had the desired effect of diverting the royal attention from itself to the country at large, and its opportunism was undoubtedly the major factor in the initiation of the general Benevolence of 1614, of which the gift of £10,000 was a part. Some members of the nobility and higher clergy had already made personal gifts to James, and so well was the Corporation's offer timed that the Archbishop of Canterbury, in a letter to the Bishop of London, referred to it not as if it were a *pis aller* for the failure of a particular loan, but as a normal demand from the Crown to the Corporation made in the normal course of raising a more general Benevolence.[21] The records of the companies suggest that some of them took the initiative in offering a free gift themselves,[22] whilst others seem to have been specifically directed by the Lord Mayor to offer a gift rather than a loan.[23] In each case, however, there can be little doubt that the idea of the gift came originally from the Corporation itself, and that the example of individual companies assessed by the Lord Mayor towards a gift as an alternative to a loan would soon spread to other companies which would then, ostensibly of their own initiative, adopt this more agreeable course. For our purpose the incidents of 1614 are significant chiefly for the fact that they suggest a loss of confidence in royal securities in the city, and from this point we proceed naturally to an examination of the loan of 1617 in which the Corporation assumed a role which was radically different from that which it had played hitherto.

4. The Loan of 1617

On 22 January 1617 the members of the Common Council of London, being 'ashamed to comme short of those that had gone before them, in expressing their loyall and dutifull affections to so gratious a Kinge', agreed to James I's request for a loan of £100,000 for one year at 10 per cent. But their apparently cheerful acquiescence could not conceal the realities of the situation, for on this

[20] Repertory, xxi, pt. ii, fo. 380.

[21] Goodman, op. cit. ii. 158. This interpretation of the relation between the Corporation's gift and the general Benevolence also has the authority of Gardiner (*History*, ii. 261).

[22] Merchant Taylors' Hall, Court Minutes, vii, fo. 128; Mercers' Hall, Acts of Court (1595–1629), fo. 133(b).

[23] Vintners' Hall, Transcripts of Court Minutes for 1610–15, p. 174.

occasion the Corporation was required to do far more than act as loan contractor, and the new loan marks a reversion to the frequent practice of the mid-Tudor era of foreign borrowing, when the Corporation lent its credit to the government. On the payment of his contribution into the Exchequer each individual lender was to receive a tally of receipt, and on delivery of this tally to the municipal authorities, was to receive in return the bond of the Corporation, which undertook that the King would make repayment with interest one year hence. On the redelivery of the tallies into the Exchequer, the Corporation in its turn was to receive a royal bond under the Great Seal as counter-security that the Crown would fulfil the conditions for which the Corporation stood bound. The pious protestations of the members of a municipal deputation that they esteemed the royal word 'farre more then all the greate seales whatsoeuer' was no more than verbiage which is totally inadequate to describe a situation, the essence of which is to be found in the deterioration of the royal credit in the city.[24]

All but a few of the contributors were secured by the Corporation in the manner which has been described above. Ten of them, however, consented to lend direct to the King, four receiving the royal bonds and the remainder simply tallies of receipt as security. But only £2,700 was subscribed in this way.[25]

It appears that it had originally been intended to raise voluntary loans of about £3,000 from some thirty-three of the wealthier citizens, but once this plan had fallen through a more general assessment was adopted by which the aldermen rated some 280 citizens who contributed sums which varied between £3,000—which was lent by five citizens, among them Sir William Cockayne and Sir Thomas Middleton—and £100, at which sum 135 citizens were assessed.[26] The new arrangements for securing lenders had not

[24] *A.P.C. (1616–17)*, pp. 122, 172–3, 203–4; Patent Roll, 15 Jac. I, pts. 8, 14, 15, 18; Coll. Sign Man. Jac. I, vol. vii, no. 59; Journal, xxx, fo. 159; Repertory, xxxiii, fos. 80, 94, 161(*b*), 220–220(*b*); Remembrancia, iv. 64. This description of the Corporation's obligations as surety is different from that given in my unpublished Ph.D. thesis (op. cit., pp. 395–407), which is based on a misreading of the evidence.

[25] C. of L.R.O. Royal Contract Estates Papers (hereafter R.C.E.P.), 4, 'A Division of the King's Debt', 'Moneys lent by divers Citizens . . .'. Sir Thomas Hewitt, who lent £500, later had this transferred to the main account and presumably received the Corporation's bond as security (C. of L.R.O. Royal Loans Ledger (1617–29), fo. 1) (hereafter referred to as Royal Loans Ledger).

[26] *A.P.C. (1616–17)*, pp. 172–3; *Chamberlain's Letters*, ii. 53; Journal, xxx, fo. 159; Remembrancia, iv. 64; Royal Loans Ledger (1617–29), *passim*.

succeeded in making the loan popular in the city, and there were
many attempts at evasion, some of which necessitated severe puni-
tive action. However, some concessions were made. John Eldred
was allowed to postpone the payment of £400 of his quota of £1,000
until the following year on the plea that 'allmost his whole estate is
in venture beyond the Seas and that hee is not able to make half the
somme but by borrowinge'. Sir Stephen Soame, who had served the
Crown so well in the loan of 1608, was allowed to make contribution in goods in lieu of his quota of £3,000, but the goods were offi-
cially valued at £5,000! And other cases called for sterner measures.
The Corporation had called upon the Privy Council to force Rowland Backhouse to submit to his assessment, to which request the
Lords acceded and were understandably enraged when the municipal authorities later took up Backhouse's case, pleading that his
assessment should be reduced. William Cater, who had fled from
London, was fetched out of hiding and hauled before the Privy
Council, who demanded that he be rated at no less than £1,500.
Fear of being sent in disgrace to follow the royal progress to Scotland was enough to loosen the purse-strings of most of the remainder, though of the five citizens who received letters to the
Privy Council in Scotland, informing that body of their recalcitrant
attitude, at least one remained obdurate and had to make the jour-
ney north with uncomfortable results.[27]

By 23 April £80,000 had been collected, but great difficulty was
experienced in providing the remainder. In the meantime conciliar
rebukes grew sharper, imputing the delay 'either to backwardnes
and ill affecion (which wee would be loath to find in you . . .) or to
the negligent and indiscrete carriage of the same'. The council
reiterated the familiar complaint that the Corporation had under-
assessed the wealthier and over-assessed the poorer contributors
with the result that the latter were unable to lend without great
hardship to themselves and delay to the royal service. A further and
related complaint was that, in response to the council's request that
the names of the recalcitrant citizens should be reported to it, those
in charge of the loan did 'after soe longe tyme of breathinge, and
that the busines hath ben thus blasted by ill handlinge, retourne
such multitudes unto us as you doe, or make this Boarde your

[27] A.P.C. (1616–17), pp. 217, 219–20, 285–6; Chamberlain's Letters, ii. 85;
Cal. S.P.D. (1611–18), pp. 449, 481; Remembrancia, iv. 79, 84; Royal Loans
Ledger (1617–29), fo. 64; R.C.E.P. 3, 7; Gardiner, History, iii. 197.

mynisters to performe that which belongeth unto you'. What the council required of the Lord Mayor and aldermen was 'no further excuses and pretences, but service and performance . . . and that with such dilligence and expedicion as may redeeme your former omission and neglect'. Failure to comply with these demands would result in the aldermen being called upon to supply the deficiency themselves, whether they had already contributed or not, and perhaps to make an additional loan whose size should be proportionate to the inconvenience which the King was suffering from the delay. These formidable threats were made on 28 May, and were reinforced on 12 June by the Lord Treasurer's warning that any further delays would be reported to the King, who 'will take it verie ill'. Even after yet another similar rebuke had been administered on 11 July James had to be content with a total contribution of £96,466. 13s. 4d.[28]

The fact that many of the lenders were not repaid until well into the 1630's has meant that the role of the Chamber of London can be much more fully documented in the case of the loan of 1617 than in that of its predecessors, for the city Chamberlain's accounts, which have not survived before 1633, and the many miscellaneous papers which were drawn up largely in connexion with the repayment operation can be used to throw light on this problem. Nevertheless, it is highly probable that, even when allowance is made for the evidential deficiencies of the earlier transactions before 1617, the Chamber did play a far more important part in the loan of 1617 than it had done in the case of any of its predecessors, for the functions which it performed stemmed naturally from the Corporation's new—or revived—role as loan guarantor.

The first of these apparently new functions was the Chamber's subsidization of individual lenders. The total extent of these subsidies is indeterminate, but the majority of the lenders appear to have borrowed some part of their contributions from the Chamber, giving their bonds to the Chamberlain for repayment within one year. Thus part of the money lent to the Crown was, in effect though not in law, due to the city treasury itself, and although there was theoretically no more need for the Chamber to forgo the repayment of these advances until the Crown repaid the individual lenders

[28] A.P.C. (1616–17), pp. 256–7, 298–9; Cal. S.P.D. (1611–18), pp. 461, 468, 470, 472, 473, 475; S.P. James I, 112/24; Remembrancia, iv. 75, 77, 82; Royal Loans Ledger (1617–29), passim; R.C.E.P. 7.

than there was for them to forbear to sue on the Corporation's bonds if the Crown did not make repayment, in actual practice both sides exercised great restraint in this matter.[29]

More obviously connected with the Corporation's role as loan guarantor was the Chamber's payment of interest to some of the lenders. When the loan was first prolonged in March 1618, the King paid one year's interest to the Chamberlain which was distributed by him to the lenders. In this case the Chamber was, of course, acting simply as a distributing agency through which royal interest-payments might conveniently pass. But hereafter further prolonga-tions were obtained by the Crown year after year, and a hope which was raised in 1620 that the lenders would be repaid by annual assignments of £20,000 on the great customs soon evaporated when it was learnt that this was little more than a bait to secure further advances, to which proposal the Corporation not surprisingly re-turned an uncompromising negative. Moreover, no further interest payments were made by the Crown. In these circumstances the payment of interest out of the Chamber to some of the lenders on 11 February 1623 and 21 June 1625 was an operation of quite a dif-ferent order. It was, in fact, a unilateral payment by the surety, and not by the principal debtor, and was probably made to satisfy the most clamorous or the most influential of the lenders. The sum of £7,850 was paid out in this way, both payments being for five years' interest, that of 1622 for the period ending 11 February 1623, and that of 1625 for the five years ending 8 March 1623. The total prin-cipal sum on which this interest was paid was £15,700, about one-sixth of the total sum which had been advanced in 1617.[30]

Between 1618 and the end of the reign of James I a few of the contributors, some of whom had lent on the Corporation's bonds and some on royal security, were repaid privately by the King, and the principal debt to the lenders which was carried over to the next reign was in this way reduced to £86,066. 13s. 4d.[31] The Corpora-tion's refusal to accede to James's requests for further loans is hardly

[29] Evidence for these subsidizations is chiefly drawn from a later document, Repertory, lv, fo. 76(b).

[30] A.P.C. (1618–19), p. 73; E. 403/2737. fos. 77(b), 90; Repertory, xxxiv, fo. 424(b); ibid., xxxv, 69–69(b); ibid., lv, fos. 76–76(b); Remembrancia, iv. 103; v. 72; Royal Loans Ledger (1617–29), fos. 1, 77; City Cash Accounts, 1/1 (1633–5), fos. 83(b)–84.

[31] Cal. S.P.D. (1619–23), p. 390; E. 403/2737, fos. 101(b), 109(b); E. 403/2741, fo. 18(b). A number of other petitioners for repayment were not so for-tunate (MS. Cal. of Sackville MSS. 635, 7572, M. 857).

surprising in the circumstances of the financial stringency associated with the business depression of the early 1620's, to which must be added the fact that in 1620 and 1622 it had to make further levies on the Livery Companies and to deplete the resources of the Chamber to provide money for the Palatinate,[32] and, above all, its obvious reluctance to advance further sums in view of the continued refusal of the Crown to honour its existing obligations.

5. *The Loan of 1625*

The arguments against further advances were apparently less powerful after the accession of Charles I. The new king was more immediately concerned with raising further sums than with meeting his inherited obligations, and accordingly, in April 1625, requested a loan of £60,000 at the new statutory maximum rate of 8 per cent. per annum. The lenders were now to be collectively secured by a mortgage of Crown lands which was to be sufficient to cover both the new loan and the still unsatisfied debt of 1617. It was originally hoped that the duration of the new loan would be for a year, but this term was later reduced to six months, and it was agreed that both loans should be repaid within the year, that of 1625 in December of that year and that of 1617 in the following June. 'The citizens', wrote the Tuscan envoy in London, 'cannot do less than advance the money', and clearly the accession of a new king who held out such promises for prompt repayment of both the new and the old debt, and who resorted to the pledging of his lands, an expedient which had been shunned by James, as an earnest of his good intentions, made refusal difficult.[33]

On 25 May the Common Council decided that the money should be raised by thirty aldermen and 100 commoners, who were to be divided into twenty groups, each of which was to be responsible for the raising of £3,000. Since the circle of contributors was relatively restricted, provision was made for the replacement of the original lenders by fresh contributors in the case either of death or of the sensible deterioration in the wealth of any of the former during the currency of the loan. In the event only 119 contributors were found,

[32] Out of a contribution of £6,666. 13s. 4d. made in 1620, £1,666. 13s. 4d. was paid out of the Chamber (Repertory, xxv, fo. 57(b)). Dietz's statement that the Corporation provided £10,000 on this count seems to be due to his having mistaken marks for pounds (op. cit., pp. 186–7).

[33] S.P. Charles I, 1/66; Patent Roll, 1 Car. I, pt. 4; Journal, xxxiii, fos. 85(b)–86(b); *Hist. MSS. Comm.*, *XIth Report*, i. 9.

one lending £200 and the remainder £500 each. The Corporation now found itself in a similar position to that of the underwriter of a loan, subscriptions for which had fallen short of the desired total. This situation was by no means novel, for the same thing had happened before in 1604, 1608, and 1617, and on each of these occasions the Crown had to be content with the sums subscribed by contributors, whereas in 1625 the deficiency of £800 was made up out of the Chamber, the money being borrowed from the Orphans' Fund at 8 per cent.[34]

This was only one of several important functions which were performed by the Chamber in connexion with the loan of 1625. In addition, it acted as a place of safe deposit for incoming contributions, upon which it also made at least one advance payment into the Exchequer—of £14,000 on 27 May 'for the speedie supplie of his Majestie's present occasions'—reimbursing itself out of the loan money as it came into its hands. Finally, and most important of all, it lent money at the rate of 8 per cent. per annum to those contributors who were unable to provide their quotas. Sixty-three lenders borrowed money from the Chamber in this way, of whom 61 borrowed their full quota of £500. Of the remaining two, one Richard Cooper borrowed the whole of his contribution of £200, while another, Jeremy Gay, borrowed £300 of his £500.[35] The position can be most conveniently expressed in the following table:

TABLE V

The Provision of the Loan of £60,000 (1625)

	£
Lenders who borrowed the whole of their contributions from the Chamber	30,700
Part of Gay's contribution borrowed by him from the Chamber	300
Remainder of Gay's contribution	200
Lenders not borrowing from the Chamber . . .	28,000
Money paid by the Chamber to make up the deficiency in the total sum	800
Total	£60,000

Thus, in effect, more than half the total of the money advanced was

[34] Journal, xxxiii, fos. 105–105(b); R.C.E.P. 12, 13, 'Debts due by King Charles . . .', 'Monyes lent to King Charles'; Royal Loans Ledger (1617–29), fo. 89; City Cash Accounts, 1/1 (1633–5), fos. 86(b), 173(b), 264(b).

[35] Repertory, xxix, fo. 226(b); Journal, xxxiii, fo. 112; R.C.E.P. 12, 19, 'Money owing to the Chamber upon the 60,000 li. Accompt for King Charles' Loane'; City Cash Accounts, 1/1 (1633–5), fos. 84(b) et seq.

provided not by individual contributors, but out of the Corporation's own resources.

Charles's promises proved to be of little more value than those of his father, and, as one prolongation of both the loan of 1625 and that of 1617 succeeded another, the city authorities, moved no doubt by the revelations of a committee which had been appointed in 1626 to examine the financial condition of the Chamber and the extent of the depredations on the Orphans' Fund,[36] became restive and action was taken in the Lord Mayor's court for recovery by the Chamberlain of the sums which had been lent out of the Chamber to individual contributors in 1625. However, on petition of these persons to the Court of Aldermen proceedings against them were stayed indefinitely.[37] Like his father, Charles I made some private settlements with lenders. Edward Sewster, who had lent £500 in 1625, and Sir Sebastian Harvey, who had lent £3,000 to James I in 1617, were both repaid, but the remainder of the lenders still remained unsatisfied at the end of 1626.[38]

6. The Loan of 1626

In the meantime, in Midsummer 1626, Charles I had approached the Corporation for yet another loan to meet the supposed dangers of a Spanish invasion, which the government probably exaggerated out of all proportion to their real significance in its attempt to find money at this time.[39] £100,000 was urgently required for the military needs of the government, and that the council would brook no delay is emphasized by the stinging letter which was sent to the Lord Mayor and aldermen, complaining that 'wee have received answere so farre from our expectation as wee cannot judge to proceede from men sensible either of the comon danger or theire owne . . . but marvell that they [such excuses] should be made to you or accepted by you'. The city authorities were ordered to behave themselves 'as appertaynes to magistrates and governors so highly entrusted, and in such a time, and not to give over easie passage to those light excuses that shalbe made unto you by persons more intentive to their private profitt then the public safety'.[40]

[36] C. of L.R.O. Misc. MSS. 166/1; M. C. Wren, 'The Chamber of London in 1633', Econ. Hist. Rev. 2nd ser. i (1948), 49–50.

[37] Repertory, xli, fos. 134–134(b); ibid., xlii, fo. 6(b).

[38] Royal Loans Ledger (1617–29), fo. 90; R.C.E.P. 11.

[39] See Gardiner, History, vi. 124.

[40] A.P.C. (1626), pp. 20–21; Repertory, xl, fos. 266(b), 272–272(b); Remembrancia, vi. 89.

Among these 'light excuses' the unhappy fate of the lenders of 1617 must certainly have been numbered. And there may have been other reasons for the Corporation's reluctance than Charles's flagrant disregard of his financial obligations. Two foreign observers in London, the diplomatic representatives of Venice and Tuscany, remark on the fact that it was the general opinion in the city that parliamentary supply was the proper means of providing for such extraordinary occasions.[41] While the comments of such observers were often based on political gossip and rumour and are therefore notoriously suspect as evidence, there is no need to assume that, in this particular case, they were very wide of the mark. If the alternative to parliamentary supply from the country in general was yet another loan from the citizens, one can be sure that such constitutional scruples as they may have possessed were reinforced by their desires not to dip heavily into their purses once again, convictions which would certainly be strengthened by annoyance at the royal dissolution of parliament early in June. Such factors help to explain two central facts about the loan of 1626. The first is that only £20,000 was forthcoming from the citizens—'scarce enough to buy a dozen points', as one contemporary puts it; the second is the fact that subscribers to the loan were limited to the aldermanic bench, perhaps for fear of inciting the popular elements in the city still further. The arrangements which had been applied to the last loan from this source in 1610, involving the liability for a portion of the loan of those who succeeded to the aldermanry during its currency, were again adopted, while any alderman who could not afford to lend his assessed quota might borrow all or part of it from the Chamber. In view of the fact that such borrowing might be done at the very favourable rate of 7 per cent., when the rate paid to the lenders by the Crown was 8 per cent., it is perhaps surprising that none of the aldermen appear to have taken advantage of this concession. Their restraint may have been due to a laudable and public-spirited desire not to tax the resources of the Chamber still further, unless this was obviously necessary, in view of the revelations of the committee of 1626.[42]

The aldermen were more fortunate than the lenders of 1617 and 1625. Their loan was secured on the farms of the petty customs and

---

[41] Cal. S.P. Ven. (1625–6), p. 468; Hist. MSS. Comm., XIth Report, i. 77.
[42] Cal. S.P.D. (1625–6), pp. 371, 392; Repertory, xl, fos. 278(b)–9; Remembrancia, vi. 90.

was repaid during the course of 1627 and 1628.[43] The loan had fallen far short of Charles's requirements, and although there may have been tentative royal overtures for further advances,[44] they were completely unsuccessful. Charles's failure to raise money in the city led him to turn his attention to the country at large and to initiate the Loan of Five Subsidies, the title of which is inappropriate in the sense that it was a loan only in name, and yet appropriate in that it betrays its true nature as a substitute for parliamentary taxation. Since this forced loan had in a real sense arisen out of Charles's relative failure as a borrower in the city in 1626, further substance is given to the view that the citizens' opposition to, and the pitifully low yield of, the loan of 1626 were not unconnected with matters of political discontent as well as their more obvious financial grievances relating to the loans of 1617 and 1625. Nevertheless, quite apart from the Loan of Five Subsidies, the city was not freed from further financial burdens in 1626 and the early months of 1627. Of the £18,000 which was the cost of meeting the demand that it should provide twenty ships for the royal service, and which was assessed upon individual citizens, more than £9,000 had to be provided out of the city Chamber.[45] In the meantime the vast bulk of the creditors of 1617 and 1625 remained unsatisfied, and the unusual and complicated arrangements which were made for their repayment, and the worsening of the relations between Crown and city which these occasioned, are in themselves sufficiently important to merit separate treatment in the chapter which follows.

[43] S.P. Charles I, 42/56, 47/55, 54/66; E. 403/2745, fo. 204(*b*); Repertory, xl, fos. 278–9.
[44] The Venetian ambassador mentions such attempts. *Cal. S.P. Ven. (1625–6)*, pp. 548, 558, 568, 603.
[45] On this episode, see Dietz, op. cit., pp. 230–1; M. C. Wren, 'London and the Twenty Ships', in *Amer. H.R.* lv (1950), 321–35.

VI

THE CORPORATION OF LONDON AS A LAND CONTRACTOR (1627-40)

1. *The Royal Contract with the Corporation (1627–8)*

THE contract which was made by Charles I with the Corporation of London in 1627–8 was not, as some historians have suggested,[1] a loan on the mortgage of royal lands, but a gigantic repayment operation, whereby the King conveyed certain lands to trustees of the Corporation in repayment of the principal and the outstanding interest on the loans of 1617 and 1625 and of a further advance of £120,000. The purpose of this chapter is to offer a detailed examination of this operation, which was the most intricate financial transaction of the reign and of crucial importance in relation both to the decline of the royal credit and to the deterioration in the relations between Crown and city in the 1630's.

From the beginning of 1627 a number of proposals were advanced whereby the outstanding debt should be repaid, by the conveyance of royal lands to the Corporation,[2] but it was not until 4 December of that year that the real germs of the royal contract in its final form can be discerned. From then onwards one proposal followed another in quick succession until, by a sort of process of elimination, arrangements which were convenient to both parties finally emerged.[3] It will be convenient to take up the story on 12 December, on which date the King, after withdrawing an earlier offer, made two proposals which were, in fact, alternatives. The first was that, in satisfaction of the two principal debts of 1617 and 1625, the Corporation was to take any royal lands of its own choosing at twenty-five years' purchase. Since no provision was made for the repayment of the outstanding interest which was deemed to be 'fully satisfied in the goodnes of the bargaine', the Common Council of London was

[1] See Gardiner, *History*, vi. 220; Dietz, op. cit., p. 243; S. J. Madge, *The Domesday of Crown Lands* (1938), p. 60. For a more correct interpretation, see Tawney, *Econ. Hist. Rev.* xi (1941), 31; Wren, *Econ. Hist. Rev.* 2nd ser. i (1948), 50.

[2] *Cal. S.P. Ven.* (1626–8), pp. 154, 350; Journal, xxxiv, fos. 80(*b*), 98(*b*); Repertory, xli, fo. 253(*b*).

[3] *A.P.C.* (1627–8), pp. 163, 167; Journal, xxxiv, fos. 191–2(*b*).

wholly justified in its rejection of this proposal on the grounds that
'the moneys are not to be accompted as interest to this Citty . . . in
regard the cittie is not the lender, but as a suretie gave there common seale for the first debtes (viz. those of 1617) and for ye seacond
debte (viz. that of 1625) it was furnished by the credite of private
men but undertaken to be secured to them by this Courte'. In object-
ing to the alternative royal proposal the Common Council was,
however, on weaker ground. According to this, royal lands of the
yearly value of £14,000 were to be sold jointly by royal commissioners and the Corporation's own nominees, and the proceeds were
to be used to satisfy the contributors for the full principal and interest down to the date of the agreement, subsequent interest being
satisfied out of the rents. Any surplus over and above the expenses
of the operation and the money needed to repay all the lenders was
to be returned to the Crown, but, on the other hand, if the sale of
the lands did not bring in sufficient money to accomplish this, more
lands were to be sold until repayment had been completed. The
price of this arrangement was to be a further advance of £120,000,
which was also to be repaid out of the proceeds of the land sales.
Since this condition was itself adopted by the Common Council in
its counter-proposal, it can hardly be cited as a valid reason for
refusing the royal offer, and the citizens' objections rested solely
upon the assertion that the proposed arrangement would mean
'putting their sales to a dependence upon the pleasure of others'.
This could mean either that they distrusted the probity of the proposed royal commission, or, more likely, that they believed that the
lands would be sold more efficiently by the unfettered use of the
machinery of the business world, a viewpoint to which the experience of the great land sales of the previous reign lent some support. These considerations apart, the rejected proposition was in a
number of respects far more equitable than the ultimate contract,
and if the Corporation's failure to accept the royal offer is viewed in
the light of its later conduct of the land sales, it is not difficult to
detect a somewhat disingenuous note in its arguments, although
it would probably be unfair to the Corporation to reason from
the events of the 1630's to its attitude at the time of the original
negotiations with the Crown.[4]

Instead the Common Council put forward alternative suggestions
which were, in essence, the same as those which were ultimately

[4] Journal, xxxiv, fos. 192–192(b).

adopted. Royal lands were to be conveyed to the trustees of the Corporation at twenty-eight years' purchase and were to be sold off to effect repayment of the principal and interest on the loans of 1617 and 1625 and the principal sum of £120,000, which was to be advanced in addition. From the date of the agreement all subsequent interest was to be discharged out of the income derived from these lands.[5] The government's immediate response to these new proposals was unfavourable, but its misgivings were finally allayed by an assurance which, since it became the bone of subsequent contention, is here printed in full and in its proper context.

His Majestie will not tie the Citty to accounte, nor put anie to survey, controll or hinder the sales, but will give them [viz. the Corporation] absolute power to dispose of them at theire pleasure and sell them at what rate they liste. Neither shall his Majestie put uppon them any trust which may or shall tye them in a Courte of equitie or otherwise housoever to aunswere any thinge to his Majestie though they gaign by the bargaine. But as the Cittie hath trusted both himselfe and his Royall father with the moneys, *soe his Majestie will expecte from the Citty that, if they shall make any gaign by the Bargaine above the principall debte and interest, ther tymes of sale and forbearance of the money till the sales considered, that they will returne the same to his Majestie.*[6]

The italicized section in the above passage is the so-called 'unexpressed trust', for the fulfilment of which the Crown relied solely upon the Corporation's word, since it was not included in the formal contract.[7] It was in fact a gentlemen's agreement, but Charles was later to form the opinion that he was not dealing with gentlemen. It was claimed at a later date that the 'trust' had been omitted from the actual contract because it had been thought that potential purchasers might be deterred by it, though it is difficult to see why this should be so. A more obvious deterrent to the sale of a part of the lands, especially in view of the notorious exploitation by the Tudors and early Stuarts of their obsolescent feudal rights, was the fact that one-third of the lands were conveyed in knight-service held in chief of the Crown. In agreeing to pay an additional £5,000

[5] Journal, xxxiv, fos. 193–193(*b*).

[6] Ibid., fos. 194–194(*b*). Italics mine. S.P. Charles I, 86/97. The State Papers version rather surprisingly omits the saving clause. For further and later evidence of the Common Council's acceptance of this principle, see S.P. Charles I, 124/70, 186/58; Journal, xxxiv, fo. 203(*b*).

[7] The Corporation's copy of the contract is in R.C.E.P. 121. There is a full transcription in *A.P.C. (1627–8)*, pp. 455–63, and a summary in Journal, xxxiv, fos. 197(*b*)–202(*b*).

over and above the £120,000 to be advanced in 1628, in return for the conversion of the tenure of these lands to free and common socage, the Corporation was probably making a very good bargain.

The debts which were to be satisfied out of the proceeds of the sale of the lands conveyed under the contract are set forth below.[8]

	£	s.
Principal and interest of the remainder of the loan of 1617. Interest computed to 20 December 1627 .	158,477	2
Principal and interest of the remainder of the loan of 1625. Interest computed as above . . .	71,420	0
Further advance of 1628	120,000	0
Total	£349,897	2

It was in repayment of this money that the Corporation, or, more correctly, its trustees, after the first of whom, Edward Ditchfield, the contract has somewhat inappropriately become known to history, was to receive lands of the annual value of £12,496. 6s. 6d. The terms of this sale at twenty-eight years' purchase are perhaps surprising in the light of recent revelations on the subject of the price of land in the sixteenth and seventeenth centuries,[9] unless it is understood that the term 'annual value' which is used in the documents relating to this transaction does not in this case represent the full economic rent of the lands concerned. The fact that many of these lands were let at uneconomic rentals is, therefore, an adequate explanation of what at first sight looks like a very high purchase price, and also to some extent of the fact that the Corporation was able to get rid of some of the lands at an even higher price.

2. The Raising of the £120,000 (December 1627–September 1628)

As soon as the terms of the contract had been finally approved by both parties, the Common Council immediately set about assessing the Livery Companies towards the first half of the additional £120,000 which it had agreed should be paid to the Crown in two equal instalments. As usual the twelve great companies provided

---

[8] R.C.E.P. Copy of the Return of the Mayor and Commonalty of the City of London to the Commissioners of the Exchequer of their proceedings in Respect to the Royal Contract Estates (1627–32) (hereafter cited as Copy of Return), fos. 2–3.

[9] See H. J. Habakkuk, 'The Long-Term Rate of Interest and the Price of Land in the Seventeenth Century', Econ. Hist. Rev. 2nd ser. v (1952), 26–45, and 'The Market for Monastic Property, 1539–1603', ibid. 2nd ser. x (1958), 362–880.

by far the greater share of the whole, their total assessments amounting to £47,556.[10] Such evidence as is available indicates that the companies adopted a wide variety of methods of raising their quotas, although most of them seem, as far as possible, to have avoided the compulsory assessment of their members. That this method of raising money was highly unpopular appears clearly from one of the very few cases where its adoption proved to be necessary, for, in the case of the Vinters, opposition to a general assessment among the brethren reached such a pitch that it required nothing less drastic than a spell in jail to make some of them yield. Their reluctance to contribute was later inflated into a constitutional issue of some importance when in May 1628 the case of one of them, Nicholas Clegate, was taken up by the Commons, who pronounced that he had been unlawfully imprisoned for making a stand against the assessment of the companies by the Lord Mayor and Common Council. It is highly probable that Clegate's voice would never have been heard if his company had chosen another way of raising the money. But, like the objections of the pertinacious Bate in a more celebrated issue, his grievances raised constitutional questions of no mean importance, for the parliamentary decision in Clegate's case struck at the authority of the Lord Mayor no less than that of the Crown.[11]

Of the ten major companies for which information is available only two adopted one single method of raising the whole of their contributions. These were the Grocers and the Haberdashers, both of whom raised their quotas entirely by borrowing, that is, borrowing by bond upon commercial terms as distinct from compulsory loans raised from members on the company's own terms. Indeed an element of commercial borrowing of this type is the one common factor among the multifarious expedients which were employed by seven out of the remaining eight major companies, and which are

[10] Journal, xxxiv, fos. 195(b)–6. The twelve major companies were rated as follows: Merchant Taylors (£6,300), Grocers (£6,000), Haberdashers (£4,800), Drapers (£4,608), Goldsmiths (£4,380), Mercers (£3,720), Fishmongers (£3,390), Clothworkers (£3,390), Vintners (£3,120), Salters (£2,880), Skinners (£2,820), Ironmongers (£2,148). The ratings of the 43 lesser companies varied between £1,500 (Leathersellers) and £30 (Bowyers, Fletchers, Woolmen, and Musicians).

[11] A.P.C. (1627–8), pp. 274, 287; Cal. S.P.D. (1627–8), p. 554; H. of Commons Journal, i. 875, 891; Repertory, xlii, fos. 59(b)–62, 99–99(b); Remembrancia, vi. 144–6; Vintners' Hall, Transcripts of Court Minutes for 1626–9, pp. 30–35, 38–39, 42–43, 48–49.

too varied to be detailed here.[12] The solitary exception to this rule was the Merchant Taylors company, which raised its quota partly by assessment and partly out of the common stock of the company. Since the rate paid to the companies by the Corporation was only 6 per cent. per annum, those of them who chose to borrow often made bad bargains, for, generally speaking, money was not to be had at less than 7 per cent., and more often than not the companies had to pay the full statutory maximum rate of 8 per cent. The Mercers were fortunate in the generosity of one of their greatest members, Sir Baptist Hicks, who lent £2,700 at 6 per cent., but no such sentiments of corporate loyalty tempered the economic appetite of Sir Paul Bayning. Bayning insisted on the full statutory maximum rate for his loan of £2,000 to the Grocers, who succeeded in raising only £1,000 of their quota at 6 per cent., and paid 8 per cent. on the whole of the remainder. Moreover, the loans on such disadvantageous terms frequently fell due before the Corporation had sufficient cash in hand to repay the companies out of the proceeds of the sales of land conveyed to it under the terms of royal contract. In these circumstances the unpleasant alternatives facing the companies were prolongation at the same disadvantageous rates or repayment of the lenders by the sale of corporate property or by the raising of further loans.[13]

In connexion with this loan from the companies the Chamber of London played its traditional role as an office of receipt and issue through which the money passed on its way from the companies to the Exchequer. It paid over its receipts in round sums into the Exchequer and on one occasion supplemented these receipts out of its own funds to the tune of £60, reimbursing itself when this money had been received from the companies. All this appears clearly in the following table.

[12] A full account is given in my 'Government Borrowing under the First Two Stuarts (1603–42)', pp. 613–19.

[13] London, Merchant Taylors' Hall, Court Minutes, viii, fos. 314(*b*)–18(*b*); Grocers' Hall, Orders of Court of Assistants (1616–39), fos. 360–1, 362, 363–4, 379, 395; Quires of Wardens' Accounts (1622–33), no foliation; Haberdashers' Office, Court of Assistants' Minutes (1583–1652), fos. 250–250(*b*); Goldsmiths' Hall, Wardens' Accounts and Court Minutes (1624–9), fos. 74–77, 86(*b*); Mercers' Hall, Acts of Court (1595–1629), fos. 320(*b*)–2(*b*), 323(*b*)–4; Vintners' Hall, Transcripts of Court Minutes for 1626–9, fos. 29–35, 37–38; Skinners' Hall, Court Book, iii (1617–51), fo. 114(*b*); Guildhall, Fishmongers' Court Ledger, ii (1610–31), fos. 649–55; A. H. Johnson, op. cit. iii. 119–20 and note; J. Nicholl, *Some Account of the Worshipful Company of Ironmongers* (1851), pp. 216–19.

TABLE VI

Dates of the Payment of the Contributions by the Companies into the Chamber and by the Chamber into the Exchequer

Date	Received in Chamber from companies[14] (£)	Paid into Exchequer[15] (£)
4 January 1628	4,060	Nil
5 January 1628	1,000	5,000
7 January 1628	9,246	Nil
8 January 1628	Nil	5,000
9 January 1628	24,184	10,000
10 January 1628	11,656	20,000
11 January 1628	8,374	15,000
12 January 1628	1,420	5,000
16 January 1628	60	Nil

It had originally been hoped that as much as possible of the second instalment of the £120,000 would be raised out of the proceeds of the sale of the royal contract estates, and that the remainder would be provided again by the companies or by other means. But two considerations were to make this impossible. In the first place, it was not until September 1628 that the first lands were sold off by the Corporation, and, secondly, the King did not wait for the stipulated six months before asking for some of the second instalment on account. Indeed the first of these royal demands was made as early as 18 February, when Charles required an instalment of £20,000. This and a further £5,000 demanded on 11 March was raised by some of the aldermen and was paid into the Exchequer between 23 February and 27 March. Some of the aldermen had to borrow to raise their contributions. At least one of them raised a loan from the Chamber, another borrowed £800 from Sir Martin Lumley at 7 per cent., while the four aldermen who raised the additional £5,000 demanded on 11 March borrowed this sum from the ever-provident Sir Baptist Hicks.[16]

The Chamber played a more active part in these arrangements than it had done in connexion with the raising of the first £60,000

---

[14] R.C.E.P. 128, 'An abstracte of the Receptes and Payments for the Land Accompte'.

[15] Exchequer of Receipt, Receipt Book, E. 401/1914, no foliation.

[16] A.P.C. (1627–8), pp. 241, 308–9, 315, 345; S.P. Charles I, 94/67; E. 401/1914; Journal, xxxiv, fo. 203; Repertory, xlii, fos. 103–4, 123–123°, 167–167(b); ibid., xliii, fos. 90(b)–91, 163; R.C.E.P. 128.

in January. Apart from lending money to at least one of the contributors, the urgent military necessities of the government and the
slowness of the contributors in paying in their quotas made it necessary for it to pay out considerable sums to the Exchequer before it
had received equivalent contributions from the lenders. The extent
of these advances which were made out of the Chamber's funds
may be seen in the following table which covers the first £15,000
of this instalment and shows that the Chamber had paid this sum
into the Exchequer before receiving all of it from the lenders.

TABLE VII

Dates of the Payments by the Aldermen into the Chamber and by
the Chamber into the Exchequer

Date	Received in Chamber from aldermen [17] (£ s. d.)	Paid into Exchequer [18] (£)
22 February 1628	733 6 8	Nil
23 February 1628	Nil	5,000
25 February 1628	3,300	Nil
28 February 1628	1,800	3,000
29 February 1628	400	Nil
1 March 1628	500	Nil
3 March 1628	Nil	2,000
5 March 1628	1,800	Nil
6 March 1628	1,800	2,000
10 March 1628	1,966 13 4	3,000

On the failure of attempts to raise the remaining £35,000 of the
£120,000 in one piece on the mortgage of some of those royal contract estates which had already been conveyed to the Corporation's
trustees, it was decided on 25 May to raise the money in two separate instalments. The first of these was to be £15,000 plus an additional £5,000 for the alteration of the tenure of one-third of the
lands from knight-service to socage. After an attempt to raise the
£20,000 at 7½ per cent. from the companies had fallen through,
together with a subsequent offer of 8 per cent. for a loan of £15,000
on mortgage from members of the Land Sales Committee and the
Court of Aldermen, the Corporation again resorted, on 7 June, to

[17] R.C.E.P. 128.   [18] E. 401/1914.

a hurried assessment of the aldermen as a means of providing the latter sum. £13,000 of this was paid into the Exchequer by 21 June and for once the Chamber made no advance payments to the Crown, which had to wait until 24 September for the remaining £2,000. The Chamber did, however, step into the breach by advancing the whole of the £5,000 for the alteration of the tenure of the lands, for which it was later reimbursed by six aldermen, each of whom contributed equal proportions, and, like the other lenders of 1628, 1625, and 1617, took their turn in the queue of creditors awaiting repayment out of the proceeds of the land sales.[19]

In the meantime the conveyance of the first batch of the royal contract estates had been completed, and on 21 June the Common Council consented to make arrangements for the raising of the remaining £20,000 of the £120,000. It was decided that this should be levied on the Livery Companies, each of which was to pay a third of its contributions to the £60,000 which had been raised in December and January 1627-8. There was, however, one important difference between the arrangements of December and those of June, for since what was from the Corporation's point of view an unfortunate precedent had been set in the case of the advances of the aldermen, the companies were to receive interest on their contributions towards the £20,000 not at 6 per cent. but at the full statutory maximum rate of 8 per cent.[20] This gave far more scope to those companies who decided to raise the money, or part of it, by normal borrowing on security rather than by assessing their members, a device which was most conspicuous by its absence. Such borrowing had been very prominent in the transactions of December and January, but it now assumed an even greater importance, and indeed offered opportunities of profit to companies such as the Grocers, who were able to borrow £1,000 of their quota at 7 per cent., and the Goldsmiths, who borrowed the whole of theirs at 7 and 6 per cent. Of the nine major companies about whose operations information is available, only one, the Drapers, failed to have recourse to formal borrowing. Of the remainder, five raised the

<hr/>

[19] A.P.C. (1627-8), pp. 464-6, 467-70; Exchequer of Receipt, Receipt Books, E. 401/1915, 1919, no foliation; Journal, xxxiv, fos. 264, 265-6, 279; Repertory, xlii, fos. 202-3, 233, 319; Royal Loans Ledger (1617-29), fo. 90; R.C.E.P. 15, 'The names of such persons as did lend Money for furnishing of the sume of Vm. li. . . . for altering the tenure of the Landes'; R.C.E.P. 128; Copy of Return, fo. 90.

[20] Journal, xxxiv, fos. 278(b)-80.

whole of their quotas by borrowing on bond, and the other three supplemented the proceeds of such borrowing by dipping into their own funds, and, in one case, into trust funds in their possession.[21]

The minor companies were obviously in a less happy position, and twenty-five of them borrowed at the statutory maximum from the Chamber, which in all but one of these cases lent the full quota assessed upon the company. In these circumstances, therefore, it was the Corporation and not the companies which was the effective lender, and even where this did not apply and the companies borrowed from private individuals, as did the Brewers and the Barber-Surgeons, the surviving evidence suggests that they were no more successful in the matter of terms.[22]

On 30 June the King wrote to the Lord Mayor, demanding that the proceeds of the loan be handed over to Philip Burlamachi to be employed by him towards the relief of La Rochelle. But there were considerable delays in doing this, one of the reasons for which was the attitude of the Mercers, who, before paying in their contribution, fought a long rearguard action against the municipal authorities, in the course of which they cited the parliamentary decision in Clegate's case against the Common Council's right to assess the companies for the present purpose. Due to these delays, the whole of the money was not paid over until 24 September, and in the course of its payment the remainder of the royal contract estates, which were scattered throughout England and Wales, were conveyed to the Corporation's trustees. At long last Charles I had satisfied his part of the bargain, and it now remained for the Corporation to sell off the lands, and to see that its own bonds were honoured out of the proceeds.[23]

[21] Merchant Taylors, Court Minutes, viii, fos. 328–328(b), 330–330(b); Grocers, Orders of Court of Assistants (1616–39), fos. 382–3; Quires of Wardens' Accounts (1622–33), no foliation; Haberdashers, Court of Assistants' Minutes (1583–1652), fo. 252; Goldsmiths, Wardens' Accounts and Court Minutes (1624–9), fos. 87, 88; Mercers, Acts of Court (1595–1629), fos. 333–6, 337–9; Vintners, Transcripts of Court Minutes for 1626–9, fos. 60–61, 63–64, 69; Skinners, Court Book, iii (1617–51), fo. 117(b); Fishmongers, Court Ledger, ii (1610–31), fos. 689–91, 692–4; Johnson. op. cit. iii. 120 and note.

[22] London Guildhall, Brewers, Court Minutes (1620–8), no foliation; Barber-Surgeons, Court Minutes (1621–51), fo. 80; Carpenters, Court Book (1618–35), fo. 193; Wardens' Accounts (1614–47), fo. 150; Turners, Court Minutes (1605–33), no foliation; Wardens' Accounts (1593–1670), no foliation; Blacksmiths, Court Minutes (1625–31), fo. 61; R.C.E.P. 128.

[23] E. 401/1915; Remembrancia, vi. 153; Royal Loans Ledger (1617–29), fo. 90; Mercers, Acts of Court (1595–1629), fos. 333–6, 337–9.

3. The Sale of the Lands and the Repayment of the Lenders (1628–41)

The sale of the royal contract estates and the repayment of the creditors of the Crown may be divided into three clearly defined stages, the first of which lasted from September 1628 to the end of 1629. By 10 December 1629 lands of the annual value of £2,907. 0s. 9½d. had been sold for a total price of £111,025. 13s. 3d., that is at more than thirty-eight years' purchase.[24] There is nothing surprising in the fact that this first batch of lands was sold at an average price which was well above that at which the whole had been conveyed to the Corporation, and the high average price of thirty-eight years' purchase can probably be ascribed to the fact that the majority of the lands sold off in this batch were among those which were more attractive to purchasers for one reason or another.

During this period the second half of the £120,000 which had been advanced during 1628 was repaid, together with the £5,000 which had been paid to the King for the alteration of the land tenure. That these creditors, who had been the last to lend their money, should be the first to be repaid was a triumph of natural convenience over natural justice. By a forced conversion operation which was itself a highly dubious piece of sharp practice the interest on the loans of 1617 and 1625 had been reduced from 8 to 5 per cent. as from 20 December 1627. Moreover, while the sums which had been raised from the aldermen and the companies between February and September 1628 had carried an interest charge of 8 per cent., it will be remembered that the first £60,000 which had been lent by the companies in January 1628 had been raised at 6 per cent. The repayment of this loan did not commence until December 1629 and was not completed until the following July, much of the money for this operation coming from the proceeds of the sale of the second batch of lands. And that the unfortunate lenders of 1617 and 1625 had to wait still longer for repayment was, as will be seen, perhaps the least of their misfortunes.[25]

The repayment of the first half of the £120,000 which had been advanced in 1628 thus bridged the gap between the first and second stages of land sales. The latter was inaugurated in January 1630 by

[24] Copy of Return, fo. 5. Many of the lands sold at far higher and many at far lower prices than 38 years' purchase.

[25] Repertory, xliii, fos. 182, 230(b)–1; ibid., xliv, fo. 81; R.C.E.P. 128; Copy of Return, fos. 90–96.

the Common Council's adoption of a new sales policy which was connected not with the repayment of the remaining sums due to the companies which was speedily enough completed by July, but with the arrangements for the repayment of the lenders of 1617 and 1625, which was now to begin. The new policy is described in a later report, which was made in 1632.[26]

It was . . . agreed that the readiest and best way to quicken the sales, (and) advance the price of the landes in sale . . . was to admitt the lenders in the first two loanes [viz. those of 1617 and 1625] to purchase for some readie monie and satisfaction of their debtes allowed by his highnes in both or either of these loanes, or to ioyne with some purchasere to receave their satisfaction out of such Landes as they should purchase, and thereupon to give discharges of their severall debtes.

Thus those creditors who were willing to obtain repayment via the purchase of lands might deliver up their bonds and have the money due to them counted as a part of their purchase price. On the other hand, those who desired quick repayment but were unwilling to obtain it by purchasing land themselves might receive payment from purchasers as part of the latters' purchase price. In the former case the normal procedure was for the creditors to approach the committee which had been entrusted with the management of the land sales, which then offered them a choice of lands.[27] The second method, which the Common Council had originally regarded as an expedient to be adopted only if the first failed to quicken the rate of sale appreciably, but which in actual practice was put into effect almost from the beginning and became a far more usual practice than the first, was to operate via private arrangement between creditors and purchasers. On presentation of a creditor's bond for repayment, a purchaser would then have the money due to the creditor reduced from the purchase price agreed upon for the lands to be sold to him. Although the Land Sales Committee reserved the right to determine the proportion between cash payments and payments by discharge of the obligations of the lenders of 1617 and 1625, no fixed ratio between the two was in fact maintained, and some purchasers paid entirely in cash and others in both cash and bonds.[28] Indeed some cash payments were necessary,

[26] Copy of Return, fo. 5; also Journal, xxxv, fo. 52.
[27] For examples, see C. of L.R.O. Minutes of Committee for Royal Contract Estates (1632–64) (hereafter cited as Minutes), fos. 5(b), 26(b).
[28] Copy of Return, *passim*; City Cash Accounts, 1/1–1/4 (1633–43), *passim*.

especially in the months immediately following January 1630, in order to pay off the remainder of the loans which had been raised in 1628, to which the new procedure did not apply, as well as to discharge incidental expenses arising out of the sales. But from the time of its adoption onwards the use of the new procedure became more and more common and, indeed, many purchasers who had made their original contracts long previously, but had not yet completed their instalments hastened to take advantage of it.[29]

That the adoption of the new policy resulted in a marked quickening of the rate of the land sales may be seen from the fact that between 10 December 1629 and 6 May 1632 lands of the total annual value of £5,816. 8s. 9½d. were sold for £195,231. 1s. 1d., that is, at about thirty-three years' purchase.[30] Among the possible explanations of the lower average price of this second batch of lands are the facts that they were probably on the whole less desirable than the first, that their price may have been forced down by the glut of lands on the market, and that the appetite for land may have been appreciably blunted by the earlier sales. Indeed, the average price of thirty-three years' purchase must have represented more than the intrinsic value of this second batch of lands. Giving evidence before the Attorney-General in the inquiry which opened in 1632, one purchaser, William Child, affirmed that he would not have been willing to pay the full price demanded of him, if he had not been allowed to discharge some of the debts due to lenders as a part of that price.[31] The unpleasant truth was that part of the burden of the price of these lands was shifted from the purchasers to the much-abused lenders of 1617 and 1625, whose bonds they discharged often, and perhaps invariably, at a very heavy discount. This fact made the terms of sale far more attractive to those purchasers who were willing to redeem the Corporation's obligations as part of their purchase price, a procedure which was looked upon

[29] Copy of Return, fo. 28; instalment buying was allowed and no interest seems to have been charged except when instalments were overdue (City Cash Accounts, 1/3 (1639–40), fo. 160(b); Minutes, fos. 18(b), 19(b), 20, 28(b), 35(b)).

[30] Copy of Return, fo. 5. The nature of the evidence makes it necessary to adopt this date in December 1629 rather than January 1630 as the beginning of this stage of the sales. The fact that it pre-dates by a few weeks the adoption of the new sales policy does not materially affect my conclusions as to the effects of this policy.

[31] R.C.E.P. 79, 'Papers touching Informacions . . . against the City for non payment of their Debtes by Sale of the Royal Contract Estates.'

with disfavour by the royal commission which was appointed in 1632 to examine the conduct of the sales.

For some time there had been official suspicions that the Corporation's conduct of the land sales was open to question,[32] but it was not until 15 May 1632 that it was ordered to give a full account of its actions to this commission. What clearly emerged from this inquiry was that the commissioners' suspicions that many of the purchasers had 'bought in the dettes of severall cittizens and others and their executors, administrators and assigns for small somes, and yet have taken full allowance upon the Sales both of principall and Interest Mony to the dishonor of his Majesty, disadvantage of the Buyer, and violation of the Originall Trust' were only too well justified.[33] One example will suffice to illustrate this distasteful process. This relates to lands in the county of Oxfordshire which were purchased by Alderman Christopher Clitheroe in 1630. For the first of these purchases, made in February, Clitheroe paid £850, of which £574. 10s. was allowed to him in satisfaction of principal and interest of £300 lent by him in 1617. The remainder he paid in cash. There was nothing shady or disreputable about this transaction, since the creditor whose claims were satisfied was himself the purchaser of the lands, and he received full satisfaction of the debt due to him. The same cannot, however, be said of the arrangements made for his purchase in May of the manor of Bensington in the same county. For this he paid an official price of £386. 5s., of which £4. 1s. 8d. was paid in ready money, and the remainder by discharging two debts—one of £190. 13s. 4d. due to William Towerson for principal and interest of £100 lent in 1617, and the other of £191. 10s. lent by John Prowde in the same year, and now due to the lender's executors.[34] Giving evidence before Attorney-General Noy, Clitheroe described the procedure which was adopted in the following terms:

Being unwilling to stay for payment of their said debtes . . . but desiring rather to have some mony for the same, the said William Towerson for one hundred poundes by this defendant [Clitheroe] to him paid and the said Habacvcke Pricket and Julian, his wife, as executors of ye last

[32] S.P. Charles I, 186/21; *Hist. MSS. Comm., XIIth Report,* i. 394-5.
[33] S.P. Charles I, 220/64.
[34] Copy of Return, fos. 36, 58. Interest on all these transactions was confined to the period ending 20 December 1617. Interest thereafter was at 5 per cent. and paid separately.

will of the said John Prowde for one hundred poundes agreed to be paid them by this defendant did by severall deeds respectively releace to the said Mayor and Comminalty and Cittizens the said Two severall debtes and interest which deedes of release with the said Common bondes for the same this defendant did deliver to the said Robert Bateman [the City Chamberlain] in satisfaction of part of this defendents said last mencioned purchase mony and the residue of (the) said three hundred (and) eighty six poundes and five shillings, being foure poundes one shilling and eight pence, he, this defendent did pay in mony to the said Robert Bateman.[35]

The other purchasers who were put on oath gave similar testimony of a procedure which was no doubt convenient to the Corporation, except in so far as its credit was damaged by the process. To the purchasers themselves it might, of course, be extremely profitable, except in so far as it resulted in their paying a higher price for their land than would have been the case if they had paid wholly in cash. The real sufferers, however, were the luckless creditors. It may be argued that the disposal of their paper at a heavy discount was a price which they might be expected to pay in return for the privilege of receiving preferential treatment and going to the head of the queue of creditors. But against this must be remembered the fact that the vast bulk of the purchase money for the lands was paid by discharge of debts rather than in cash, a procedure which was grossly unfair to those lenders who chose to wait rather than have their paper discounted by purchasers. Moreover, this in itself made it all but inevitable that more and more creditors would choose the latter expedient rather than wait for what looked like being an interminable period for full satisfaction out of the diminishing receipts in cash which were the inevitable result of the adoption of the new policy of land sales. As time went on, recourse to this method of repayment became inevitably not a method of securing preferential treatment, but, in effect, the creditors' only hope of securing repayment at all, at least as far as the lenders of 1617 were concerned. The lenders of 1625 were rather more fortunate. Down to Michaelmas 1632 the principal sum of £34,855 of this loan was repaid with some small parcels of interest, and of this sum only £2,825 was repaid through the medium of purchasers of land. Thereafter, it is true, the whole of the remaining debts of 1625, like those of 1617, were discharged by purchasers, but by this time the trans-

[35] R.C.E.P. 79.

actions had come under the close scrutiny of the government, in which circumstances it is probable that the opportunities for abuses arising out of the despair of the lenders were lessened appreciably.[36]

As a result of the investigations of the royal commission, a number of charges were formulated against the Corporation by the government. The first of these was that the Corporation was now denying its liability in the so-called 'unexpressed trust' of the royal contract to return any surplus to the Crown over and above its expenses and the money required to pay off the debts. To this the city fathers replied that since a debt of £89,000 still remained to be paid off, and the remaining lands of the annual value of £3,323. 13s. 9d. were unlikely to sell at more than twenty years' purchase, it was highly improbable that there would be any surplus to return, a contention which seems somewhat implausible in view of the later history of the sales. The second royal charge was that certain city officials and members of the Land Sales Committee had feathered their own nests by making purchases both for themselves and for other privileged parties at undervalues, a charge which was, needless to say, hotly denied by all those concerned. Thirdly, and with some justice, it was argued that since the lands had been conveyed to the Corporation as a means of repaying the Crown's creditors, it was a violation of the agreement that the Corporation's debt to those aldermen who had furnished the £5,000 which had been paid to the Crown for altering the tenure of one-third of the lands from knight-service to socage should be honoured out of the proceeds, since this was a purely private debt of the Corporation. And finally it was objected that the King's promise to the lenders was being dishonoured by the arrangement whereby their debts were discharged by purchasers of land at a heavy discount.[37]

That the inquiry of the royal commissioners had uncovered shocking abuses was undeniable, but the royal complaints against the conduct of the Corporation and its dishonouring of the royal word, while they might have been amply justified in an unprejudiced observer, smack of that brand of sanctimonious hypocrisy which was one of the less agreeable traits of early Stuart governments. For the main responsibility for the tardiness of the repayment, which alone had rendered the unsatisfactory expedient of the royal contract acceptable to the Corporation, rested squarely upon the royal shoulders.

[36] R.C.E.P. 128.
[37] S.P. Charles I, 251/24; Journal, xxxv, fos. 465(b)–6; R.C.E.P. 79.

While the Corporation certainly cannot be acquitted of blame for the undoubted abuses which had arisen out of the close connexion between the land sales and the repayment technique, the fact that so many of the creditors had already waited so long that they were willing to forgo a large part of the money due to them was primarily and preponderantly the fault of no one but the Crown. Moreover, the latter's claim that the existing surplus from the land sales over and above the amount needed to pay off the debt should immediately be paid to it was grossly unreasonable for the obvious reason that the Corporation was unable to tell whether the transaction had been carried through at a profit or a loss until all the lands had been sold off.

The dispute over the royal contract estates represents yet another, and by no means the least important, of the influences which exacerbated the relations between Crown and city in the 1630's. To it must be added the more familiar royal charges about the management of the Ulster Plantation, disputes over tithes, the spread of the London suburbs and the growth of the new building, and the city's opposition to the collection of Ship Money.[38] The Corporation's decision in December 1633 to compound with the Crown for a settlement of some of these issues, including the question of the sale of the lands and the repayment of the lenders, was no more than the line of least resistance and was decidedly not an act of genuine contrition. There were few things in early Stuart England which could not be bought, but the King's price for his honour and the quieting of his scruples about the treatment of the unhappy lenders was so high as to delay final agreement on this matter until 1638. With £12,000 to pay for a settlement of this and other issues, the city was in no mood to welcome with patriotic effusion the new royal demands for assistance which were shortly to follow with the beginning of the Scottish war.[39]

The opening of the dispute between the Crown and the Corporation marks the end of the second and most prolific period of land

[38] Gardiner, *History*, vii. 375–6; viii. 59, 287–90; T. W. Moody, *The Londonderry Plantation (1609–1641)* (Belfast, 1939), pp. 238–66, 287–93, 355–405; C. Hill, *Economic Problems of the Church* (Oxford, 1956), pp. 275–88.

[39] S.P. Charles I, 251/24; Repertory, xlviii, fos. 46(b)–47, 60–60(b); Journal, xxxvii, fos. 193, 202(b), 257–8; ibid., fos. 103–4(b), 161. The chief issue was the Londonderry Plantation. After much haggling, the Corporation decided to forfeit the Ulster lands and pay a composition of £12,000 for the settlement of the dispute over the Ulster and royal contract lands and other minor matters. See Moody, op. cit., pp. 380–9.

sales. The prolonged dispute greatly slowed down the rate of sale, so that in the decade which succeeded Michaelmas 1632 lands of the total annual value of only £1,726. 5s. 2d. were sold for a total price of £55,068. 4s. 9½d., that is at rather more than thirty-one years' purchase. During the five years when the dispute was at its height, from Michaelmas 1633 onwards, lands of a mere £256. 8s. 3½d. annual value were sold. The accounting year beginning at Michaelmas 1638, by which time the dispute was virtually settled, saw a considerable improvement, which was sustained into the following year, but over the next two years the deterioration in the political situation and the Corporation's and the citizens' preoccupation with the raising of further loans meant a renewed decline in the effective demand for land which was continued into the troubled period of the Civil War.[40]

The slowing down of the land sales naturally retarded the process of debt repayment, so that by Michaelmas 1642 there still remained £12,500 of the principal and £13,074 of the interest to be repaid to the lenders of 1617, and £24,300 principal with £5,980 interest to those of 1625. The excess of interest over principal due on the earlier loan is explained by the fact that many of the lenders had received their full principal (nominally at least), but only part of the interest. The slow liquidation of the principal debt of 1625 from the figure of £25,145, at which it had stood at Michaelmas 1632, is explained by the fact, which is, however, rather odd in itself, that the bulk of the repayments of the lenders of 1625 which were made after this date was for interest only.[41] With the onset of the Civil War, sales, especially of those lands in royalist territory, were bound to fall off, and neither these nor the repayment of the lenders had been completed by as late as October 1657.[42]

The interest due on these loans as stated in the above account was computed only down to 20 December 1627, and it is unfortunate that no evidence has survived which might throw light on the method whereby the subsequent interest at the converted rate

---

[40] City Cash Accounts, 1/1 (1633–5), fos. 75(b)–78, 164–5(b), 256(b)–7; 1/2 (1636–8), fos. 65–65(b), 230; 1/3 (1639–40), fos. 67–72, 160–3; 1/4 (1641–3), fos. 65(b)–67(b), 170(b)–2.

[41] Figures obtained from R.C.E.P. 8, 'Monyes Resting Unpayed to the Creditors of King Charles', and R.C.E.P. 9, 'Debtes Resting unsatisfied to the Creditors of King Jeames', supplemented and amended by City Cash Accounts, 1/3 (1639–40), fos. 80(b), 163(b), 165(b), 166(b), 169; 1/4 (1641–3), fos. 65(b)–67(b), 170(b)–2.

[42] Journal, xli, fo. 165(b).

of 5 per cent. was discharged. If, as seems likely, these interest
charges were paid out of the money which came into the Corporation's hands from the rents and miscellaneous profits of the lands
between the dates of their conveyance to the Ditchfield trustees
and the dates of their sale, this raises the interesting question of
whether these rents and profits might be more than sufficient to
pay off both the interest charges and the unaccustomed expenses
incurred by the Corporation in maintaining semi-permanent
machinery for collecting rents over such a widespread area. If such
was indeed the case, rapid sale might not be in the Corporation's
interest, a suggestion which casts a sinister, if only a very flickering,
light upon the slow process of repayment. It is unfortunate that
such speculations cannot be removed from the realm of conjecture
into that of statistical fact. Not only would the calculations which
would be required to establish the truth in this matter be highly
complicated on account of the wide divergence between the dates
at which the lands were sold off and those on which the lenders
were repaid, but, in addition, any figures which might emerge from
such a calculation would be positively misleading in view of the
fact that the full details of the extent to which the rents were raised
by the Corporation when leases fell in during the period when it
had possession of the property are not available.

One creditor whose claims have not yet been mentioned in this
account of the process of repayment was the Chamber of London
itself. Before and during the great repayment operation money was
due to the Chamber on a number of counts. The first of these in
order of priority relates to expenses incurred in selling off the lands,
which were, of course, a first charge on the cash receipts from the
land sales. The second was the subsidies made by the Chamber to
the smaller companies for their contribution to the £20,000 lent by
the companies in the summer of 1628, and these were repaid with
the repayment of that loan in 1629. The remaining debts to the
Chamber were of much longer standing, and the first of these was
the unilateral interest payments which the Chamber had made in
1623 and 1625 upon the loan of 1617.[43] These, it will be remembered, had originally amounted to £7,850, but by March 1641 this
sum had been reduced to £3,950, for as soon as the lenders themselves had been repaid in full principal and interest, at least as far
as the face value of their debts was concerned, they had to pay back

[43] See above, p. 126.

such unilateral interests payments as the Chamber had formerly paid to them. No one, however, took very seriously the city Chamberlain's claim that these lenders should pay interest to the Chamber on this count, for, in making these payments, the Corporation had done no more, and, in fact, very much less, than might be expected of a surety when the principal debtor had defaulted. Interest, however, might more reasonably be demanded, and was, in fact, obtained on all the other items due to the Chamber, that is the subsidies to the lenders of 1617 and 1625 and the £800 which had been paid in 1625 to make up the total sum which was raised by subscription in that year,[44] the latter being simply a book debt due to the normal account of the Chamberlain from the land sales account. Interest on these items, of course, ran at the rate of 5 per cent. from 20 December 1627, for the Corporation's quasi-conversion operation had in equity to be made to apply to itself no less than to the lenders.[45]

The report of a committee of the Court of Aldermen which had been appointed to examine the debt due to the Chamber, and which was presented on 16 March 1641, recommended the adoption of a form of clearing-house procedure whereby the debts to those lenders who still remained unpaid should be offset against their debts to the Chamber for the sums in which it had subsidized them. In the case of those contributors to the loan of 1625 who had been subsidized to the full extent of their contributions, this operation simply involved a book transfer to the Chamber of the claims of these lenders, and was little more than a formal recognition of an already established procedure. In that of other lenders, however, to whom the total debt due was far greater than their own debt to the Chamber, the difference between these two sums was to be reduced as far as possible by adding to the Chamber's claims upon them any sums which they might owe as fines for refusing to take up municipal office. They were to receive the remainder when sufficient proceeds were available from the sales of the royal contract

---

[44] See above, pp. 125–6, 128–9.

[45] Repertory, lv, fos. 75(b)–77(b); City Cash Accounts, 1/4 (1641–3), fos. 72(b)–73, 77; R.C.E.P. 19, 'Mony owing to the Chamber'. Of the subsidies to the lenders of 1617, £300 was still due to the Chamber by lenders who had not yet been repaid by 16 March 1641. This sum probably does not include interest. By the same date £22,866. 13s. 4d. was due in principal and interest for subsidies to the lenders of 1625, while the £800 paid to make up the £60,000 lent in 1625 had accumulated an interest debt of £720 by Michaelmas 1641.

estates. The chief significance of this arrangement, which was adopted as from 24 March, was the curtailment of the widely adopted practice whereby purchasers of land discharged the debts of lenders as part of their purchase price. The bonds of that great majority of lenders who had been subsidized by the Chamber were to be delivered up by them to the Chamber, and the Corporation would in future demand full cash payment from purchasers, as opposed to payments partly in cash and partly in bonds. The only persons to whom the latter procedure might still apply were those lenders who had not been subsidized by the Chamber.[46]

The long delay in the repayment of the lenders of 1617 and 1625 and the unsatisfactory nature of the measures which were ultimately taken to give them satisfaction have a double significance for the historian of government borrowing. Neither the sale of royal lands as an expedient of debt redemption nor the use of the machinery of the business world, though not, it is true of the Corporation itself, to effect these sales were new devices, as the events of the period of heavy land sales in the early years of the previous reign clearly show.[47] The novelty of the royal contract of 1627–8 lay in the fact that the loan contractor itself was entrusted with the sale of the lands and the repayment of the lenders. The abuses to which this expedient gave rise via the procedure whereby purchasers of land were allowed to discount the debts due to lenders as part of their purchase price provides one more indication of the fact that the bond of the Corporation offered no greater security to the lenders than that of the Crown, at least in cases where the latter was the principal debtor. The inevitable result was that the financial reputation of the Corporation to some extent sank with that of the Crown.

The second significance of the royal contract lies in the fact that, while this cumbersome repayment operation was in progress, and especially while the protracted disputes between the Crown and the Corporation about the malpractices involved remained unsettled, the Crown could not use the Corporation as a source of loans, and this is one of the reasons for the heightened importance of the customs farmers as lenders in the 1630's. The example of many of the lenders still waiting for repayment of money which

---

[46] Repertory, lv, fos. 75(b)–77(b); Journal, xl, fos. 1–1(b).

[47] See Dietz, op. cit., pp. 123–5, 147–8; Tawney, *Business and Politics under James I*, pp. 109–13, and *Econ. Hist. Rev.* xi (1941), 30–31; Ashton, *Econ. Hist. Rev.* 2nd ser. x (1957), 20–23.

they had lent as long ago as 1617, and the shocking treatment received by many of them when they were repaid, was hardly conducive to a further loosening of the citizens' purse-strings. It was
not until 1639, therefore, when the Crown could plead an emergency, and when the disputes had been settled, though hardly in a
manner likely to re-establish harmonious relations between Crown
and city, that a further loan was demanded. These last royal demands came at a time when the credit of the Crown had reached its
nadir and to discuss them in their proper context it will be most
convenient to turn to the next chapter, which attempts to chart the
main stages by which this position was reached.

VII

THE COURSE OF ROYAL BORROWING AND THE DECLINE IN THE ROYAL CREDIT

THE subsequent disasters of Jacobean finance have perhaps tended to obscure the fact that the financial history of the reign of James I began auspiciously enough with the King's promise to honour his inherited obligations, a gratis loan from the Livery Companies—though for a lesser sum than that originally requested—and a relative easiness in the Crown's relations with the money market. By contrast, the period of Charles I's personal government ended with a spate of quasi-forced loans, an undignified scraping after funds in London and the provinces, and arbitrary financial actions such as the seizure of the bullion deposited in the Mint and the threat to coin brass money if the Corporation of London did not meet the royal demands. Even if we grant that the opening years of James's reign were a period of remarkable economic expansion and buoyant commercial and financial confidence when, in addition, the royal demand for loans was not unduly heavy, while 1640 saw the beginning of a long depression coinciding with a peak period of the royal demand for funds, the contrast between the two situations is impressive, and reflects to some extent a decline in the royal credit between the death of Elizabeth and the calling of the Long Parliament. It is true that Charles's loans in 1640 were not formally Forced Loans in the old-fashioned sense of loans on letters of Privy Seal dispatched to gentlemen all over the country; whereas in 1604 James raised a Forced Loan of this type. But it is easy to attach too much importance to this fact. In the first place, a strong element of compulsion lurked only very thinly disguised behind many of the loans raised during the emergency which was created by the Scottish war in 1639–40. Secondly, at the opening of the Stuart period, Forced Loans in the usual sense of the term were significant not simply—or even chiefly—for the fact that they were forced, but rather as the only known method of raising loans from the country at large as opposed to the London money market in particular. This was the use to which they had been put by Elizabeth, and, although her punctiliousness in the observance of her obligations was certainly far less marked in the last decade of her reign than it had been previously, her use of this form of borrowing reflects not the desperate state of her credit, but rather the inadequacy of the financial machinery of the metropolis. By 1640 the scandalous treatment of the holders of Jacobean Privy Seals and the still more significant Caroline development of the Forced Loan into a tax in all but name had resulted in its abandonment as a financial expedient whose advantages were more than offset by the political irritation which it caused. Paradoxically enough, therefore, the very absence of the use of the traditional Forced Loan on letters of Privy Seal after the 1620's was a sign not of an improved state of the royal credit which rendered such pressure unnecessary, but of the previous misuse of a useful, even if administratively rudimentary, fiscal device which had outlived its usefulness because it had been so grossly abused. It is an index of financial no less than of political decline.

Here, then, is one sign of the decline of the royal credit between 1603 and 1640, though at the most a minor one, and perhaps a symptom as much as it is a cause. But if the difference between the financial reputation of the Crown in 1603 and in 1640 is relatively easy to see, the developments which were responsible for this change are elusive to trace. One of the main difficulties here is the poverty of literary information on the state of the royal credit at different times, and, indeed, the difficulty of finding satisfactory criteria against which the financial reputation of the Crown can be measured.

To the solution of this problem the rate of interest has little to offer. Interest rates should, of course, fluctuate according to the prevalence of monetary stringency or monetary abundance, and a large-scale invasion of the money market by the Crown might well send the market rate up. But it is not so much the level of interest rates as the difference between the royal and the market rate which should provide some sort of information about the state of the royal credit. The Crown ought to have been able to borrow at around the same rate as the ordinary private borrower when its credit was relatively good, while it should have found its borrowings more expensive when its credit was relatively bad. But the consistency of royal borrowing at the statutory maximum rate in conditions of both monetary stringency and abundance, and despite other indications that the royal credit may have been deteriorating, suggests that differential rates of interest are an unsound guide.

It was shown earlier[1] that this consistency of royal interest rates is explicable partly in terms of the prevalence of a strong convention as to the level of interest rates which rendered the rate of interest less responsive to changed conditions in the money market than it is today, and partly in the Crown's use both of additional forms of inducement and its application of quasi-political pressure to lenders. *Ceteris paribus*, one would expect the prevalence of these factors of privilege and pressure to be more pronounced when the royal credit was declining. Even this criterion is, taken by itself, somewhat untrustworthy, however, for it is conceivable that the prevalence of these factors may reflect not so much a decline in the royal credit, as an expansion of the royal demand for loans. When such demands were exceptionally heavy—even in times when the royal credit was relatively good—the sources of loanable funds available to the Crown might be grossly insufficient without the use of additional forms of inducement or the application of pressure. In such periods one would expect to find institutionalized forms of borrowing, notably through the medium of the Corporation of London and the farmers of the customs, especially prominent. It is true, of course, that the need to borrow heavily from such sources—the need, that is, to bring the factors of privilege and pressure into greater prominence—may result in a decline in the royal credit. In certain circumstances it may also reflect the previous existence of such a decline, but, on the other hand, it may reflect an expansion of the royal demand for loans in absolute terms.

A more reliable criterion is the Crown's punctual observance of its financial obligations. But here again there are formidable difficulties, for it is necessary to distinguish between those prolongations which were willingly and those which were reluctantly conceded. The prevalence of the former is an index of good rather than bad credit; the proliferation of the latter must surely have affected adversely the financial standing of the government. But in actual practice it is more often than not extremely difficult to decide from the evidence whether a particular lender viewed prolongation as a means of turning a sound short-term into an equally sound medium-term investment, or whether he was grudgingly conceding renewal because he had virtually no choice in the matter. Difficult, except perhaps in one case. The surviving material relating to the

[1] See above, pp. 68–78.

loans raised through the Corporation of London is very abundant, and provides a number of cases where reasonable certainty of the facts and attitudes behind prolongation is possible. Nor is this so narrowly based a criterion as might appear at first sight, for the Corporation, as was shown in the two preceding chapters, did not supply the money required by the Crown out of its existing stock, but raised it from the money market at large. With reasonable caution, therefore, and with reference to other considerations where possible, the financial relations of the Crown with the Corporation of London may be used to throw light upon the royal credit in the city in general.

Bearing these facts in mind the first significant date in this connexion is April 1611, when the Crown obtained the first of two prolongations of the loan of £100,000 raised from the aldermen in 1610, for there is clear and indisputable evidence that a considerable degree of pressure had to be brought to bear upon a number of the lenders before they agreed to prolong their loans.[2] In the cases of the two previous loans raised through the Corporation, that of 1604 was paid off, except in the case of two of the companies, within nine months of the originally stipulated date, and that of 1608 punctually at the appointed time. Moreover, in the latter year the repayment of the loan of £60,000 which Elizabeth had raised in 1599 was completed.[3] All this was a more than tolerably good beginning, and although James had to raise a somewhat unpopular Forced Loan, which yielded £111,891 in 1604,[4] this, as we have seen, was the time-honoured method of tapping provincial in addition to metropolitan sources of capital. More serious, perhaps, were the first signs of financial laxity in the repayment of this loan, on which £20,000 was still due as late as December 1609.[5] But even here the relatively fast rate of liquidation of this loan as compared with the Forced Loans which were raised later in the reign is in itself suggestive.

In the years following 1606 there had been a notable expansion of the royal demand for loans. This was the period during which

[2] S.P. James I, 63/60.
[3] For the repayment of the loans of 1604 and 1608 see above, pp. 117, 118; for the repayment of the Elizabethan loan, Exchequer of Receipt, Issue Book (Pells), E. 403/1703, no foliation; Order Book (Pells), E. 403/2726, fos. 116(b), 152; Cal. S.P.D. (1603–10), p. 439.
[4] Dietz, op. cit., p. 115.
[5] S.P. James I, 50/75.

the carefree extravagance which had marked the opening years of
the reign was beginning to bear fruit in the form of an alarmingly
enhanced debt which had risen to about £735,000 by the beginning of 1606. The period down to 1611 saw a formidable attempt to
reduce the debt, beginning with the parliamentary grant of 1606
and ending with the extensive sale of Crown lands from 1609 onwards.[6] The need to borrow both to bridge the deficit and to anticipate the proceeds of the parliamentary grant was correspondingly
increased, and these years—and more especially 1607–8, when
about £350,000 was borrowed—were a period of relatively heavy
borrowing. It is difficult to decide how far the Crown was able to
borrow upon normal commercial terms and how far it had to have
recourse to additional forms of inducement at this time. The fact
that loans from privileged concessionaires were very prominent is
more likely to be indicative of a substantial increase in the royal
demand for funds than of the state of the royal credit. Such loans
were the advance payments of rent made between 1609 and 1611 by
a number of syndicates of contractors for Crown lands, the £30,000
from a coalition of contractors from different syndicates in the
autumn and winter of 1609, and the £120,000 advanced by the
customs farmers in 1607. In all these cases the fact that the lenders
were government concessionaires is obviously important, while in
the cases of the £69,000 and £100,000 borrowed through the Corporation of London in 1608 and 1610 respectively and the £116,381
borrowed on Privy Seals in 1611–12 royal pressure is obviously a
factor to be reckoned with.[7] Many other cases are indeterminate.
Sir Baptist Hicks, for instance, may well have been influenced by
the fact that he had lucrative contracts with the Court, and that
royal payments to him on this account were long overdue. On more
than one occasion he wrote to his brother, Michael, in tones of
despair at the dilatoriness of the royal debtor,[8] and it may well be
true that, like Burlamachi in the 1620's, he saw in further lending
the only hope of ultimately getting back what was due to him. If so,

    [6] For the policy and technique of debt reduction in these years, see Ashton,
Econ. Hist. Rev. 2nd ser. x (1957), 21–23.
    [7] For the loans from the contractors for lands, Exchequer of Receipt, Order
Books (Pells), E. 403/2728, fo. 252; E. 403/2732, fo. 32; *Hist. MSS. Comm.*,
Sackville MSS. i. 183; from the customs farmers, above, p. 84; from the Cor-
poration of London, above, pp. 117–21; for the Forced Loan, Dietz, op. cit.,
pp. 149, 159, note.
    [8] B.M. Lansdowne MSS. 89, nos. 73, 106; Lansdowne MSS. 90, no. 3.

he was not the first merchant to make the discovery that the role of contractor to the Court was likely to be supplemented by that of lender to the Crown.[9] Hicks was also a member of a syndicate of merchants which lent £120,000 to James I in a number of instalments over 1607 and 1608, and since a number of the members of this syndicate were actual or potential government concessionaires, it is difficult to rule out the possibility that their advances may have been connected with their other economic interests. Some, like Nicholas Salter and William Garway, were already customs farmers, while others, like Hicks and John Eldred, were shortly to become contractors for Crown lands. One is left with a number of minor cases, the most important of which is the relatively small loan of £14,500 made by certain 'merchant strangers' in 1607, where there is no obvious possibility of a connexion between the loans and the existence of additional forms of inducement. And even here certainty is precluded.[10]

From this maze of conjecture and uncertainty it is a relief to turn to the loan of 1610 from the aldermen and its sequel. For here, as we have seen, prolongation was very grudgingly conceded by some of the lenders, and the fact that six—and only six—of the aldermen proved willing to lend £2,000 apiece in the summer of 1613 after the loan of 1610 had been repaid is of relatively minor importance beside the other significant repercussions of the two prolongations of the loan of 1610. For on the next occasion when the Crown sought to borrow on a large scale in June 1614, the Corporation preferred to make a gift of £10,000 rather than to lend £100,000. Moreover, it will be remembered that when it finally could not avoid raising a loan for the government in 1617, the lenders did not receive the royal bonds as security, but the Crown borrowed the credit of the Corporation.[11] All this evidence points clearly to a decline in the royal credit between 1611 and 1617, and an additional though minor factor in this decline was the failure to honour the

[9] For an interesting continental example, see Pierre Jeannin, 'Les Relations économiques des villes de la Baltique avec Anvers au XVIe siècle', *Vierteljahrschrift für Sozial- und Wirtschaftsgeschichte*, 43 Band (1956), 216–17.

[10] For Hicks's loans, Exchequer of Receipt, Order Books (Pells), E. 403/2727, fos. 69(b), 247(b); E. 403/2731, fos. 139(b), 160(b); S.P. James I, 26/103, 32/68, 36/42, 38/46–47, 60, 40/67; for the syndicate of 1607, Close Roll, 6 Jac. I, pts. 41, 43, Close Roll, 7 Jac. I, pt. 29; Warrant Book James I, vol. ii, fo. 76; E. 403/2728, fo. 67(b); for the loan from the 'merchant strangers', B.M. Lansdowne MSS. 151, fo. 83.

[11] For a detailed treatment of these developments, see above, pp. 120–3.

Forced Loan of 1611–12, of which as much as £112,000 remained to be paid as late as July 1618.[12]

However, the shock to the royal credit, though appreciable, was not paralysing in its effects. The royal failure with the Corporation of London in 1614 apart, down to 1617 the royal demand for loans was not sufficiently great for the Crown to experience any unusual difficulty in the raising of funds. About this time Cranfield had been disturbed about the effects of the heavy sales of royal land and the level of royal borrowing in inducing financial stringency in the city and raising the rate of interest for commercial borrowing,[13] and while there may be much that is valid in his diagnosis as far as the former factor is concerned, the invasion of the money market by the Crown at or about the time when Cockayne's project—the real villain of the piece, one suspects—was in the air was of very modest dimensions as compared with the years before 1611, and especially with the 1620's. Among its most important borrowings in these years were the £8,000 raised from Sir Noel de Caron, the Dutch ambassador, Robert de la Barre, and Philip Jacobson in January 1616 on the security of the revenues of the Hanaper of Chancery and the fines for alienations, the £7,500 on the same security from Hicks, Sir Paul Bayning, and William Herrick in December of the same year, the £10,000 from Thomas Stockton in 1615, and £18,500 from William Courteen in the course of 1613–14. None of these loans was for a very spectacular sum, though the farmers of the great customs were also providing short-term accommodation on a far larger scale than hitherto at this time.[14]

1617 was a heavier and more difficult year. The heavier borrowing of this year appears originally to have arisen from the government's determination to reduce the debt which had risen rapidly since 1610. As a preliminary to further permanent debt reduction the government planned to manage the debt by borrowing more than £220,000, the bulk of which was to be raised from the Corporation of London and the farmers of the great customs. The plan

[12] P.R.O. MS. Cal. of Sackville MSS. M. 1047.

[13] R. H. Tawney, *Business and Politics under James I* (Cambridge, 1958), p. 128.

[14] For Caron, &c., and Hicks, &c., see Patent Roll, 15 Jac. I, pt. 5; Coll. Sign Man. Jac. I, vol. viii, no. 15; Exchequer of Receipt, Order Book (Pells), E. 403/2736, fo. 109; for Stockton, E. 403/2734, fo. 184(*b*); for Courteen, *Cal. S.P.D. (1611–18)*, p. 197; S.P. James I, 115/115; Exchequer of Receipt, Receipt Books (Pells), E. 401/1890, 1892; Order Books (Pells), E. 403/2733, fo. 163; E. 403/2745, fos. 11, 13(*b*), 22(*b*); for the customs farmers, see above, pp. 88–91.

failed for two reasons. In the first place, the farmers, who since 1613 had been persuaded to grant substantial—and in 1615 spectacular—short-term loans by allowing the Crown to overdraw its rent, were now seeking to draw in their horns, as is clear enough from the reduction in the size of their overdrafts between 1616 and the expiration of their lease in 1621.[15] Accordingly, the projected loan from the farmers was a damp squib, and the official reason given for its failure was the fact that the farmers were unwilling to anticipate their rents to this amount, and that suitable alternative assignments were not available. The Corporation's contribution did not fail, though it fell short by over £3,000. In these circumstances loans such as the £3,000 provided by Vanlore and the £20,000 negotiated by the Dutch ambassador, Caron, from the Dutch merchants in London were quite inadequate to bridge the gap. But the plan would probably have failed anyway for the additional reason that the royal progress to Scotland precipitated an onrush of extraordinary charges which swallowed up the proceeds of such loans as were negotiated successfully. So much for the management of the debt![16]

In 1617, therefore, as in 1614, the Crown experienced some difficulty in its search for loanable funds. The refusal of the customs farmers to lend, the need to borrow the credit of the Corporation of London for the loan in the city, and the failure of this loan to be fully paid up all suggest a decline of the royal credit since the period of Salisbury's administration. Indeed, the conduct of royal financial policy, and especially the gross financial maladministration associated with Suffolk's tenure of the white staff were probably at least as important as the two prolongations of the aldermen's loan of 1610 in bringing about this state of affairs.

The Crown certainly experienced some difficulty in 1617, but almost every line of inquiry points to a worsening of the financial situation in the 1620's, and especially after 1624, when England was at war and the need to borrow was enormously increased. The years 1620–1, when well over £100,000 was borrowed, were a time of

---

[15] See above, pp. 88–92.

[16] For the failure of the farmers' loan, *Cal. S.P.D. (1611–18)*, p. 485; Spedding, op. cit. vi. 254–5; for the Corporation, see above, pp. 122–5; for Vanlore, Exchequer of Receipt, Order Book (Pells), E. 403/2737, fo. 87; MS. Cal. of Sackville MSS. M. 1047; for the Dutch merchants, *Cal. S.P.D. (1611–18)*, p. 447; S.P. James I, 91/1; MS. Cal. of Sackville MSS. M. 1047; B.M. Lansdowne MSS. 165, fos. 282–3(b).

relatively heavy borrowing, but this was trifling compared with what was to come. Between 1624 and 1628 more than a million pounds were borrowed. When the fact that during these years England was only slowly struggling out of an exceptionally severe economic depression is taken into consideration, the continued resilience of the money market offers just grounds for amazement and suggests that the exceptional rise of the royal demands might well have been an important factor in retarding the rate of economic recovery. Moreover, a further consideration, more germane to our argument, arises—that is, whether the successful borrowing by the Crown of such vast sums is compatible with the thesis of a decline of the royal credit. Yet some decline there must have been in the 1620's. We have seen that the position of 1617 had its roots in the prolongations of 1611 and 1612 and the incompetence of financial policy in the years before the second commission of the Treasury. The effect had been the relative failure of the loan operations of that year, and its most striking outward and visible sign, the need to borrow the credit of the Corporation of London. In the early 1620's the royal finances were directed along more efficient lines, but the circumstances of that time, with its greatly increased extraordinary charges, due to the greater embroilment of England in international affairs, meant a rise rather than a reduction of debt, and, as one prolongation of the loan of 1617 and other loans raised in and after this year followed another, the royal credit must have suffered still further.[17] Indeed, the continued and growing clamour of the more vociferous of the lenders of 1617 cannot but have had a profoundly deleterious effect upon the royal credit in the city. The Corporation cited the royal default as an excuse for not lending further sums. 'His Majesty', suggested the Venetian ambassador in August 1621, 'is not well pleased with this City, which has grown tired of paying out money on loan, being creditor for large amounts',[18] while Chamberlain suggested that the last loan had so impoverished the citizens that they were unable to lend again even if they had been willing to do so.[19] The ultimate creditors were, of course, not the Corporation itself, but individual citizens who constantly bombarded the Corporation and the Crown with complaints of the in-

---

[17] For financial policy and the state of the debt in these years, see Dietz, op. cit., pp. 182–213; Tawney, op. cit., pp. 184–228; Ashton, *Econ. Hist. Rev.* 2nd ser. x (1957), 20, 23–24.

[18] *Cal. S.P. Ven. (1621–3)*, p. 108.

[19] *Cal. S.P.D. (1619–23)*, pp. 456–7.

convenience caused to them by the latter's refusal to pay up.[20] One of their number, a Mr. Alington, stressed the fact that he had lent money on more than one previous occasion, and that the Crown's delay in the matter of repayment was a poor reward for the services of one who had served it well in the past.[21] Here, indeed, is the crux of the matter, for many of the individual citizens who had contributed to the corporate loan of 1617 were also potential sources of individual loans. In these circumstances it is not improbable that the Crown's continued default on its obligations in 1618 and after had a more generally damaging effect on its credit in the city than is indicated simply by a study of its financial relations with the Corporation of London. That there was a revival of heavy borrowing through the Corporation in the early years of Charles I's reign, connected with the needs of war finance, does not materially affect this argument. For institutionalized borrowing of this type represents one of the most notable examples of the importance of the factors of privilege and pressure. There is, therefore, every reason to believe that the Crown's failure to repay the loan of 1617 had a more damaging and lasting effect on its ability to raise loans on commercial terms than on its ability to borrow through the Corporation itself.

To these difficulties must be added the financial stringency associated with the depression of the early 1620's. It was certainly fortunate for the Crown that its unprecedented invasion of the money market in the war years did not coincide with the worst of the depression. Yet, on the face of things, inducements to lenders to provide this vastly increased amount of money would appear to have been lessened by the reduction of the statutory maximum rate of interest to 8 per cent. in 1624. Although this affected the private no less than the royal borrower, the scale of royal borrowing over the succeeding five years was so vast that it is difficult to see how the royal demands could be met by offering less inducements in the way of interest than ever before. Were additional forms of inducement more prevalent? The evidence is not particularly helpful in this respect. Down to 1627 at least, non-institutionalized borrowing was more prominent than borrowing from the customs farmers and the Corporation of London. The accession of Pindar's syndicate to the great farm in 1625 was obviously prompted mainly by royal

---

[20] Remembrancia, v. 72; vi. 1, 54, 125, 140.
[21] MS. Cal. of Sackville MSS. 635.

dissatisfaction with its predecessor, whose advances had been for paltry and insignificant amounts by comparison with those of the first syndicate, which it had succeeded in 1621.[22] Nevertheless, the period of really spectacular advances by the customs farmers is undoubtedly the 1630's, and not the late 1620's, when the Crown needed money most. The Corporation of London was adamant in refusing to raise money for James I after 1617, though it was again active in 1625, 1626, and 1627–8.[23] What of the other lenders? With a decline of the relative importance of institutionalized borrowing can it be said that the consequently enhanced significance of other forms of borrowing can be ascribed to the growth of the importance of additional inducements to lenders or to the fact that royal pressure to force them to lend was more in evidence than at previous times?

To this question it is impossible to return a firm reply. While in the case of the institutionalized borrowing from the Corporation of London and the farmers the connexion between royal borrowing and both privilege and pressure is clear and indisputable, in dealing with other forms of borrowing we move on to more difficult ground, for here such a connexion cannot be established almost *ex defitione*, and even when there is a strong probability of its existence, evidential certainty is almost invariably precluded.

With these qualifications in mind we can now consider the main characteristics of the borrowing of the 1620's. In the first place the element of pressure can be seen most clearly in the Forced Loans of 1625–7, which aroused fierce opposition from unexpected and influential quarters.[24] Secondly, in this decade some money was borrowed abroad, notably the 300,000 rixdollars—in English money more than £70,000—raised from Christian IV of Denmark in 1620–1 at the extremely favourable rate of 6 per cent., and the £58,400 obtained at Amsterdam on the pawn of jewels in 1626, though the yield of the latter loan fell far below the royal expectations.[25] But the era of extensive foreign borrowing was now long

---

[22] See above, pp. 94–95.

[23] For borrowing from the farmers and the Corporation, see above, pp. 97, 126–41.

[24] Gardiner, *History*, vi. 143–4, 148–50, 154–8, 178–9, 202–3, 212–19; Dietz, op. cit., pp. 227–8, 235–8.

[25] For the Danish loan, S.P. Foreign, Denmark (S.P. 75/5), bdle. v, fos. 215–215(b), 217–18, 244, 261–2; MS. Cal. of Sackville MSS. 1111, 6920–1; Rymer, *Foedera*, vii, pt. iii, p. 208. For the loan at Amsterdam, see above, pp. 64–65.

past, and these loans were of small importance compared with those raised in London. Thirdly, and most important of all, despite the fact that the importance of non-institutionalized borrowing was enormously enhanced in the 1620's, there was no corresponding expansion of the circle of individual lenders. Relative to the expansion of the volume of lending to the government, there was, in fact, a most marked contraction. The same names recur over and over again in the records, and of these names two, in particular, strike the eye by virtue of the frequency with which they appear and the size of the financial operations with which they are connected. The names are those of Sir William Russell, the naval treasurer, and Philip Burlamachi.[26] Burlamachi may have been, as Mr. Cooper has recently suggested,[27] 'a somewhat shady financier', but the Crown could not afford to be fastidious at this juncture, and, indeed, it is difficult to see how it could have kept its head above water during these years if it had not been for his loans and the 'surplusages' which he allowed it in connexion with his numerous quasi-official assignations abroad. By no means inconsiderable in earlier years, the scale of his services expanded enormously with the onset of war, beginning with the £55,000 lent in conjunction with Sir Ralph Freeman at the end of 1624, and totalling more than £90,000 on his own account in 1625 alone, and at least as much as £40,000 between 1626 and 1629. These figures relate only to his conventional loans; his incidental disbursements in advance of his receipts as paymaster and his over-payments of his account all helped to swell this total considerably. If ever a financier could be said to be indispensable to a government at a particularly critical stage in its affairs, that financier was Burlamachi. During the same period Russell was making advances of a similar order, largely in connexion with the navy. Too small and too few the advances of such lenders may have been for the successful conduct of war in the seventeenth century; nevertheless, as contributions from individual financiers they were staggering, and deserving of more worthy recipients than the feckless Mansfeld or the vain-glorious Buckingham.

On a lesser, but by no means inconsiderable, scale, Russell's services to naval finance were paralleled by those of one of the

[26] For a detailed treatment of Russell and Burlamachi's operations, see Ashton, *B.I.H.R.* loc. cit., pp. 162–74; for Burlamachi, Judges, *Economica*, loc. cit., pp. 285–300.

[27] J. P. Cooper, 'The Fortune of Thomas Wentworth, Earl of Strafford', *Econ Hist. Rev.* 2nd ser. xi (1958), 238.

Surveyors of Marine Victuals, Sir Allen Apsley, who is probably best known through the praise bestowed upon him by his celebrated daughter.[28] Apsley helped to fill some of the gaps in naval finance both by lending money and by pledging his credit to supply naval victuals. There was nothing new about this type of operation, except possibly its scale, which was enormously increased by the demands of war. In August 1626 Apsley reported that he had become engaged for £25,000 for naval victuals on credit, but 'for want of paiement his creditt would extend no further', and the resultant dearth of provisions had precipitated the wholesale desertion of seamen. The royal debt to him in 1627 amounted to more than £41,000 and was repaid in the next year by the grant of royal lands, the conveyance of a part of which was closely modelled on that of the more famous transaction of the same year with the Corporation of London. With the financial entanglements following Apsley's death and resulting from the suspiciously belated discovery that it was he who owed money to the Crown and not vice versa we need not concern ourselves, beyond noting that the royal argument turned to a considerable extent upon the legalistic point that the victuallers' disbursements for the year 1626 must be totally disallowed on the grounds that they had obtained the signatures of only three, instead of the required four, naval commissioners. The dispute between the Crown and Apsley's creditors, to whom he had conveyed the lands in satisfaction of his debts, had still not been settled by as late as the end of 1639.[29]

Such financial conduct was not likely to render responsible service in government disbursing departments a very popular occupation—at least in war-time, when the scale of the financial services which the Crown required of its disbursing officials was of sufficient magnitude to break all but the most powerful. In peace-time, of course, such posts had very real compensations, not the least of which was ready access to government funds in the form of unused balances. Both the advantages of peace-time and the difficulties of

[28] Lucy Hutchinson, *Memoirs of the Life of Colonel Hutchinson* (ed. C. H. Firth) (1906), pp. 7–10, 14.

[29] *Cal. S.P.D.* (1627–8), p. 499; (1628–9), pp. 139, 197, 204, 247, 442, 580; (1629–31), pp. 33, 94; (1634–5), pp. 459–60; (1637), pp. 69, 173; (1637–8), p. 120; (1638–9), pp. 33, 538, 598–600; (1639), pp. 101–2, 132–3; (1639–40), p. 39; S.P. Charles I, 92/9, 18, 176/53, 224/62, 317/93(ii); *A.P.C.* (1626), pp. 165, 178; (1628–9), pp. 13–14, 25; P.C.R. (1633–4), fos. 379–81, 614; (1637–8), pp. 341–2; (1638), pp. 566–8; (1639), pp. 136–7, 294–5, 339, 346, 380–1; Exchequer L.T.R. Declared Accounts, E. 351/2428.

war-time service help to explain the prevalence of business men like Russell and Burlamachi in offices which today would be occupied by salaried civil servants. But there were also occasions when military or semi-military officers themselves were called upon to pay out money before the funds which had been appropriated for the purposes for which their advances were made had become available. In 1631 the unpaid balance of the sums due to Lord Vere for his disbursements when commanding foreign troops in the Palatinate, as well as for later advances for victuals, amounted to £5,071. In order to obtain immediate payment of this long-overdue debt, Vere announced that he would be satisfied with £5,000, an offer which the Crown accepted with alacrity, thus finding itself in the enviable position of receiving interest on money which it had borrowed. The post of Admiral of South Cornwall was perhaps an office which might be expected to yield emoluments rather than burdens. But not in war-time. Between February 1626 and October 1628 the then admiral, Sir James Bagg, disbursed £26,491. 0s. 3¾d. above his total receipts of £25,118. 11s. 1d.[30]

Loans by privy councillors, peers, courtiers, and other notabilities were far more prominent in the 1620's than in earlier decades, and these, like the examples just considered, can hardly be classed as normal commercial borrowings. The loans made by Sir Francis Crane and James Maxwell have already been considered in another context.[31] The arch-courtier Buckingham also lent quite freely. Destined not to receive back in his lifetime the sums which he had disbursed in connexion with his Spanish escapade of 1623 and which, it was claimed, amounted to more than £30,000,[32] he was, nevertheless, prominent as a lender towards the charges of the military preparations which the failure of that dismal and irresponsible episode had been partly responsible for precipitating. Early in 1624 he lent at least £10,000 for naval purposes, and either at the end of the next year or the beginning of 1626 borrowed a further £10,000 from Sir Paul Bayning for the fleet. A lesser example of enlightened self-interest on the part of a courtier with a finger in a number of economic pies and ambitions to obtain further concessions is the £3,700 lent by Sir George Goring in 1628. The

[30] For Vere, Coll. Sign Man. Car. I, vol. xii, no. 63; for Bagg, *Cal. S.P.D. (1629–31)*, pp. 305–6, 335.

[31] See above, pp. 62–64, 66–67.

[32] These advances were not repaid until 1629.

advances of the future customs farmer can certainly be connected with his desire to obtain the privilege of issuing licences to retail wine.[33]

Scepticism as to the motives of well-born and influential lenders can, of course, be carried too far. There were peers who eschewed the gaudy attractions of the Court, and sought to serve the Crown by applying their talents to more serious matters. Such a man was Lord Digby, later Earl of Bristol, who was one of the ablest members of his class, and a diplomat of considerable eminence. In September 1621, when returning from Vienna where he had been conducting some delicate diplomatic negotiations, he pledged his plate to certain bankers in Nuremberg in order to keep together the allied armies in the lower Palatinate, and was repaid after his return to England. On occasions the members of the Privy Council lent money as a body partly in order to set a patriotic example to the rest of the realm, as in 1628, when twenty-eight members of the council lent £9,600 towards the charges of the La Rochelle expedition.[34]

So far we have dealt with titans like Burlamachi and Russell, office-holders, courtiers, and other social notabilities. In turning to those moneylenders who were men on a smaller scale than Burlamachi and Russell but who, nevertheless, had provided the main source of non-institutionalized loans during the first two decades of the century, it is far more difficult to be categorical about the extent to which their loans were raised on normal commercial terms. Nevertheless, while it is difficult to find unequivocal evidence of the connexion of these loans with one form or another of additional inducement over and above the interest received by the lenders, there are some indications that this connexion may have been applicable in a number of the cases. For example, while there is no obvious reason for doubting that the loan of £30,000 made in the autumn of 1621 by Hicks, Vanlore, and Cockayne, for use in connexion with the Palatinate was other than a normal commercial transaction, in the case of the first two of these lenders its repay-

[33] For Buckingham, S.P. Charles I, 145/7; Coll. Sign Man. Car. I, vol. vi, no. 36; Exchequer of Receipt, Order Book (Pells), E. 403/2747, fo. 52(b); Cal. S.P.D. (1623–5), pp. 206, 212–13; (1625–6), p. 557. For Goring, S.P. Charles I, 87/63; Cal. S.P.D. (1627–8), p. 517.
[34] For Digby, Cal. S.P.D. (1619–23), p. 300; Gardiner, History, iv. 222–3. For the Privy Council, P.C.R. (1628), fo. 205. Buckingham supplied £2,000 and the other contributions varied between £500 and £200.

ment, when already long overdue, was made conditional upon their making further advances. Vanlore had to lend a further £10,000 in July 1625 and Hicks an equivalent sum in May 1626 in return for receiving assignments for both their old and new debts.[35] The Crown exploited a similar situation in precisely the same way in the case of Bayning, whose contribution to the £7,500 lent in conjunction with Hicks and Herrick in 1616 had still not been repaid in October 1626, when he was persuaded to advance a further £7,500 as a condition of obtaining fresh assignments for both loans. Bayning's other notable contributions as a lender in the mid and later 1620's have already been noticed as being perhaps connected with the peerage which he had long coveted and finally obtained in 1628.[36] An associate of Bayning's and an executor of his will was one Jeffrey Kerby, 'an Aldermen's fellow in London, who was servant to old Mr. Bayning',[37] and who lent £24,000—of Bayning's money?—to Charles I in the course of 1629, but here there is no obvious tie-up between loans and privileges.[38] Sir William Courteen, the famous merchant, financier, and colonizer, lent £13,500 to Charles I in July 1625, notwithstanding the fact that the loans which he had made to James I more than a decade earlier had not yet been repaid, and in August 1628 he followed this up with a further loan of £3,000. In the meantime the bulk, and perhaps the whole, of his Jacobean loans had been repaid, but of his two loans to Charles I the principal sum of £7,250 still remained due to him as late as April 1635. It is by no means improbable that these last two loans were connected with Courteen's desire to obtain royal support for his current West Indian plantation schemes, and the latter, in particular, may well have been designed to stave off the opposition which had developed in the previous year, from a rival group in Barbados, headed by the Earl of Carlisle. If so, its

[35] P.R.O. MS. Cal. of Sackville MSS., Lord Treasurer's Warrant Book (1621–2), fos. 4–5, 20–21; Coll. Sign Man. Car. I, vol. i, no. 76; Exchequer of Receipt, Issue Book (Pells), E. 403/1736, no foliation; Order Books (Pells), E. 403/2745, fos. 10(b), 21, 177(b), 214(b); E. 403/2746, fo. 131; A.P.C. (1621–3), pp. 83–84, 92–93, 99–100; (1625–6), pp. 466–7; Cal. S.P.D. (1625–6), pp. 579, 580. For another form of inducement in Hicks's case, see above, p. 74. Hicks lent a further £2,500 in 1628 (B.M. Harleian MSS. 3796, fo. 22).

[36] S.P. Charles I, 42/56; Docquets, Charles I, bdle. xiii; Exchequer of Receipt, Order Books (Pells), E. 403/2745, fo. 126; E. 403/2747, fo. 52(b). And see above, pp. 73–74.

[37] Viz. Bayning's father.

[38] Coll. Sign Man. Car. I, vol. xi, no. 63; Cal. S.P.D. (1629–31), pp. 30, 54.

aim was unsuccessful.[39] It is less likely that privileges were an important factor in the £8,000 lent by Nicholas and Ellis Crispe and Abraham Chamberlain in 1625,[40] although Nicholas Crispe's interest in the Guinea trade certainly pre-dates by a good many years his successful flotation of a company in 1631. Chamberlain was interested in the petty farms, but Nicholas Crispe was not to turn his attention to the profitable business of customs farming for more than another decade. Finally, we come to a number of cases where extraneous forms of inducement were clearly involved. Sir Cornelius Vermuyden's loan of £10,000 in May 1628 was definitely connected with his land reclamation schemes;[41] £5,000 of the £7,000 lent by Lawrence Halstead in 1627-8 may well have been advanced as a means of obtaining repayment of a debt due to him from the Crown for French wines seized by the Commissioners for Sale of French Goods,[42] and, substituting naval victuals for French wines, the same is probably true of the £5,000 lent by John Bland and Hugh Perry in July 1628.[43] Apart, then, from the cases of Kerby, and perhaps that of the Crispes and Chamberlain, we are left with the £7,000 lent by Charles Harbord and the £5,000 by Alexander Stafford in 1629[44] as the only cases where there is no obvious reason to suspect a possibility that the loans may have been raised on other than normal terms. In all the other cases cited above either the evidence is too suggestive or the economic connexion of the lender with the Crown too intimate for us to be able to postulate with confidence that the non-institutionalized loans of the 1620's were—by contrast with the loans from the customs farmers and the Corporation of London—raised upon ordinary commercial terms.

If it is true—as it may well be—that the factors of privilege and pressure were more important in connexion with royal borrowing

[39] S.P. Charles I, 4/128, 112/67, 286/43, 90; Exchequer of Receipt, Order Book (Pells), E. 403/2749, fo. 109; B.M. Harleian MSS. 3796, fo. 22. For Courteen's West Indian schemes, see V. T. Harlow (ed.), *Colonizing Expeditions to the West Indies (1623-1667)* (Hakluyt Society), 2nd ser., no. 56 (1925), pp. xxix–xxxiii; V. T. Harlow, *A History of Barbados (1625-1685)* (Oxford, 1926), pp. 3-13.

[40] Docquets, Charles I, bk. xiii.   [41] See above, p. 61.

[42] S.P. Charles I, 186/90; Coll. Sign Man. Car. I, vol. viii, no. 23; Exchequer of Receipt, Order Books (Pells), E. 403/2747, fo. 114(b); E. 403/2748, fo. 15(b); A.P.C. (1628-9), pp. 24-25.

[43] Coll. Sign Man. Car. I, vol. viii, no. 45; Exchequer of Receipt, Order Books (Pells), E. 403/2747, fo. 126(b); E. 403/2748, fo. 12; A.P.C. (1628-9), p. 64.

[44] S.P. Charles I, 186/90, 286/43; B.M. Harleian MSS. 3796, fo. 22.

from individual moneylenders in the 1620's than they had been in the two previous decades, it is perhaps surprising that the Crown did not make greater use of syndicates of privileged concessionaires as sources of loans at this time. Apart from the advances of the farmers, which, as we have seen, were less substantial in the 1620's than in the following decade, the only important example of such a loan is the £10,000 which was raised from the East India Company in October 1623, and even this fell short by £2,000 of the sum originally required by the Crown.[45] On 2 July 1628, when Charles I was scouring London for money to finance Buckingham's expedition to La Rochelle, he demanded a further loan of £10,000 from the company. Despite the fact that the loan was stated to be for only three weeks until the receipts of the first subsidy voted by parliament were available, the King's request was rejected politely, but very firmly, on the grounds that 'it never came more unseasonably, for they were now on a new subscription for prosecution of the trade, and, if his request should be known, it would utterly overthrow the whole business'.[46] The implications of these excuses are interesting. These are either that a loan to the Crown, even for the absurdly short term of three weeks, was likely to reduce catastrophically the demand for East India stock, or that it was the fact that the loan was unlikely to be repaid within the originally stipulated time which would bring about this effect. Neither suggestion is in the least absurd in view of the great difficulties which the company was experiencing in raising subscriptions to its third joint stock at this time. Indeed, the fact that one of the main causes of its lack of success was Thomas Smethwicke's attack on the alleged maladministration of the company authorities, and his allied proposal to admit the King as an adventurer for one-fifth of the stock gratis—or, at least, in return for royal protection to the company[47] —probably rendered refusal to lend to the Crown the product of pious indignation at least as much as of financial necessity. Here certainly was the main reason for the company's refusal. In addition, it is not unlikely that the raising of the last £60,000 of the £120,000 paid by the Corporation of London to Charles I under the terms of the royal contract had annoyed some of the merchants who had been asked to contribute. Such events were hardly conducive to dutiful and cheerful compliance when asked for a further loan

[45] *Cal. S.P. East Indies (1622–4)*, p. 159.
[46] Ibid. *(1625–9)*, p. 521.   [47] Scott, op. cit. ii. 109–10, 112.

through a different medium, and the incident demonstrates clearly that the Crown might experience very considerable difficulty in borrowing even from a privileged syndicate.

We are now in a position to draw some general—although necessarily rather tentative—conclusions about the role of non-institutionalized borrowing in the third decade of the seventeenth century. It has been shown that during this period the importance of this type of borrowing increased, both in absolute terms and relative to the borrowing through the Corporation of London and from syndicates such as the customs farmers, and that the loans of two of the lenders, Russell and Burlamachi, dwarf those of the others. But despite this relative and absolute increase in the importance of loans raised from individuals, there was by no means a corresponding expansion in the number of the lenders, and a fairly definite number of regular lenders were assuming an increasingly heavy load. It is, however, possible that this constriction in the number of private individual lenders relative to the general expansion of borrowing from individuals may mask an effective expansion of the range of loanable funds tapped by the Crown. Just as the decline of the royal credit by 1617 was manifested in the need to borrow the credit of the Corporation of London for the loan of that year, so its further decline in the 1620's may have manifested itself in the royal inability to tap directly sources of loanable funds which might have been available, if the Crown had been able to borrow upon strictly commercial terms. Hence those lenders whose names recur more and more frequently in the records may sometimes have been acting as financial intermediaries who, in effect, lent their credit and other people's money to the Crown, thus enabling it to lay its hands upon funds which would hardly have been available to it if it had tried to borrow direct from the money market, as opposed to the regular lenders. It must be pointed out that the evidence for this hypothesis is anything but conclusive, but it does suggest, nevertheless, that after about 1620 there was a notable increase in the practice of borrowing and relending to the Crown on the part of these lenders.[48]

This period is also marked by a decline in borrowing from large *ad hoc* syndicates. Large numbers of merchants could apparently no longer be persuaded to combine resources for the purpose of making substantial loans to the Crown, as a number of merchants

---

[48] For examples, see above, pp. 24–25, below, pp. 183–4.

of the city had done in providing the enormous sum of £120,000 in
1607–8, and as groups of aliens had done in 1607 and 1617. Institutionalized borrowing from the Corporation of London and—though
to a lesser extent—from the customs farmers became important
again in the early years of Charles I's reign, but it is extremely
doubtful whether the Corporation's renewed willingness to lend
after its prolonged inactivity since 1617 reflects a real revival of the
royal credit. Just as the beginning of the commercial revival in those
years was sluggish, so was the response of the money market as
a whole, as opposed to that of the restricted circle of recurrent
lenders. Neither the royal credit nor the level of commercial activity
was restored to its former state of the years before the Crown's first
prolongation of the loan of 1617 from the Corporation of London,
and the economic difficulties which had been consequent upon the
opening of hostilities in the Thirty Years War.

It is possible to be more definite about the borrowing of the
1630's, partly because the end of the war ushered in a quieter period
during which the royal finances were—to some extent at least—
recovering from the strains to which they had been subjected
during the war years. During this period the Crown appears to
have borrowed exclusively from persons and syndicates who were
intimately connected with it by economic or other ties. Moreover,
as compared with the individuals who had lent money regularly
in the 1620's, the circle of lenders became even more constricted.
Many of the familiar lenders of the 1620's had by now disappeared.
Hicks, Vanlore, and Bayning had all died in the late 1620's, and
Burlamachi, now long past the peak of his activity, was to go
bankrupt in 1633. But in a period when its demands were enormously reduced, the Crown could afford to do without them. When,
in the previous decade, it had needed the services of Burlamachi
most, it had shown itself fully cognizant of the need to preserve the
credit of that remarkable man. It is not improbable that its sudden
disregard of these once essential conditions owed something to the
fact that it no longer viewed these services as necessary. A similar
argument may be adduced in explanation of the fact that the
Crown did not borrow from the Corporation of London over these
years. It may be true that—after 1633 at least—this can be ascribed
to the royal dispute with the Corporation over the disposal of
the royal contract estates and other matters. But the very fact
that the Crown felt that it could indulge in the luxury of such a

dispute in itself suggests that, once it had become certain that the now greatly increased credit operations of the customs farmers plus a little supplementation from other sources of loans were adequate to meet its greatly reduced demand for loans, the services of the Corporation were now no more essential than those of Burlamachi.

In other words, the royal demands might comfortably be met by a greatly reduced number of lenders, among whom easily the most important were the customs farmers, who were spurred on to greater efforts than ever before by their shorter leases and by the judiciously dropped hints that the Crown might again consider the resumption of direct customs administration. Loans from privileged corporations were also quite prominent. Such were the advances of rent obtained in the years following 1633 from the two successive monopolistic companies of soapmakers.[49]

On the whole the individual lenders of these years were smaller men than their counterparts of the 1620's. To this rule there is, however, one exception. After a brief period from 1627–9, when the naval treasurership was in the hands of Sir Sackville Crow, Russell resumed office. Although Crow had made a number of loans during his first year of office, he had subsequently been found unsuitable, partly because of tightness upon his purse-strings, and perhaps partly, as Dr. Aylmer suggests,[50] because of his dishonesty. Although naturally less active than during the war years, Russell was again prominent as a lender, notably in anticipation of the receipts of Ship Money after 1635, while in all but one of the years 1630–4, he was prepared to pay out sums in excess of his receipts of revenue. But as an individual lender Russell was a survivor from an earlier and more hectic decade. More typical of the new period was Sir John Winter. In return for an option on the grant of the right to cut wood in the Forest of Dean, similar to that held by the Earl of Pembroke, who had made a number of small advances of rent in the later 1620's, Winter lent £4,000 in 1633, this being an advance payment of two years' rent and containing a stipulation that he would receive back the money with interest, if the ultimate grant were made to another. Another such lender was Sir George (now Lord) Goring, who advanced £6,000 in the course of 1637 at about

---

[49] For the farmers, see above, pp. 97–99; for the soapmakers, above, p. 72.
[50] G. E. Aylmer, 'Attempts at Administrative Reform, 1625–40', *Eng. Hist. Rev.* lxxii (1957), 236.

the same time as he was attempting to form a syndicate to make his successful bid for the farm of the customs.[51]

The financial tranquillity of the age of Thorough was shattered by the war with the Scots in 1639. From 1638, when preparations for war were being made, we enter another period of very heavy borrowing, which was characterized partly by an expansion of borrowing from individuals, most of whom had strong vested interests in the survival of the old régime. Among such persons, few had more to fear from the summoning of parliament than the farmers of the customs, and Sir Paul Pindar, the greatest of the farmers, though temporarily displaced after Christmas 1638, now made a supreme effort. 'This Sir Paul', remarked Sir Edmund Rossingham, 'never fails the king when he has most need', and although he had borne his share of the very large syndicated loans made by the customs farmers in 1637–8, Pindar now ventured forth as an independent lender on a truly remarkable scale. In view of the fact that his syndicate was to lose control of the great and other farms after Christmas, his loans may have been in some measure intended as a display of fireworks to demonstrate his indispensability to the Crown. On 22 May 1638 he had purchased for Charles I a large pendant diamond for £8,000, for which he was willing to accept payment by assignments on the royal alum farm, falling due between Christmas 1642 and February 1643. Although the estimate of one contemporary that Pindar lent £100,000 is an exaggeration, it is not a hopelessly wild one, and his provision of £85,000 in 1638–9, quite apart from the transaction concerning the jewel and his participation in the syndicated loans of the farmers in 1638 and 1640, was a very remarkable feat. These loans were secured upon numerous branches of the revenue which were due to mature between Michaelmas 1639 and Christmas 1645, so that many of these sums were never repaid to him. Yet the Long Parliament, which had contributed to his ruin by its fine on the farmers and the sequestration of their lease in 1641, was to demand a further £20,000 from him in 1643, to which request he returned a conciliatory but temporizing reply. Indeed, far from lending money to the parliament in that year, he was engaged in shipping gold to Oxford for the use of the

[51] For Russell and Crow, see Ashton, *B.I.H.R.* loc. cit., pp. 165–6. For Winter, S.P. Charles I, 266/69, 286/43. I am indebted to Mr. G. Hammersley for drawing my attention to the former reference, and for information about the grants to both Pembroke and Winter. For Goring, Exchequer of Receipt, Order Book (Pells), E. 403/2757, fos. 19–19(*b*); *Cal. S.P.D.* (*1637–8*), p. 418.

King. It is unnecessary to be a Marxist to appreciate that there are a number of individual cases for which the economic interpretation of choice of allegiance in the Civil War provides a wholly satisfactory explanation, and, in view of the circumstances, it would have required a quite extraordinary degree of altruism on Pindar's part for him to have been anything but a royalist.[52]

John Harrison, whom we have already observed in his ambivalent roles as customs farmer and as an informed and determined advocate of the nationalization of the customs, made one very substantial loan to Charles I in November 1640 at a time when he too had already lent very considerable sums through the syndicated loans of the farmers. The King required money urgently for the royal army and the relief of the north, and to await the proceeds of a parliamentary grant with its usual attendant delays might prove fatal unless something could be provided on account. In Harrison's absence from London, his son had consented on his behalf to a royal request for a loan of £50,000, an act of unfilial presumption which greatly displeased his father, who, however, rather grudgingly acquiesced in the arrangements which had been made for him. He later claimed that this loan, for which and other services he was knighted by the King, helped to encourage the Corporation of London to supply a second instalment of the £200,000 which it had consented to lend to the King.[53]

Outside the now greatly constricted range of normal lenders on the money market were many peers, gentlemen, courtiers, and great and petty officials who were no less interested in the preservation of the old régime than were the farmers to whom the victory of parliament spelt ruin. It was to such classes that Charles turned at the end of 1639, when it was planned to borrow £300,000 for the defence of the realm against the Scottish rebels. Charles had agreed that he would call parliament in April 1640, but the loan was intended to fill the gap until parliament itself could make a grant.[54] After the

---

[52] Patent Roll, 4 Car. I, pt. 44; S.P. Charles I, 410/108, 443/10; B.M. Sloane MSS. 3515, fo. 27; *Cal. S.P.D. (1638–9)*, p. 540; *(1639)*, pp. 3, 147; *A Brief Narrative of the Cases of Sir William Courteen and Sir Paul Pindar; A Declaration of the Marquis of Hertford. . . . Together with the Desires of the House of Commons to Sir Paul Pindar, with Sir Paul Pindar's answer to the same* (1643) (I am indebted to Professor R. H. Tawney for drawing my attention to this document); T. Rymer, *Foedera* (3rd edn., The Hague, 1735–45), ix, pt. ii, pp. 197–8.

[53] B.M. Stowe MSS. 326, fos. 90(b)–91.

[54] *Cal. S.P.D. (1639–40)*, pp. 148–9.

long interval of personal government the promise to call parliament was greeted with understandable scepticism in some quarters. 'Between you and me', wrote Thomas Smith to John Pennington on 12 December, 'few men believe it, but think it will be put off from time to time.'[55] However, the arrangements went on apace, and the Short Parliament was indeed called in April, by which time the bulk of the loan had been subscribed. Prominent at the head of the contributors were the Duke of Lennox, who lent £30,000, and Strafford, who lent £20,000. Archbishop Laud, with characteristic consistency, refused to receive interest on his £5,000, but his example was not followed by another eminent member of the episcopal bench, William Juxon, the Lord Treasurer and Bishop of London. Most of the loans were secured separately by assignment on many branches of the revenue, but, in view of the impending catastrophe, those few lenders who, like Lord Keeper Finch, had their contributions deducted from money due by them to the Crown,[56] could count themselves extremely fortunate. Some excuses were inevitably made. The Earl of Danby pleaded that, being of a very advanced age, he had already conveyed most of his estates to his heirs, but stated his willingness to lend £5,000. The excuses of this former opponent of Ship Money were not likely to cut any ice with the Privy Council, who compelled him to supply the whole of his quota of £10,000. By these and other methods, the council succeeded in raising £232,530 between 20 December 1639 and 15 May 1640, so that this loan was by no means the dismal failure that Professor Dietz suggests.[57]

Humbler persons too were prepared to make sacrifices to finance the Crown in this, the hour of its greatest need. Thus the King's saddler, Thomas Smithsby, in the latter part of 1640, not only disbursed more than £5,000 from his own resources for the pay of several of the King's servants, but also made an additional loan of £4,500 to Charles I.[58]

It is hardly fanciful to suggest that the character of the non-institutionalized borrowing in the last years of the effective reign of Charles I reflects the political division of the country at the end of

[55] Ibid., p. 159.
[56] In Finch's case a wardship and marriage fine.
[57] S.P. Charles I, 539/6, 453/74, 468/125, 487/74; *Cal. S.P.D. (1639–40)*, pp. 158, 333, 337, 461; *(1640)*, p. 149; Dietz, op. cit., p. 285.
[58] *Cal. S.P.D. (1640–1)*, pp. 96, 252. A more celebrated lender was the great architect, Inigo Jones, who lent £500 to Charles I in 1643 (ibid. *(1641–3)*, p. 362).

the period of personal government. No better illustration could be found of the fact that the only lenders upon whom the Crown could henceforth rely were persons whose interests were in one way or another inextricably bound up with those of the monarchy than a letter written by Charles in September 1642 after he had set up his standard at Nottingham. In this letter the King requests a loan from the Earl of Kingston, and is at pains to stress the fact that 'all persons of your fortune and quality . . . are not altogether unconserned in my necessety'.[59]

Remarkable as the efforts of individual lenders and the customs farmers had been, they were not by themselves sufficient, and they had to be supplemented by applying pressure to potential lenders who stubbornly refused to perceive an identity between their own interests and those of the monarchy. The desperation with which the government turned its attention to the East India Company is admirably summed up in a dispatch from the Venetian ambassador, written on 7 September.

> Not knowing where else to go, they have tried to obtain on credit from the India Company all the pepper brought by the ships . . . with the idea of selling it afterwards to the merchants at a loss, who will readily supply the money.[60]

This refers to instructions which were issued in August to Sir Nicholas Crispe and Sir John Nulls to buy East Indian commodities on credit to the value of about £120,000. The sellers were to receive tallies on the customs revenue, and the goods were to be immediately resold, the Crown being prepared to sustain 'Considerabull Los' on the transaction. But in face of the company's opposition to this plan, Charles instructed Cottington in November to seize 2,310 bags of pepper belonging to the company for £63,283. 11s. 1d. The sellers, however, were not to receive this sum in cash, but in tallies on the customs revenue, and were to be repaid, without interest, in five instalments, falling due between March 1641 and December 1642. The urgency of the royal needs necessitated the immediate resale of the pepper, the consequent glutting of the market and the receipt of only £50,626. 17s. 1d. from sale to seven London merchants. The sequestration of the customs farmers' lease by the Long Parliament in 1641 meant that not all the lenders' tallies could be

[59] B.M. Stowe MSS. 154, fo. 10.
[60] *Cal. S.P. Ven. (1640–2)*, p. 74.

honoured. Some payments were certainly made, but the bulk of the money was not repaid until after the Restoration.[61]

It has been argued [62] that Charles I's action in the pepper business was less arbitrary than might appear at first sight. It is quite true that the company had originally offered the pepper for sale to anyone who was willing to pay a stipulated price, which, as it turned out, only the Crown was prepared to pay. Nevertheless, there can be no doubt whatever that the company was acutely embarrassed by the royal offer, despite the arguments of one of its representatives that, 'if any Strainger had made the same offer, hee shold have had it, nor Can it bee worse for the Company because the King hath the bargayne'.[63] And it is not necessary to seek far for the reasons for its embarrassment. Charles I's support for Courteen's East India association in the later 1630's had subjected the already difficult relations between the Crown and the company to further severe strains. Moreover, it is misleading to treat the Crown's offer for the pepper as if it were the equivalent of any ordinary private transaction. The length of the credit which the company had originally been willing to grant was extended, and, given the current state of the royal finances, the chances were that it would be prolonged still further. No interest was payable on the loan, and to describe the security given by the Crown as 'excellent',[64] is to ignore the realities of the situation. It has already been remarked that the lenders received tallies on the great customs, and, in addition, they obtained the bonds of a number of private sureties, among them prominent customs farmers. Tallies might easily be dishonoured, and, as the past history of royal borrowing on the bonds of sureties demonstrated, and the future course of this particular transaction was to confirm, many forms of pressure could be applied to lenders to prevail upon them not to prosecute such bonds. If there is any validity in the central argument of this book, an account of royal financial operations which treats them as directly analogous to those of the private business man must inevitably be suspect. Charles's action in the pepper business was, no doubt, less high-handed than

[61] S.P. Charles I, 465/64, 473/83, 478/83; A.O. 1/1948/1; *Cal. S.P.D. (1641–3)*, p. 365; *Cal. S.P. Ven. (1640–2)*, p. 74; *Cal. Treasury Books (1660–7)*, p. 386. *Cal. Court Minutes, East India Company (1640–3)* (ed. E. B. Sainsbury) (Oxford, 1909), pp. 80–84, 242–3, 247, 256, 269, 325, 333, 343, 370.

[62] W. Foster, 'Charles I and the East India Company', *Eng. Hist. Rev.* xix (1904), 456–63.

[63] Ibid., p. 459.   [64] Ibid.

his outright seizure of the bullion in the Mint in the same year. But the element of compulsion in this transaction, however discreetly veiled, is hardly in doubt.

Long before it had approached the East India Company, the Crown had begun a long battle of threats, cajolings and evasions with the Corporation of London. The disputes over the royal contract estates and other issues which had brought about a marked deterioration in Charles's relations with the Corporation now began to bear their bitter fruits. A half-hearted attempt to raise money for a voluntary contribution in the wards early in 1639 had failed dismally, yielding hardly more than £200,[65] but armed with the oversanguine hope that a loan might succeed where a gift had failed, Charles again approached the Corporation on 4 June 1639 with a request for a loan of £100,000. The result of his action was the exact reverse of his intention, for his demand was met with the tactics of 1614, that is, the substitution of a gift of £10,000 for a loan of £100,000.[66] The naïve comment of the historian of the Corporation on this incident that 'the citizens were not indisposed to assist the king, if left to themselves and not subjected to threats and intimidation' hardly merits serious consideration, and we can readily agree with Mr. Harper that the substitution of a gift for a loan, in 1640 as in 1614, reflects the deterioration of the royal credit in the city.[67] But it reflects far more than this, for there can be no doubt that the reluctance of many of the citizens to risk their money was reinforced by their political dispositions. Both the greatest historian of the politics of the early Stuart period and the historian of the Corporation itself are agreed that, despite the existence of an important royalist party in the city, the war was even more unpopular there than elsewhere in the country.[68]

This view seems to be borne out by the Corporation's reception of the King's demands in the next year. By 14 April 1640 Charles had already consulted the Lord Mayor three times about a loan of £100,000 to be raised from the aldermen, to which some of the richer commoners might also contribute. 'The City', suggested the Lord Privy Seal with all the characteristic arrogance of Stuart

---

[65] Journal, xxxviii, fos. 209–209(b), 215, 297.

[66] S.P. Charles I, 423/102, 424/30; Journal, xxxviii, fo. 303; Cal. S.P.D. Addenda (1625–49), p. 609; Cal. S.P. Ven. (1636–9), pp. 565, 568.

[67] R. R. Sharpe, London and the Kingdom (1894), ii. 121; W. P. Harper, Public Borrowing (1640–1660), p. 16.

[68] Gardiner, History, ix. 39; Sharpe, op. cit. ii. 120.

governing circles, 'was rather beholding with his Majesty to take their money than his Majesty should be beholding to the City for lending it.' At this state in the Crown's affairs his statement could hardly be farther from the truth. Further delays ensued and the King raised his demands to £200,000, threatening to increase them by a further £100,000 if the citizens did not comply quickly. But compliance was not so easy. Many of the aldermen had, it is true, consented to assess the citizens in their wards, but four of them[69] had refused to do so, and had been consigned to separate prisons. During the period between the dissolution of the Short and the final decision to summon the Long Parliament the King obviously thought that stern measures would pay dividends, and during July he threatened to issue brass coins and to give them a forced circulation if no loan was forthcoming. When this threat failed, he treated separately with the Livery Companies at the end of July, and, although the Salters and the Barber-Surgeons expressed their willingness to lend £2,800 and £300 respectively, the remainder were adamant, most of them pleading the charges of the Ulster Plantation.[70]

No further progress was made until 24 September, when, at a council of peers held at York, the King finally decided that he would call parliament on 3 November, and that the Corporation was again to be approached for a loan of £200,000 which would serve as a stop-gap until an adequate parliamentary grant was available. The proceeds of the loan were to be used for the maintenance of an army for so long as the Scots retained an armed force on English soil, and for its demobilization after the emergency had passed. Since all branches of the revenue were heavily pledged already, the security offered was the joint bond of five peers of the realm—the number was later raised to ten. The peers, one of whom was Goring, a rather unfortunate choice, were sent to London to add their personal persuasions to those contained in letters which had been dispatched from York. On 3 October they were able to report that some progress had been made, and that although the Corporation had not yet formally consented that £200,000 should be raised in three instalments, it had at least agreed to raise the first £50,000 by

[69] Aldermen Atkins, Rainton, Geere, and Soame.
[70] *Cal. S.P.D. (1640)*, pp. 31–32, 41, 142–3, 155, 168, 497, 500, 513, 514, 521–2, 535; Remembrancia, viii. 226; Goldsmiths' Hall, Court Minutes (1634–42), fos. 70–70(b); Grocers' Hall, Orders of Court of Assistants (1640–68), fo. 6; A. H. Johnson, op. cit. iii. 145–7; J. Nicholl, op. cit., pp. 247–8.

levying it upon the Livery Companies, which were assessed by the Lord Mayor on the same day.[71]

There can be no doubt that the attitude taken by the Corporation over this loan played an important part in inducing Charles I to make the fateful decision to call the Long Parliament. By September 1640 the King's intransigence had changed to a willingness to consider whether his object might not be better secured by the substitution of concessions for threats. Giustinian, the Venetian ambassador, wrote in August that the King had already thought good to emphasize at his third time of asking for the £200,000 that the money was required 'not . . . for warlike purposes but to establish a beneficial peace in this kingdom'.[72] The qualification was probably necessary on account of the wide sympathy for the Scots then prevalent in London—'itself as sure to you as the good town of Edinburgh. Their purses, which have been shut to their King, doubt not but you shall find open to you'[73]—the current hostility to royal ecclesiastical policy in the city, which led at least one person to assert that the proceeds of the loan money would be used to further the cause of Popery,[74] and the further fear, which was intimately connected with this, that the hostilities against the Scots might mark the beginning of the extension of the Thirty Years War to England. It was only with the royal decision to call another parliament that moderation won the day—at least, temporarily—and the citizens could subscribe to the loan with full purses and easy consciences. Giustinian had remarked, on 7 September, that the Corporation would not consent to raise money in the absence of any prospect of parliament.[75] A similar view was held by the Earl of Bristol, one of the most sagacious of the peers at York,[76] and, as if to emphasize the strength of the Corporation's position, a petition of citizens of London was presented on 24 September, reciting a num-

[71] S.P. Charles I, 468/14, 29(a); Cal. S.P.D. (1640–1), pp. 96–97, 101, 113, 128, 133–5, 146; B.M. Harleian MSS. 1219, fos. 26–26(b), 165–73; Remembrancia, viii. 233; Hist. MSS. Comm., XIIth Report, pt. iv, p. 525 (John Amye to Thomas Loate. This writer's statement that the consent of the Livery Companies was obtained before that of the municipal authorities is incorrect).

[72] Cal. S.P. Ven. (1640–2), p. 65. See also Cal. S.P.D. (1640), p. 554.

[73] Ibid., p. 612. This quotation is drawn from a royalist pamphlet, but the view which it expresses, though exaggerated, was by no means divorced from reality.

[74] Cal. S.P.D. (1640–1), pp. 126–7.

[75] Cal. S.P. Ven. (1640–2), p. 74. Giustinian actually says 'without a vote of parliament'.

[76] Gardiner, History, ix. 209.

ber of grievances which included impositions, monopolies, religious innovations, and 'the seldom calling and sudden dissolving of parliaments'.[77] In the Corporation's refusal to lend until parliament had been summoned lay the germs of parliamentary control of the government's ability to borrow, and with the loan of 1640, we pass into a new stage of financial no less than of political history.

Between the desperate measures of 1640 and the much wider circle of lenders upon whom James I could draw in the earlier years of his reign there is a notable contrast. In the intervening process of the decline of the royal credit the crucial events were probably the two prolongations of the aldermen's loan of 1610, the need to borrow the credit of the Corporation in 1617, the failure to repay the loan of 1617 for more than a decade, the prolongations of other borrowings in the 1620's, and the Crown's disregard for the need to husband its credit in the 1630's when times were quieter. It has already been suggested that the rather strange coincidence of the expansion of the importance of borrowing from a relatively few individuals in the 1620's, at a time when the royal demand for loans was expanding prodigiously and when, by all other criteria, the royal credit ought to have been declining, may mask an actual expansion of the effective sources of loanable funds tapped by the Crown; that at this time it may have been forced to adopt a more indirect approach to the money market through the medium of a limited circle of direct lenders. Certainly the most prolific individual lenders of the period, Burlamachi and Russell, Hicks, Cockayne, and Vanlore seem to have been borrowing regularly in the city and, in the case of Burlamachi, drawing bills of exchange on correspondents abroad in order to re-lend to the Crown. Such operations might prove to be very profitable with the rate of interest on the best securities—except in times of acute financial stringency—well below the statutory maximum. For those lenders who had few or no connexions with the city, however, it was a very different story. Sir Francis Crane had raised the whole of the £7,500 which he lent to Charles I in 1628 by borrowing, becoming 'bound and ingaged to other men, and is to pay the utmost rate of interest'.[78] Many of the contributors to the great loan of 1639–40 found themselves in the same unenviable position. Secretary Windebank raised his contribution of £3,000 by borrowing £1,000 from Sir Paul

---

[77] *Cal. S.P.D. (1640–1)*, p. 94; J. Rushworth, *Historical Collections* (1712), iii. 1263.   [78] Coll. Sign Man. Car. I, vol. vi, no. 2.

Pindar and £2,000 from Peter Ricaut on the bonds of his son and nephew and at the statutory maximum rate.[79] The Earl of Bridgewater probably fared no better. He tried to raise his quota by borrowing from friends and by negotiating a loan through certain London scriveners, with whom he had apparently had dealings on former occasions. He doubled his originally intended contribution of £5,000 at the King's request, managed to scrape together some of the original £5,000 by the methods described above, and, for the remainder, expressed the hope that Charles himself would find him a lender who would be prepared to accept a mortgage of his lands, 'for other securities I cannot give'.[80]

These examples have naturally been drawn from the 1620's and from the years 1638–40, both periods of very heavy government borrowing. The early and mid-1630's had seen a further reduction in the number of direct lenders, resulting from the death of some of the most prominent lenders of the previous decade and the bankruptcy of the greatest of them all. But, largely because of the very remarkable expansion of the credit operations of the customs farmers and because of the greatly reduced need to borrow this did not present any very acute problems in the years before 1638. The Crown must have sorely missed the services of the now penurious Burlamachi in the two years which followed. There is no better index of the weakness of the royal financial position in 1640 than the recourse to the pepper loan, the threat to coin brass money, the seizure of the bullion in the Mint, and—the most desperate expedient of all—the calling of parliament.

[79] S.P. Charles I, 473/58–59.
[80] *Cal. S.P.D. (1639–40)*, pp. 301–2, 309, 391, 416–17.

VIII

CONCLUSION

FROM the time of the closure of Antwerp, the English Crown had been thrown back preponderantly upon native English resources for its loans. From at least the time of the Armada, when the royal need to borrow was enormously increased, it had been by far the most important borrower in London, and certainly the only borrower the size of whose demands was sufficient to affect sensibly the terms on which private borrowers might raise money. That royal invasions of the money market might result in a general stiffening of the terms upon which money might be obtained by private borrowers in London was certainly the opinion of Cranfield, and, although, as we have seen,[1] there are reasons for questioning the efficacy of his diagnosis when applied to the first half of the second decade of the seventeenth century, the monetary stringency about which so many contemporaries complained during the 1620's was not simply due to a diminution in the supply of funds connected with depression and sluggish economic recovery, but also—at least after 1624—to an unprecedented expansion of the royal demand for loans.

In such times as these the operations of a borrower on this enormous scale might be expected to stretch the resources of the money market to their limits. The relatively small number of regular lenders was inadequate, and more general sources of loanable funds had to be tapped via the utilization of the machinery of the Corporation of London, and the growth of the practice of borrowing in order to re-lend to the Crown on the part both of individuals and of syndicates. The most important developments in the history of the relationship between the Crown and the money market in the early seventeenth century were three. The first was the growth of the importance of the Corporation of London as a loan contractor —a growth which stretches back to the financial difficulties of the 1590's—and its assumption from 1617 onwards of a new role as a guarantor for domestic loans. Secondly, there was the government's

---

[1] See above, p. 160.

recourse to the farming of the customs on a larger scale than ever before, an expedient which was connected from the first with the need to anticipate revenue, but which had developed by the 1630's into the provision of loans of a quite different and more substantial order. And, finally, there was the heightened importance of Englishmen as lenders.

Each of these developments obviously had its roots in a situation in which the royal demand for loans had greatly increased and the supply of these funds had become virtually restricted to home resources. Ever parsimonious, Elizabeth's need to borrow had been reduced by her ability to maintain a surplus of revenue over expenditure during the period between the closure of Antwerp and the opening of the Spanish war. Thereafter, the need to borrow was greatly increased, but the return of peace in 1604 did not bring with it a return to peace-time economy. Unlike his predecessor, James did not live in constant terror of his overdraft. His attitude to matters financial was no less naïve than that of the housewife who is unable to resist the financial importunities of the hire-purchase man, and it was fraught with serious consequences, among which were heavy borrowing and an alarming rise of the debt in peacetime. 'The want of parsimony in time of peace', warns Adam Smith, 'imposes the necessity of contracting debt in time of war.'[2] Elizabeth and Burleigh might protest—if the anachronism be permitted—at the inadequacy of this *obiter dictum*, for the most grinding parsimony in the matter of ordinary expenditure in peace-time had been pathetically inadequate to prepare England for the financial crisis of war when this came. On the other hand, Salisbury, Cranfield—and ultimately even James himself—all learnt that the fruits of royal improvidence in peace-time ripened long before the national financial unpreparedness was glaringly revealed in the early years of the Thirty Years War. The rise of the debt in Jacobean England indicated that, unlike the situation of the previous reign, heavy royal borrowing was no longer confined to situations of national emergency, though from the financial point of view the very presence of James on the throne was emergency enough in itself.

The significance of the increased importance of the Corporation of London as loan contractor and loan guarantor, and the growth of the intimate connexion between revenue farming and government

_____
[2] *Wealth of Nations* (Everyman edn.), ii. 391.

borrowing, does not lie in the fact that they in some measure provided models for the credit institutions which were utilized by later
governments. Although borrowing from the Corporation and the
farming of revenues were certainly not unknown in Common-
wealth, Protectorate, and Restoration—as, indeed, in medieval—
England, the pattern of the royal relations with the money market
was to change significantly in the closing decades of the seventeenth
century and some of the features of this change were foreshadowed
by the use of goldsmith bankers by Cromwell and Charles II, and
in the latter's experiments in the use of paper money. Herein lies,
as Dr. Shaw showed many years ago,[3] the origins of the national
debt, and it is with the national debt that modern finance begins.
The expedients of the early seventeenth century whereby the
Crown sought to establish permanent machinery (the customs
farmers), and to adapt pre-existing machinery (the Corporation of
London), to meet its financial demands are significant, therefore, not
as prototypes of modern credit institutions—for this they obviously
were not—but rather as the early stages of a process of elimination,
and the first attempted solutions to the problems arising out of a
situation in which the requirements of a modern State had to be
financed almost entirely without having recourse to foreign capital.

   Nor can it be claimed that royal financial practice exerted a
marked influence upon the development of private credit institutions and techniques. In not having recourse to those classes of
lenders who were eventually to become the originators of banking
in England, the Crown was merely following the general practice
of most private borrowers. These raised loans from unspecialized
moneylenders who frequently borrowed from others in order to
relend, and occasionally ran deposit businesses of their own as a
sideline to their main economic interests. But the way of advance
in the development of banking, as in other sectors of economic life,
was to be via the specialists, and there can be no doubt that those
classes of lenders who were later to become professional bankers
were used by private borrowers long before the Crown discerned in
them a useful source of loans, although their rise to importance in
both the public and the private sectors of the money market lies

---

[3] W. A. Shaw, 'The Treasury Order Book', *Econ. J.* xvi (1906), 33–40; 'The
Beginnings of the National Debt', *Historical Essays in Commemoration of
the Jubilee of Owens College, Manchester* (ed. T. F. Tout and J. Tait) (Manchester, 1907), pp. 391–422.

outside our period. Similarly, there is no reason to believe that the cheque and the inland bill owed anything to the earlier example of the Exchequer tally. The techniques evolved by the Exchequer, the customs farmers, the Corporation of London, and individual lenders were essentially specific responses to specific financial exigencies, and there is neither the evidence nor even an *a priori* case for assuming that they were copied by private bankers. That in each case the underlying problems and the resultant techniques might be similar is hardly proof of the existence of such a connexion. The development of government and private borrowing and credit techniques might run along roughly parallel lines, but each was, in a real sense, *sui generis.*

The heightened importance of Englishmen both as individual lenders, as subscribers to the loans raised through the Corporation of London, and as members of loan syndicates, of which the customs farmers were by far the most important, might not be worthy of remark if it were not for the fact that the early seventeenth century was a period when both the royal need and the royal inclination to borrow were substantially increased. It is true that the period produced its borrowings abroad, notably the loans from Christian IV of Denmark and the £58,400 raised in Amsterdam in the 1620's. But these were of very minor importance. More significant, certainly, were the services rendered by merchant-financiers of foreign origin, resident in England and possessing useful financial contacts abroad; though the last advantage was not, of course, confined to aliens. Such services were highly valuable in the cases of lenders like Courteen and Vanlore; indispensable in that of Burlamachi, the greatest financier of the age. But great men arose from the ranks of English merchants too. The services of Russell and Pindar were second only to those of Burlamachi, while the loans of Hicks and Bayning were certainly not less substantial than those of Courteen and Vanlore. In addition to this, the directors of the great farm of the customs, the most considerable financial concession of the period, were English to a man. 'I would wisshe', Gresham had written in 1569, 'that the Queene's Majestie in this time shuld not use anny strangers but her owne subiectes [viz. as lenders] whereby . . . all other Princes may se what a Prince of powr she ys.'[4] His advice, offered in connexion with a particular emergency on the eve of the closure of Antwerp, was to move several substantial steps nearer to

[4] B.M. Lansdowne MSS. 12, no. 8.

permanent realization in the early seventeenth century, although
the same cannot be said of its political corollary.

In assessing the contribution made during any age to the solution
of practical economic problems, the expedients which were rejected
by contemporaries are frequently no less illuminating than those
which they adopted. The methods of borrowing described in these
pages were more likely to be successful—at least, temporarily—than
more exotic and sophisticated schemes which had not the advantages of indigenous growth. Numerous projects for the establishment of a national bank—one of them by the great Burlamachi
himself three years after his bankruptcy[5]—were put forward during
this period, but none of them seems to have been taken very
seriously by anyone save the projectors. The much-travelled English financier, Sir Paul Pindar, may have considered himself free
from the grosser economic prejudices of his countrymen. At any
rate he advanced, at some time during the mid 1620's, a project for
the establishment of a public bank in London, which owed something to his observation of the working of the Bank of Venice. This
proposal, penned in an appropriately Italianate hand, claimed that
through such a bank 'ye Prince and State mighte haue exacte knowledge of the trewe estate of everye particular man, by meanes
wherof dewties might be Imposed proportionable to ye effectuall
valliditie of mens trewe Estates'. Still more alarming and significant,
even to the undertaxed citizens of London, was the author's observation that in the money lodged by depositors in the bank there
would be a source of loanable funds 'uppon which his Majestie may
prevayell at pleazure eyther by Consente or withoute ye privite of
ye Propryetaryes at all tymes'.[6] And it is here, of course, that we
meet with the most fundamental obstacles to the establishment of
a national bank in conditions other than those in which the power
of the State is either limited or absolute. As long as the Stuarts continued to resort to arbitrary methods of finance, the existence of the
minimum degree of public credit compatible with the successful
working of such an institution was precluded, and potential depositors would obviously be unwilling to entrust their funds to a bank
which was helpless to resist the royal demands. On the other hand,
to force merchants to deposit funds in the bank would be a task far
beyond the powers of a monarchy whose tendencies towards
absolutism were severely limited by the inadequate machinery of

[5] S.P. Charles I, 329/34.   [6] B.M. Lansdowne MSS. 108, no. 90.

enforcement at its command. It was not until the attempts of the Stuarts to establish absolute monarchy on the French model had received their final *coup de grâce* in 1688 that the conditions were present under which a national bank could flourish. 'Dutch finance' and limited monarchy were complementary.

Thus, in the absence of more formalized financial institutions the Crown was forced back upon simpler methods of borrowing, and, in particular, upon the three resources mentioned above—the use of private capitalists to administer and anticipate the most important branch of the revenue, of the Corporation of London to canalize widespread sources of loanable funds in periods of very heavy borrowing, and of a comparatively small number of wealthy individual lenders in London. It is pertinent to inquire whether it viewed each source of loans as appropriate to a particular type of accommodation. Apart from the obvious connexions between its use of the Corporation and the existence of a need to borrow heavily to finance deficits or to manage the debt, this question is not easy to answer, for as we have seen, few royal borrowings were nominally long-term obligations, in which circumstances the Crown had to rely for its longer-term borrowings chiefly upon prolongations of short-term loans. In its borrowings from individual moneylenders there are many examples of such prolongations, and it is therefore reasonable to conclude that it used such lenders as sources of both short- and longer-term loans as the exigencies of particular occasions required; in that of the Corporation of London, however, from 1608 onwards all but one of the loans, though nominally raised at short-term, were in effect long-term obligations. In so far as renewals were willingly conceded, there was no great harm in this procedure. But in so far as pressure had to be applied to lenders to persuade them to concede renewal, the royal credit was bound to suffer accordingly. This is obviously true of the Corporation's loans of 1617 and 1625; and, though to a much lesser extent, of that of 1610 also.

In the case of the farmers of the customs, the type of accommodation provided was predominantly short-term under James I, but under Charles I the farmers became important as longer-term lenders. It was shown that this development was connected with the fact that the Crown was unable to borrow from the Corporation of London in the 1630's, and that many of the individual lenders upon whom it had become accustomed to rely were no longer available. The essence of this situation is that the Crown was now borrowing only from those persons or syndicates to whom it had granted privileges or could easily apply pressure. The more indispensable a lender could make himself, the tighter his hold upon his privileges became, and the more likely he was to obtain additional concessions. Down to 1638 the Pindar syndicate of farmers was able to maintain its hold upon the customs revenue, to triumph over schemes to abrogate the system of farming in favour of direct royal administration, and probably also to augment its profits on account of the fact that the Crown did not obtain an increase of rent during a period of revived commercial activity. It did so by virtue of the fact that it expanded the scope of its credit operations, and became a regular long-term lender. As long as the country remained at peace and the royal demand for loans was not unduly heavy, the situation was happy enough for all concerned. But there were dangers in it, and these quickly became apparent after 1638, when, under the pressure of war again, there was a notable expansion of the royal demand for loans. By the end of our period, with the farmers stretched to the utmost limits of their resources, and the Corporation of London unwilling to lend immediately more than £50,000 of the required £200,000, and that only after receiving a political *quid pro quo* in the form of a guarantee that parliament would be called, Charles was forced to such desperate measures as the pepper loan and the seizure of the bullion in the Mint. The bankruptcy of the régime had become glaringly apparent. But the suddenness of the financial collapse in 1640 must not be allowed to obscure the fact that the weakness of the position of the royal borrower can be traced back at least as far as 1618, and perhaps to 1611. Such precarious financial stability as had existed in the 1630's had depended upon the continuance of peace for two reasons. The first is that the process of cumulative hypothecation which was such an important feature of these years was bound to break down under the weight of a renewal of heavy royal borrowing. Secondly, the Crown's disregard of the need to preserve its credit in the city had brought about a situation in which the available sources of loans were patently inadequate to meet such needs. The response of the restricted circle of lenders in 1638–40 had been truly magnificent, but further expenditure was necessary at the end of 1640 and the resources of these lenders were nearly exhausted.

Given the preponderant role of the Crown as a borrower, if

financial capitalism developed apace in the early seventeenth century, the royal financial needs provided an important stimulus to that development. It may, perhaps, be argued that to describe the moneylenders of this period as financial capitalists is positively misleading, since, with the exception of Burlamachi, who was the nearest thing that the period produced to a professional financier in the modern sense, finance was unspecialized and the source of financial capital is to be found in the alternative, and usually preponderating, non-financial activities of the lenders. Nevertheless, granting the validity of this objection, the size of royal demands for funds was perhaps the main factor in causing finance to loom larger on the economic scene than in any previous period, so that large-scale and regular lending to the Crown might result in a partial shift of resources from commerce to finance on the part of individual lenders. This process can be observed, for example, in Sir William Russell's shedding of many of his East India investments before assuming the office of Treasurer of the Navy in 1618.[7] Inquiries into the origins of particular forms of economic capital have not normally been particularly fruitful, especially when tied to schematic formulae such as that propounded by Sombart in the case of commercial capital. Working within the English empirical tradition, the approach of George Unwin to the problem of commercial capital in the Elizabethan period and the inquiry of Professor T. S. Ashton into the sources of industrial capital in the eighteenth century have demonstrated that such questions are rarely susceptible of a simple answer.[8] The same is true of financial capital in the early seventeenth century. That financial capital can, to use Professor Ashton's famous description of industrial capital, be in some measure its own progenitor, especially via the process of deposit banking, is, of course, true, but not especially relevant to early Stuart conditions when banking was relatively unimportant, though the use of government funds by revenue collectors perhaps provides a significant analogy. But just as capital flowed in both directions between commerce and industry, so was there a similar two-way traffic between commerce and finance. That the profits of the Levant, Eastland, and Guinea trades might fertilize finance is shown by the investments of the Garways, Salter, Pindar, Cockayne,

[7] See Ashton, *B.I.H.R.* loc. cit., p. 163.
[8] G. Unwin, *Studies in Economic History* (ed. R. H. Tawney) (1927), pp. 192–6; T. S. Ashton, *The Industrial Revolution* (1948), pp. 94–109.

and Crispe in the farms of the customs. But the case of Sir Francis Jones, whose commercial investments were small before he acquired an interest in the great farm and expanded afterwards, together with the practice of revenue collectors and farmers of using receipts of revenue as sources of mercantile loans should remind us that the flow was not all in one direction; while the accession of Lord Goring to the farm provides an example of the accession of capital to finance from activities connected with economic concessions which had been obtained via influence at Court.

The last example is characteristic of the age. Influence was one of the most precious of all forms of capital. In the days when economic concessions were showered upon the business world, those who were well connected with the Court went to the head of the queue. Almost every aspect of the economic history of this period provides any number of variations upon this basic theme, to illustrate which it is necessary to turn only to those most sought after of all concessions, the farms of the customs. The connexion with the Court might take the form of a sublease by the managing syndicate of business men from a courtly intermediary such as the Earl of Southampton, in the case of the sweet-wine farm, Robert Cecil in that of the silk farm, or the Earl of Suffolk in that of the currant farm.[9] Alternatively, where the practice of subletting did not obtain, the most important factor in the acquisition of a lease might well be the degree of influence which each rival syndicate could bring to bear at Court—influence which, of course, had a cash price. That Swinnerton's success in obtaining the support of the Earl of Northampton for his designs on the great and the French and Rhenish wine farms in the early years of James I's reign availed him nothing does not prove that such influence was of negligible importance, but rather suggests—as was in fact the case—that the successful rival syndicate had succeeded in obtaining still more powerful backing. Again the triumph of Goring's syndicate over the well-tried Pindar group in 1638 was not due to the deficiencies of the latter, which had, in fact, served Charles I exceptionally well, but to the fact that Goring was a force to be reckoned with at Court. The influence of such connexions on the economic history of the period is still a relatively unexplored subject.

[9] *Cal. S.P.D. Addenda (1580–1625)*, pp. 427–8; *Cal. S.P.D. (1603–10)*, p. 161; S.P. James I, 7/15; *Hist. MSS. Comm., Salisbury MSS.* xv. 96, 115, 124; xvi. 354; *Sackville MSS.* i. 57–59, 122–5.

In private financial transactions in London, while merchants of
one sort or another were always the most prominent lenders, members of the legal profession probably came a by no means con-
temptible second. Certainly the early seventeenth century was a
period when legal fortunes were being made, but the movement of
capital from legal profits into royal as opposed to private financial
securities was not a feature of the age. Perhaps lawyers knew too
much about the law for them to consider lending to the Crown as
an attractive proposition. More probably, they were far less interested than merchants in obtaining the sort of economic concessions
to which lending might form one avenue of approach, and, at the
same time, less susceptible to pressure as a form of persuasion. This
study has laid great stress on the importance of these factors. In an
age of clientage the Crown was the greatest of all patrons, and
economic concessions created a form of clientage in the business
world which was no less important than its more familiar manifes-
tations in other sectors of seventeenth-century society. Loans might
be instrumental in securing or retaining privileges, and these privileges in turn formed a tie of economic interest between the Crown
and the recipient, though the former by rash acts of ill-advised and
precipitate economic statecraft, such as the Cockayne and Courteen projects, might alienate a number of powerful groups—in these
cases the Merchant Adventurers and the East India Company—
who in other circumstances might have given it their support in the
coming trial of strength. No one today would seriously insist upon
the validity of that deceptively simple thesis of a mutual antagonism
between Crown and city, which used to be a standard component
of the historiography of the Civil War. With the advance in our
knowledge of the economic history of the period, it becomes more
and more apparent that a significant and powerful minority in the
London business world possessed a compelling interest in the survival of the old régime. In the creation of that minority, royal borrowing and the network of intimate business connexions between
the Crown and certain forms of private enterprise, arising out of the
royal relations with the money market, are factors which no historian of the Great Rebellion can afford to neglect.

NOTE ON SOURCES AND BIBLIOGRAPHY

THE very wide range of primary materials, printed sources, and mono-graphs used makes a full account of sources and a complete bibliography of secondary material impracticable. The most important classes of sources used for general purposes were the *State Papers Domestic* and the records of the Exchequer, and more particularly, the *Receipt, Issue, and Order Books* of the Exchequer of Receipt (E. 401/1872–1927; E. 403/1698–1755; E. 403/2723–60).

There is no general history of the money market for this period. By far the most useful source of secondary information are treatises, of which G. de Malynes, *Consuetudo vel Lex Mercatoria* (1622), is the most useful. R. H. Tawney's Introduction to T. Wilson, *A Discourse Upon Usury* (1925), is an outstanding modern description of the money market in Elizabethan times, many of whose conclusions apply to the early Stuart period. The account of the bill market given by R. de Roover, *Gresham on Foreign Exchange* (Cambridge, Mass., 1949), is useful for its analysis of the mechanism of the exchanges and its discussion of contemporary theories, but R. D. Richards, *The Early History of Banking in England* (1929), is better on the later than on the early seventeenth century. Much important material relating to the legal status of securities can be derived from W. Holdsworth, *A History of English Law* (3rd ed., 1922), T. F. T. Plucknett, *A Concise History of the Common Law* (1948), and J. M. Holden, *The History of Negotiable Instruments in English Law* (1955). A great deal of material in the opening chapter has been drawn from recent works on the economy of landed families, and, in this respect, M. E. Finch, *The Wealth of Five North-amptonshire Families 1540–1640* (Oxford, 1956), is especially illuminating.

Extensive details, as opposed to stray pieces of information relating to the careers of individual moneylenders are not easy to find. Burlamachi has already been treated by A. V. Judges, 'Philip Burlamachi: A Finan-cier of the Thirty Years War', in *Economica*, vol. vi (1926), and in my own 'The Disbursing Official under the Early Stuarts: the Cases of Sir William Russell and Philip Burlamachi', in the *Bulletin of the Institute of Historical Research*, vol. xxx (1957). A good deal is known of Sir Baptist Hicks because of the survival of the papers of his brother in the *Lansdowne Collection* in the British Museum, while another British Museum Collection the *Sloane MSS.* (vol. 3515) yields much information about the life of Sir William Courteen. The latter can be supplemented by G. Carew and others, *A Vindication of the Several Actions of Law brought against the Heirs of Sir Peter Courteen and Peter Boudaen*, and *Hinc Illae Lacrimae, Or an Epitome of the Life and Death of Sir William Courteen and Sir Paul Pindar*. The papers of Lionel Cranfield, 1st Earl of Middlesex, both in their published form (*Hist. MSS. Commission, Sackville MSS.*, vol. i (1940)), and in the manuscript calendar compiled by the late Professor A. P. Newton, are an outstanding source of information relating to both public and private finance in the reign of James I, as is R. H. Tawney, *Business and Politics under James I* (Cambridge, 1958).

For the financial situations out of which the royal need to borrow arose, I have relied extensively upon F. C. Dietz, *English Public Finance 1558–1641* (New York, 1932), and on the numerous sections dealing with royal finance, in S. R. Gardiner, *History of England from the Accession of James I to the Outbreak of the Civil War, 1603–1642* (1883–4). Neither of these authorities, however, arrange their material in a manner which facilitates significant generalization about the role of borrowing in royal finance, in which circumstances it was usually found necessary to reconstruct the royal financial situation at particular times from original materials. For the reign of James I this was attempted in my 'Deficit Finance in the Reign of James I' in the *Economic History Review*, 2nd ser., vol. x (1957), based largely on scattered accounts in the State Papers and the Lansdowne (down to about 1612) and Harleian collections in the British Museum. For the reign of Charles I the most important single source was the accounts of anticipated revenue in the State Papers.

An important source of information in Chapter III was the enrolments of royal obligations on *Close and Patent Rolls* in the records of Chancery. For information relating to Exchequer tallies, there are the numerous articles on medieval tallies cited in the footnotes, my most important source of information on the seventeenth century being Dr. C. D. Chandaman, who is shortly to publish an article on this subject. The document in *Exchequer Miscellanea E. 407/71/29*, was of crucial importance in understanding the changes in the use of the tally, as was a careful comparison between entries in both Receipt and Issue Books of the Exchequer. On the customs farms, A. P. Newton, 'The Establishment of the Great Farm of the English Customs', in *Roy. Historical Society Transactions*, 4th ser., vol. i (1918), deals with the creation of the great farm, and my own 'Revenue Farming under the Early Stuarts' in the *Economic History Review*, 2nd ser., vol. viii (1956), with its development down to 1640 with special reference to the needs of government borrowing. Two important primary sources, hitherto unmentioned, were important here. The first of these is statistical, the declared accounts of the farmers, enrolled in the office of the Lord Treasurer's Remembrancer (*E. 351/609–42, 667–77*), most of which are duplicated in the records of the Audit Office (*A.O. 1/594–602* and *A.O. 3/297*). The second is a magnificent collection of contemporary treatises and chronological descriptions of the development of the customs farms in the reign of Charles I, some of which are anonymous and some of which are by John Harrison (*B.M. Stowe MSS.*, vol. 326).

For the chapters dealing with the Corporation of London, use has been made of the archives of the Corporation and those of the Livery Companies. Of the latter all the surviving *Court Books* and *Wardens' Accounts* of the companies in this period have been examined, except in those rare cases where permission to search was refused. In the case of the records of the Corporation, the chief sources were the *Repertories of the Court of Aldermen* (vols. xxv–lvii), the *Journals of the Court of Common Council* (vols. xxiv–xl), the *Remembrancia* (letters to and from the Lord Mayors and aldermen) and the *City Cash Accounts* (vols. 1/1–1/4), of which the surviving volumes do not pre-date 1633. These last are essential in interpreting the sales of the Royal Contract Estates as are the numerous *Royal Contract Estates Papers* (which include the invaluable *Royal Loans Ledger, 1617–29*), the *Royal Contract Estates Deeds*, and the *Minutes of the Committee for the Sale of the Royal Contract Estates, 1632–1664*.

INDEX

Abbot, George, Archbishop of Canterbury, 92, 122.

Abbot, Sir Morris: becomes Lord Mayor, 93; business interests of, 92–93; commissioner for trade and taxation, 93; engaged in commercial diplomacy, 93; inactive as a customs farmer, 93, 96–97; relinquishes interests in customs farming, 93; undertakes farming of great customs, 92, 94, 107.

Addled Parliament, *see* Parliament.

Aldermen, *see* London.

Aleppo, 96.

Alienations, fines for, 160.

Aliens: attempt to include in city loans, 115; brokers, 13; customs privileges to, 72; loans to Crown by, 20–22, 22, 72 (*bis*), 159, 161, 173, 188; prolongation of loan by, 72; refusal of export licence to, 72.

Alington, Mr., 163.

Alum, farm of, 96, 175.

Alva, Duke of, 15.

Amsterdam: borrowing by Charles I at, 16 & n., 40, 41, 58–59, 64–65, 66, 164, 188; borrowing by Elector Palatine at, 65; Burlamachi's connexions in, 20; refusal to guarantee royal loan by, 58–59; sale of bills on, 3.

Amye, John, 182 n.

Anne of Denmark, Queen of England, 66, 106.

Annuitants, debts due to, 34.

Anticipation, *see* Borrowing; Revenue.

Antwerp: closure of, 185, 186, 188; credit of English Crown at, 68; decline of, 15–16; early sixteenth-century trade with, 16; letter of Gresham from, 56–57; Tudor borrowing in, 15–16, 68.

Apsley, Sir Allen, Surveyor of Marine Victuals, 19 n., 165–6.

Armada, Spanish, 185.

Army: arrangements for pay of regiments in Dutch service, 20, 50;

billeting of soldiers, 39; debts due to soldiers, 34; expenses of maintaining English and Scottish, 44; loan by commander of, 167; loan for troops in Palatinate, 168; money required for troops to fight Scots, 176, 181; provision for demobilization of (1640), 181.

Ashton, R., 5 n., 10 n., 15 n., 19 n. (*bis*), 21 n., 25 n., 35 n., 37 n., 79 n., 82 n., 84 n. (*ter*), 85 n., 99 n., 107 n., 114 n., 118 n., 123 n., 137 n., 152 n., 158 n., 162 n., 165 n., 175 n., 192 n., 195, 196 (*bis*).

Ashton, T. S., 192 & n.

Ashwell, William, 108.

Assignments, 50, 52, 68, 91 n., 95 n., 169, 175; *see also* Household; Tallies; Wardrobe.

Atkins, Alderman, 181 & n.

Aylmer, G. E., 77 & n., 174 & n.

Backhouse, Rowland, 124.

Bacon, Sir Francis, 12 n., 34 n.

Bagg, Sir James, Admiral of South Cornwall, 167.

Bank of England, xvi, 71.

Bankers, Case of the, 55.

Banking: banking institutions almost unknown, 10; Crown and evolution of, 187–8; deposit banking, 13–15, 187–8, 192; loan by bankers of Nuremberg, 168; loans by bankers to Crown, 14; origins of, 12–15; proposals for national bank, 96, 189–90; varieties of, 12–15; *see also* Bank of England; Customs (Farmers of); Goldsmiths; Revenue (Collectors of); Scriveners.

Barbados, 169–70.

Barber-Surgeons, Company of, *see* London.

Bardi, the, 20.

Barre, Robert de la, 22, 160.

Bate, John, case of, 136.

Bateman, Robert, Chamberlain of London, 146.

Bayning, Paul, senior, 169 & n.

Digby, Sir John, Lord Digby, Earl of
Bristol, 18 & n., 50, 168, 182.
Digby, Sir Kenelm, 77.
Ditchfield, Edward, 135.
Dorset, Earls of, *see* Sackville, Edward; Sackville, Thomas.
Drapers, Company of, *see* London.
Dry exchange, 3–4, 5.

Earth, Joseph, 106 n.
East India Company: bad relations of, with Charles I, 179; Courteen's rivalry with, 21–22, 179, 194; disputes of, with Dutch company, 93; loans to Crown by, 23, 171; members of customs farming syndicates prominent in trade of, 92, 93, 103; 'Pepper Loan' from, 44, 45, 178–80, 184; projected loans from, 76, 171–2; proposal to admit Charles I as adventurer in, 171; refusals to lend by, 171–2; sales of stock of, 103; Smethwicke's attack upon administration of, 171; subscription to, jeopardized by royal borrowing, 171.
Eastland, trade with, 192–3.
Edinburgh, 182.
Egerton, John, Earl of Bridgewater, 184.
Ehrenberg, R., 68 n.
Eldred, John, 124, 159.
Elizabeth I, 39, 57, 80, 186; able to maintain ordinary surplus, 186; advised to use English lenders, 188; and Merchant Adventurers, 70–71; borrowing at Antwerp by, 15; death of, 154; debt left by, 114; decline in prompt observance of obligations by, 154–5; Forced Loans used by, 154; gives counterbonds, 59; loans raised by, 61, 114, 157; needs to look for new sources of loans, 15; parsimony of, 186; restrictive commercial policy of, 17; seizure of Genoese treasure by, 15; subsidies voted to, 114.
Epstein, M., 98 n.
Equity of redemption, 8–9, 9 n., 60.
Exchanges, foreign, 3–4, 4 n.; *see also* Amsterdam; Dry exchange; Fictitious exchange; London; Security.
Exchequer, 14, 18, 28 (*bis*), 32, 47,

48, 49 & n., 52, 67, 88 n., 95, 109, 123.
By-passed by assignment, 52.
Discounting of tallies by official of, 53.
Financial techniques evolved in, 188.
Issue Books, 195.
Loan money paid into, 116, 117, 118, 123, 128, 137–8, 139, 140.
Of Pleas, 51.
Order Books, 88, 97, 195.
Orders of, 12, 195.
Receipt Books, 88, 97, 195.
Receipt Rolls, 49.
Records of, 195.
Tallies:
— as instruments of receipt, 48.
— as security, 48–53.
— changes in use of, 48–50, 196.
— compared with bills of exchange, 9, 48, 188.
— compared with cheques, 188.
— complaint of Clerks of Tally Court, 49, 50.
— discount of, 52, 53.
— dishonouring of assignments by, 51, 52, 68, 110–11, 178–9, 179.
— drawn on customs farmers, 32, 50, 82, 91, 110–11, 119, 178–9.
— drawn on impositions, 50.
— evolution of, 48–50.
— levying of, 48.
— materials on, 48 n., 196.
— negotiability of, 50–51.
— of 'pro', 49–50, 51, 67.
— of 'sol', 48–50, 50 n., 51, 67, 123.
— reassignment by, 52, 53.
— used for purposes of issue, 48.
— used in conjunction with bonds, 50–51, 54, 119.
Tellers of, 50.
Expenditure, royal, xiv, 31, 33, 34, 42, 191.
Extraordinary expenditure, 41.
— heavy periods of, 39, 43, 162.
— swallows up proceeds of loans in 1617, 161.
Ordinary expenditure:
— bills due on ordinary account, 34.
— economy of Cranfield in respect of, 38–39.

PRINTED IN GREAT BRITAIN
AT THE UNIVERSITY PRESS, OXFORD
BY VIVIAN RIDLER
PRINTER TO THE UNIVERSITY